WA 1329035 5

# Permanent Family Placement for Children of Minority Ethnic Origin

*of related interest*

**The Dynamics of Adoption**
*Edited by Amal Treacher and Ilan Katz*
ISBN 1 85302 782 0 pb

**Lesbian and Gay Fostering and Adoption**
**Extraordinary Yet Ordinary**
*Edited by Stephen Hicks and Janet McDermott*
ISBN 1 85302 600 X pb

**State Child Care**
**Looking After Children?**
*Carol Hayden, Jim Goddard, Sarah Gorin and Niki Van Der Spek*
ISBN 1 85302 670 0 pb

**The Adoption Experience**
**Families Who Give Children a Second Chance**
*Ann Morris*
ISBN 1 85302 783 9 pb

**Issues in Foster Care**
**The Personal, the Professional and the Organisational**
*Edited by Greg Kelly and Robbie Gilligan*
ISBN 1 85302 465 1 pb

**Child Welfare Policy and Practice**
**Issues and Lessons Emerging from Current Research**
*Dorota Iwaniec and Malcolm Hill*
ISBN 1 85302 812 6 pb

**First Steps in Parenting the Child who Hurts**
**Tiddlers and Toddlers**
*Caroline Archer*
ISBN 1 85302 801 0 pb

**Early Experiences and the Life Path**
*Ann Clarke and Alan Clarke*
ISBN 1 85302 858 4 pb

**Effective Ways of Working with Children and their Families**
*Edited by Malcolm Hill*
ISBN 1 85302 619 0 pb
*Research Highlights in Social Work 35*

**Child Development for Child Care and Protection Workers**
*Brigid Daniel, Sally Wassel and Robbie Gilligan*
ISBN 1 85302 633 6 pb

# Permanent Family Placement for Children of Minority Ethnic Origin

*June Thoburn, Liz Norford
and Stephen Parvez Rashid*

Jessica Kingsley Publishers
London and Philadelphia

All rights reserved. No paragraph of this publication may be reproduced, copied or transmitted save with written permission of the Copyright Act 1956 (as amended), or under the terms of any licence permitting limited copying issued by the Copyright Licensing Agency, 33–34 Alfred Place, London WC1E 7DP. Any person who does any unauthorised act in relation to this publication may be liable to prosecution and civil claims for damages.

The right of June Thoburn, Liz Norford and Stephen Parvez Rashid to be identified as authors of this work has been asserted by them in accordance with the Copyright, Designs and Patents Act 1988.

The research on which this book is based was undertaken by the University of East Anglia which receives funding from the Department of Health; the news expressed in this publication are those of the authors and not necessarily those of the Department.

First published in the United Kingdom in 2000 by
Jessica Kingsley Publishers Ltd,
116 Pentonville Road, London
N1 9JB, England
and
325 Chestnut Street,
Philadelphia PA 19106, USA.

*www.jkp.com*

Learning Resources
Centre

© 2000 Crown Copyright – Copyright Department of Health

**13290355**

**Library of Congress Cataloging in Publication Data**
A CIP catalog record for this book is available from the Library of Congress

**British Library Cataloguing in Publication Data**
A CIP catalogue record for this book is available from the British Library

ISBN 1 85302 875 4 pb

Printed and Bound in Great Britain by
Athenaeum Press, Gateshead, Tyne and Wear

# Contents

# Acknowledgements

The research on which this book is based has had a long gestation period, having its origins in a 'chance' conversation between Jane Rowe and June Thoburn at the British Agencies for Adoption and Fostering conference in 1985 when enthusiasm about 'permanence' through adoption for children in care was at its height. The willingness of 24 voluntary adoption agencies to expose their work to independent evaluation and to complete questionnaires on all children placed between 1980 and 1984 provided the opportunity to look in more detail at outcomes for children of minority ethnic origin. We take this opportunity to acknowledge Jane Rowe's contribution not only to this study but to the body of knowledge on family placement which owes so much to her meticulous and probing approach to research, and her determination that it should result in improved services to children, and their parents and carers.

Next we thank Marilyn Charles who took up the challenge of visiting all the agencies to gain more information about the children included in the survey, scrutinised the records, was all geared up to start on the interview programme when Laurence's imminent arrival intervened. Without the help of the staff of the adoption agencies and the London Borough this research could not have even got off the ground. They helped to locate the records and contact the families on our behalf. But they also were generous with their insights on the subject of the research and shared not only their experience but their warm hospitality, and, at times their homes, as we made our way to the further reaches of the UK.

To Dr Carolyn Davies of the Department of Health we say a special thank you for sticking with the project for so many years. In the phase represented by this book she chaired the Advisory Group, and provided sound advice and encouragement. Academic colleagues, especially Elaine Arnold and Roy Parker, have provided encouragement and insights. we thank them and members of the Advisory Group who gave generously of their time, advice and probing questions.

In chronological order in terms of their involvement in the research, but foremost in terms of their contribution to our study, we thank the parents and young people who shared their joys and sadnesses and helped us to understand something of what it means to be born to one family and grow up in another.

At UEA, our colleagues have as ever been generous with their advice, insights and encouragements. Special thanks go to Dr Peter Moffat of the School of Economic and Social Studies who gave generously of his time and advice and undertook the statistical analysis, and Jacquie White and Margaret Woolgrove for turning the quantitative data into tables and charts. Special thanks also go to Anne Borrett who has stuck with the project with enthusiasm, provided encouragement when we were flagging, and made a contribution way beyond what we had a right to expect from her. Lali Jayasooriya and Erica Barr came in at a crucial stage to transcribe tapes and type up the final report to the Department of Health. We thank them for their interest, patience, care and willingness to press on after closing time.

All have played essential parts in the preparation of this book, but we alone take responsibility for the contents, and for any opinions, and interpretations, as well as for any errors or omissions.

*June Thoburn, Liz Norford and Stephen P. Rashid*
*University of East Anglia*
*January 2000*

# Notes on language and terminology

**Special needs** is often used to refer to learning or physical disability. As used in this book it includes children and young people whose 'special needs' result from being placed with substitute parents when past infancy. The reason for this broader definition is that there is ample evidence in earlier studies that children placed from care will almost all have suffered some adversity beyond that of being separated from their family of origins which may well be reflected in their social, intellectual, emotional or behavioural development.

Much has been written about the meanings given to the words **race** and **ethnicity**. sometimes these are used interchangeably, sometimes with a more specific meaning.

The term **race** refers in this report to visible differences based on characteristics such as skin colour and hair. It is acknowledged that this has no scientific basis and that race is best understood as a social rather than a biological construct. However, given its popular usage to distinguish people who are visibly different from the white ethnic majority in British society, its usage is retained, usually in terms such as 'mixed race (or racial) parentage' and 'mixed race partnerships'. **'Ethnicity'** refers to people, usually of the same racial origin, who share a common culture or way of life.

The children were all of **minority ethnic origin** in that they were born to families who belonged to ethnic groups which are in a minority in the UK population. This term is used when the whole cohort is referred to. When appropriate, the area of origin of the child's parents in used ('South Asian, African–Caribbean' or 'Jamaican', 'Bangladeshi').

**Black** is mainly used to refer to children of African or African–Caribbean descent. However, since the majority of the children were of African–Caribbean descent, 'black' is sometimes used instead of the more accurate but clumsy 'of minority ethnic origin', especially in the tables. In using the term in this way, we do not wish to deny the importance of diversity, to which our interviewees frequently referred.

**Mixed race parentage.** Much, and conflicting, advice was received on how to describe children who had one white parent and one parent of minority ethnic origin. Children whose parents were both of minority ethnic origin, but of different racial backgrounds (e.g. African mother, African-Caribbean father) are not included in the 'mixed race parentage' group. When the point being made is a broader one, including culture as well as skin colour or country of origin, 'dual heritage' is sometimes used.

**Mixed partnership** is used to refer to a birth or substitute family where one parent is of minority ethnic origin and one parent is white.

**Parent/family/mother/father.** Because the study principally concerns the lives of the children in their substitute or new families, the terms 'parent', 'family', 'mother', 'father' usually refer to the adoptive or foster parents. If the family of origin is referred to the terms 'first' or 'birth' are used unless the meaning is clear from what has gone before. 'Parents' (in the plural) is used as a collective term since only a small number of the adoptive or foster families were single parent families. There were no same sex partnerships in the interview sample.

**Foster placement/family/child.** These terms include three groups:

- children placed with foster parents not previously known to them, with the intention, from the start of the placement, that this should be a 'family for life', but adoption was not thought appropriate;

- children placed initially as foster children prior to adoption but the family never applied to adopt (in a small proportion of these a Residence Order was made);

- the small number of children placed by the London Borough with short term foster families before a decision was taken that they would remain on a long-term or 'permanent' basis with those parents.

**Adoptive placement/family/parents; adopted child.** Includes four groups:

- children placed directly for adoption under adoption agencies' regulations;

- children place initially as foster children with parents who planned from the start to adopt them (sometimes referred to as fostering **prior** to adoption);

- children (usually in the older age groups) placed as foster children with a view to adoption if all went well;

- a small number of children placed initially with the intention that this would be a 'permanent' foster placement, who were adopted, usually in their late teens.

Most of the adopted children were in the first two groups.

**All names have been changed to maintain confidentiality.**

# CHAPTER 1

# The Context of Permanent Family Placement for Black Children

Media comment and academic and professional writing on race, identity and child placement are dominated by arguments surrounding transracial and same race placements. The history of this debate, at times acrimonious and still reverberating, has been described at length by Rhodes (1992) and in more condensed form by Gaber (1994), Stubbs (1987), Berridge and Smith (1993), and Rushton and Minnis (1997). It is summarised in this chapter and placed in the context of other research on permanent family placement in order to set the scene for the research described in this book. This will in turn contribute to the debate about the contested nature of 'black identity' as described in recent research, and cultural studies writing (Gilroy 1993; Modood et al. 1997).

The study described here was commissioned by the Department of Health because the ready-made cohort of 244 children of minority ethnic origin who had been placed over ten years ago provided an opportunity to add to the very sparse empirical data – thus contributing to this important debate. The cohort of adoption and permanent foster care placements from which the sample was mainly drawn resulted from a survey of 1165 placements made by 24 British voluntary child placement agencies between 1980 and 1984 (Thoburn 1991). A file search conducted by Charles, Rashid and Thoburn (1992) gave grounds for optimism that it would be possible to interview a sample of these young people and their adoptive or foster parents in order to add depth to our understanding of the survey findings. For reasons of feasibility, and because that is another study requiring a different methodology and raising different ethical questions, no attempt was made to contact the birth parents. They appear, to a very limited extent, through the words of the adopters and young people, and as they are pictured (mostly very unsatisfactorily) in the files. It remains one of the glaring gaps in our understanding of adoption that the experiences of birth parents are under-represented in the literature and our book does little to remedy this.

## The psychology of adoption and the special challenges of adoptive family life

The most useful source on the psychology of adoption, which refers mainly to the placement of babies, is the collection of papers edited by Brodzinsky and Schechter (1990). Following on from the earlier work by Kirk (1964) these authors write of the special challenges, but also special rewards, of adoptive parenting. Kirk's work is most relevant to baby adoption, particularly when the adopters are involuntarily childless. He argues that both the adoptees and the adopters join together in a 'shared fate' in that each has suffered a loss – for the adopters, the loss of the child they would have liked to have had by birth; for the child, the loss of the family into which he or she was born, and the consequent loss of knowledge of roots and connections with past generations. Kirk and other writers argue that the most successful adopters are those who, at some level, understand that sadness and loss brought them together with their child, and that this presents them with special opportunities as well as challenges. Thus, these authors postulate, those who accept, but do not over-emphasise, the differences between adoptive parenting and parenting by birth are most likely to find adoptive parenting a rewarding experience.

It has thus been argued that adoptive parents take on the special challenge of helping their children to overcome a series of 'jeopardies' and to accomplish additional tasks as they grow up. For the infant placed early, after experiencing good ante- and post-natal care, the single jeopardy will arise from the need to come to terms at some stage with 'being given up', 'not being wanted' by the biological parents. A short placement with a foster carer is unlikely to add to the potential difficulties, but if the infant stays with either the birth parent or foster parent beyond around six months, there will be a second 'risk' factor because of the loss of an attachment figure. Maltreatment, neglect or multiple caretakers will add to the risks. Many children placed over the age of 12 months will have been exposed to all these 'jeopardies' and, if the adoptive parents had hoped to have a child by birth and been unable to do so, there is an additional loss. It is against this background that adoptive parents take on the task of helping their children to grow into competent young adults, who have a sense of self-worth and feel comfortable with their biography and identity as members of two families. When children in addition live with a family of a different race and cultural heritage, there is an additional task to be accomplished so that the young adults can have a sense of pride in themselves as persons who are visibly different from the other members of the families they have grown to love.

It is a tribute to the resilience of most adopted children, and the competent parenting, love and determination of most adoptive and foster parents, that, as we shall see from the overview of research in the next section, the majority of the young people successfully negotiate these hurdles and, slightly later than average, grow into mature adults.

## Outcomes of permanent family placement

Before turning specifically to the question of the likely success of adoption or permanent foster placement for children of minority ethnic origin, we summarise briefly the growing volume of more general literature on substitute family placement.

Earlier studies in the UK and overseas were mostly either of the adoption of infants, or foster placement of children in care. More recently less work has been undertaken in the UK on infant adoption, and research has tended to concentrate on placement of older children. All these studies are relevant since the children and young people in our sample range in 'age at placement' from a few weeks to 19 (a young man who remained in the care of the local authority until the age of 19 because he had a severe learning disability). Different studies use different outcome measures, and follow the children up for different periods of time after placement. The research on adoption has recently been summarised by Triseliotis, Shireman and Hundleby (1997) and Department of Health (1999) and on adoption and foster care by Sellick and Thoburn (1996).

The outcome measure most often used is placement stability. It is generally agreed that around 95 per cent of children adopted as infants remain with their adoptive families until they reach adulthood, although some of these will need out-of-home placement because of emotional or behavioural difficulties. The rate of placement breakdown increases with age at placement. Thoburn (1991) found that, of the 1165 children (from whom this present sample of 297 children of minority ethnic origin is largely drawn), around one in five of those placed at the age of eight, and around half of those placed at 12 years of age, left their substitute families before they reached adulthood. It has long been held that those placed in long-term foster care are more likely to experience placement breakdown. However, when age at placement was held constant, that study found no difference in breakdown rates between adoptive and permanent foster placements. The proportions breaking down in the study by Berridge and Cleaver (1987) of long-term foster care of older children are similar to the breakdown rates for those placed for adoption described in recent studies in the UK and America (Barth and Berry 1988). Most children who are older at placement have usually experienced a range of adversities, and even with the use of complex statistical techniques it is hard to be sure whether the explanation is to be found in age itself, or in the emotional and behavioural difficulties of these older placed children.

Smaller scale studies use a range of other outcome measures, including measures of well-being, and satisfaction of parents and children. There is consistency across time in terms of satisfaction rates for adopters and adoptees. McWhinnie (1967), and Raynor (1980) concluded that around 80 per cent were generally satisfied with the experience of being an adoptive family. In terms of mental health, it is generally agreed that a slightly higher proportion of adopted children than non-adopted children are referred to the child mental health services. (See Howe 1997a and 1997b; Quinton *et al.* (1998) and Department of Health (1999) for a summary of the research on emotional and behavioural problems in adopted children). Much has been learned about long-term outcomes from adopted adults who have sought assistance in contacting birth parents as well as from the small number of research studies which include interview data from adult adoptees. (Triseliotis and Russell 1984; Howe 1996; Beek 1997). It appears that a proportion of those who are generally satisfied by the experience of growing up adopted live with some discomfort around issues of identity, which in some cases leads to emotional distress. Because of the difficulties of identifying a representative sample of adopted adults, it is not possible to know what proportion of adopted adults come into these categories.

Some studies, for which data are collected from interviews with the young people, use self-esteem and sense of identity (including identity as an adopted person) as outcome measures. Because numbers are small, and the children involved are placed at different ages with a range of different problems, the findings cannot be easily summarised. It appears that most adopted children are comfortable with being adopted and have reasonably high self-esteem. The minority who are low in self-esteem often also have emotional or behavioural problems which, for older children, sometimes pre-date the placement. Howe (1997a and 1997b) concludes, from a review of the research and interviews with a non-random sample of adopters, that adoption risks increase for children placed when over the age of around six months. There is evidence from two smaller scale studies that those placed when under the age of five who have been maltreated (Gibbons *et al.* 1995) or spent their earlier years in institutions (Rutter, Tizard and Whitmore 1981; Hodges and Tizard 1989) may experience difficulties in making relationships. Triseliotis and Russell (1984) found that, on a range of measures, 44 young adults placed for adoption between the ages of two and ten were doing better on a range of measures of well-being than were 40 young people who remained in foster care.

Researchers on foster care and adoption have sought to identify variables in the children, their early experiences, and their adoptive families which appear to be associated with more or less successful outcomes. Apart from age at placement and behavioural or emotional disturbance in the children at the time of placement, there are inconsistencies in their conclusions. Children who have physical or learning disabilities appear to fare as well, if not better, in placement than those who do not. Those placed with a sibling appear in most, though not all, studies to be less likely to experience breakdown than those placed alone. Although most studies find that older parents who have parented children born to them are more successful, some find this is not the case. Wedge and Mantle (1991) found that younger parents who had no children by birth appeared to be doing better with sibling groups than older experienced parents. Owen (1999) noted that single parents appear to have much to offer older children placed from care. Most researchers conclude that an 'own child' younger and near in age to the placed child is a risk factor. Smaller scale studies point to aspects of parenting style and behaviour (Rushton, Treseder and Quinton 1989, 1993, 1995; Quinton *et al.* 1998) or aspects of personality such as flexibility, or persistence (Thoburn, Murdoch and O'Brien 1986; Thoburn 1990; Howe 1996). Some (e.g. Nelson 1985) have found church membership and attendance to be associated with more successful adoption of older children.

Several quantitative studies (Fanshel and Shinn 1978; Barth and Berry 1988; McRoy 1991 in America; Grotevant *et al.* 1994; Grotevant and McRoy 1998; Thoburn 1991; Borland, Triseliotis and O'Hara 1990 in the UK) have found continuing parental contact to be either associated with lower disruption rates or a neutral factor in adoption or long-term foster care stability. Smaller scale studies differ in their conclusions about birth family contact. Rushton *et al.* (1995) found that in some cases parental visiting was associated with placement instability, but Berridge and Cleaver (1987) came to the opposite conclusion. The detailed interviews conducted by Ryburn (1994), Fratter (1996), McRoy (1991), Grotevant *et al.* (1994); Logan (1999) and Neil (1999a and 1999b) suggest that contact can help placement stability and contribute to the adopters' 'sense of entitlement'.

Most researchers have considered the possible impact on long-term outcomes of aspects of child placement **practice** and some have made tentative recommendations about how practice might be improved based on the opinions of adopters or young people. (See especially Thoburn *et* al. 1986; Quinton *et al.* 1998; Lowe *et al.* 1999; and Thomas and Beckford 1999). It is impossible to control statistically for the many different aspects of child placement in order to identify clearly which placement practices are associated with more successful outcomes. However, conclusions drawn from interviews list the following: workers being available when needed; well informed and honest about the particular needs of the child; supporting the family members to find their own way of doing things, and ensuring that a range of therapies (physical and emotional) is available to the children when they need them.

The opportunity to interview young people and their foster and adoptive parents twelve or more years after placement has allowed us to explore in this book some of these issues and add more data to what will always remain a very complex puzzle with many possible answers rather than a single solution.

## The literature on race and identity

The notion of a positive black identity emerged in British anti-racist social work during the 1980s and runs through the writing of Small (1986), Ahmad (1990), Association of Black Social Workers and Allied Professions (ABSWAP) (1983b) and Maximé (1986 and 1993). It may be summarised as consisting of positive identification of oneself as black and feeling pride in one's black roots and culture. Its importance in the child placement debate lies in the argument put forward by advocates of same race placements that a positive black identity is essential for black children in order that they can deal effectively with growing up in a racist society. This, they argue, is best done within black families, hence the necessity of same race placements. The theoretical underpinnings of this view derive from the work of American black psychologists on nigrescence, such as Cross (1971, 1980, 1991), Parham (1989) and Ponterotto (1989), which are summarised in the British social work literature by Robinson (1995, 1997). Failure to develop a positive black identity in the face of racism can lead to low self-esteem, identity confusion and ultimately self-hatred (Baldwin 1979). These arguments are supported by clinical studies (Maximé 1993) and by the Childline Study (MacLeod 1996) which describes the impact of racist bullying on black children:

> They felt hated and they felt despised. These feelings were exacerbated by the sense that the views embodied in the harassment were widely held. It is extremely difficult to maintain a sense of self-worth against such relentless persecution as the children have described. So it was not

surprising, though disquieting, to find that a number of youngsters described feelings of self-hatred and rejection of their colour or culture, and sometimes of their family or parents. These feelings brought their own shame. (MacLeod 1996, p.24)

The concept of a homogenous black identity has been criticised by Tizard and Phoenix (1993), Macey (1995), Katz (1996) and Owusu-Bempah and Howitt (1997) for being prescriptive and too simplistic. Modood (1988) has argued that 'when Asians are encouraged to think of themselves as black, [they]...have to define themselves in a framework that is historically and internationally developed by people in search of African roots'. (p.5)

Consequently, he argues, the political construction of 'black', whilst valuable for 'effecting a unity between very diverse, powerless minorities that is necessary for an effective anti-racist movement' has its limitations in failing to acknowledge the diversity of interests subsumed under it. The themes of diversity and difference are pursued by Katz (1996), who criticises ideas of 'black identity' as being rooted in a tradition that fails to take account of the reformulations of notions of racism and anti-racism and racial identity in the light of post-modernist developments. He cites Gilroy (1987, 1992, 1993), Brah (1992) and Rattansi (1992) as anti-racist thinkers and cultural theorists who see notions about 'the black family' and 'positive black identity' as essentialist and over-simplified. According to Katz these writers 'note that the relationship between race, culture, class and gender are complex and fractured rather than hierarchical. Racism too is seen as a more complex phenomenon '...rather than seeing a totalised, unitary institutional racism they see different racisms which are local, context bound and time limited. Anti-racism, they claim, must therefore address racism on a local and appropriate level' (Katz 1996, p.189). These notions, which have been circulating in the anti-racist debate in education, have had little impact in social work and still less in child placement, where their implications are only beginning to be worked out.

In a similar vein a recent anthropological study by Alexander (1996, p.188) draws on post-modernist perspectives to examine the creation of black British identities amongst two groups of young black adults in London. Her purpose is to describe in detail how these young adults lived out their black identities in various areas of their lives, such as home, work and leisure. Her focus is 'not to dwell excessively on the obvious structural constraints on black Britons, but on the ways in which in everyday experience these constraints are encountered'. She notes that her informants, chiefly young men aged between 18 and 24, were very aware of the collective images and stereotypes of 'the black community'. They were prepared to make use of these 'as a means of identification or distinction, fusion or fission, as the occasion required... The meanings and values attached to these images are fluid and constantly shifting' (pp.193–194). Alexander emphasises 'a degree of ambiguity (amongst her informants) around the creation of identities'. Indeed, one young man stressed to her 'You have to be able to adapt, or you're fucked' (p.194). At the same time the self-identities created had to be acknowledged by the group as appropriate. Alexander quotes Brah's (1992) description of identity formation as a kaleidoscope, as an appropriate metaphor. She acknowledges that her informants' behaviour, communal and individual, contained contradictions and concludes that:

> It would be both distorting and unfair to reduce the complexities of my informants' lives to the vagaries of theory ... In asserting their freedom to create their identities, the constraints must also be acknowledged ... My informants both eschewed essentialism and enacted it, constructed themselves and were constructed – sometimes at the same time. The dichotomous clarity of theory becomes inescapably blurred when related to lived experience... (Alexander 1996, p.195)

Such a view of black identity, as situational, relational and changing, leads one to expect that, especially when there is the added dimension of adoptive identity, black children and young people will respond in a variety of ways which may be contradictory and unpredictable.

Material from the *Fourth National Survey of Ethnic Minorities in Britain* (Modood *et al.* 1997, p.342) provides empirical evidence for changing patterns amongst and between British ethnic minority communities. In looking at the structural position of the various ethnic minorities within British society the survey argues that different minorities are very differently placed. Thus Pakistani and Bangladeshi communities 'are consistently at a disadvantage with respect to white people and often with respect to other minorities.' In terms of employment, unemployment, income levels, they are severely disadvantaged, and they tend to have the worst housing. 'People of Caribbean and Indian origin (excluding African Asians) are often found to experience disadvantage, though it is less serious for these groups than for Pakistanis and Bangladeshis.' By contrast 'Chinese people and African Asians have reached a position of broad parity with the white population – behind on some indicators perhaps, but ahead on others' so that 'it would not be appropriate to describe them as disadvantaged groups.' This brief summary suggests that it may be increasingly inappropriate to use the homogenous term 'Black' for all these ethnic minority communities, whilst recognising the evidence that it has provided a focus for the determination to challenge policies and practices which face disadvantaged black social service users, including children needing placement and their families.

Hutnik (1992, p.134) identified four strategies of ethnic self-identification, namely:

> **dissociative**, where individuals categorise themselves by their ethnic minority status and not by other ethnic majority; **assimilative**, where individuals categorise themselves by ethnic majority and deny their ethnic minority roots; **acculturative**, where individuals categorise themselves by both ethnic majority and minority status; **marginal**, where neither ethnic minority or majority status is used, but some other category e.g. job, leisure activity, etc.

When analysed in this way the answers of the survey's respondents showed that overall 30 per cent of respondents followed a dissociative strategy; 63 per cent followed an acculturative strategy, and 6 per cent an assimilative one. Only 1 per cent of all respondents followed a marginal strategy.

The research on the identity of children of mixed race parentage has taken place mainly outside the child placement literature but its relevance to child placement decisions has been emphasised by researchers such as Tizard and Phoenix (1993) and Katz (1996). These authors follow Wilson (1987) in arguing from their very different studies that children with one black and one white parent appear to develop a range of identities, which may include 'politicised black identity' or a sense of dual heritage/or bi-racialism (Tizard and Phoenix 1993). Wilson's study is concerned with children aged 6–9, that of Tizard and Phoenix with adolescents and Katz's study with young adults. All three studies report little evidence for identity confusion in their samples, but each has some bias in terms of sample. Wilson's sample of 39 families with 51 children was recruited through inter-racial support groups and is unlikely to have been representative. In Tizard and Phoenix's sample of 58 adolescents, 61 per cent came from social classes 1 and 2 and 55 per cent attended independent schools. Katz used a mixture of methods, all involving very small numbers. All three studies are concerned with children in birth families, and there are dangers in assuming that the findings can be transferred to children in substitute families. Their major point is that children of mixed racial parentage can and do develop positive views about themselves without necessarily developing a specifically black identity, and that this should be borne in mind when placement decisions have to be made. This view received some support from Banks (1995) who describes children of mixed race parentage as 'black' but argues that:

> white social workers tend to see mixed parentage children of both South
> Asian/white origin and African-Caribbean/white origin as closer to
> white society or to 'white self'. Likewise black social workers do not
> appear to have a full social acceptance of mixed parentage children as
> undoubtedly being a part of the central core of the black community.
> (Banks 1995, p.21)

Therefore, in Banks' view, 'the black community is not a homogenous group
and is not perceived as such' and 'assertions of blackness as being "all one" do
not exist when the "psychological reality" is separated from the "political
facade"'.

The *Fourth National Survey* (Modood *et al.* 1997, p.355) provides evidence
of increasing rates of intermarriage and cohabitation between the white
majority and members of the ethnic minority communities. Thus the survey
reports that 'for people born in Britain half of Caribbean men, a third of
Caribbean women and a fifth of Indian and African Asian men had a white
partner.' The survey recognises that 'this will have a direct effect, not only on
the life-styles of the men and women concerned, and also on their children
and on other members of that generation'. The survey notes that 'getting on
for half of 'Caribbean' children have one white parent' and since 'no-one has
studied mixed-origin adults in any detail...important questions will be
raised about the nature of Caribbean, and eventually Asian, identity.' These
findings are particularly important to child placement policy since an
important issue for debate has been ethnic self concept and esteem, and since
a high proportion of children of minority ethnic origin needing placement
are of mixed race parentage. On a practical note, the increase in mixed-origin
marriages and cohabitations could lead to more recruitment of mixed origin
substitute families.

## The literature on substitute family placement
## for children of minority ethnic origin

It is commonly accepted that black children were generally not regarded as
'suitable' for adoption or long-term family placement until the 1970s.
Braithwaite (1962) recalls that as a child care officer working for the London
County Council in the late 1950s, he had to fight for black children's right to
'a happy family life'. Interestingly, black families were not sought,
Braithwaite's assumption being that African-Caribbean children living in
Britain were considered to need white British families. The British Adoption
project was set up in 1965 and was the first significant attempt to place
children of African-Caribbean, Asian or mixed race parentage for adoption.
Most were placed with white families. The follow-up reports from this

project (Raynor 1970; Jackson 1976; and Gill and Jackson 1983) form a major element of the sparse British research literature on the placement of black children. The last of these, by Gill and Jackson (1983), is discussed below, since the debate prompted by its publication crystallised much of the argument on same-race and transracial placement.

The *Soul Kids* campaign of 1975 represented the first dedicated attempt to recruit families, from the black communities, with whom to place black children. It marked a major shift in British recruitment policy in that it made use of specially designed publicity material aimed at black families and had wide coverage on radio, television and in the ethnic minority press. Based in London, the campaign was influenced by Rowe and Lambert's (1973) findings that 26 per cent of children 'drifting' in residential care were black. Weise (1988) has argued that this study initially prompted an increase in transracial placements on the grounds that a white family was preferable to continued residential care, but it also served to raise the awareness of black professionals about black children within the child care system. Thus one black social worker cited in the ABAFA (1977) report of the *Soul Kids* campaign noted that:

> ...given the precarious state of race relations at the present time and the vulnerability of West Indian children growing up in care without a clear sense of the positive values of their origins and of how they can fit into a predominantly white society, a definite challenge emerges for those of like origin...particularly where they share the responsibility of planning for the care and development of these children.

Thus, unlike the British Adoption Project of a decade earlier, the *Soul Kids* campaign regarded a child's sense of racial identity as one of the more important factors in deciding on a home. The explicit reference to 'the precarious state of race relations' indicates the growing sense of the importance of the wider social context for child placement. Put another way it links professional activity and ultimately family life with wider socio-political currents. These links became more pronounced in the debates of the following decade. The campaign prompted 50 enquiries from members of the black communities, and nine families proceeded through the assessment process to approval. Its importance reached beyond the number of families recruited. As Brunton and Welch (1983) argued, it inspired social workers and local authorities in their efforts to recruit families of African-Caribbean and other minority ethnic groups. The creation of the New Black Families' Unit in Lambeth in 1980 (Arnold 1982) and its success in recruiting black families and placing children took this further and weakened arguments for transracial placements on the grounds of a lack of suitable black applicants. Success in recruiting families from black communities was not restricted to London. Gambe *et al.* (1992) quote figures from Sheffield Adoption Agency, which in 1979-80 placed 35 black children, of whom 25 were placed transracially and 10 with families of the same race. Between 1985 and 1988, 17 black children were placed, of whom two were placed transracially (in 1985) and the remaining 15 were placed in families of the same race. The authors comment that:

> ...at the time of writing, no black children were waiting. Hence, with commitment and belief in both themselves as professionals and the black community as carers, practitioners in Sheffield have managed successfully to tap the resources available within the black communities for black children in care. (Gambe *et al.* p.70)

Rhodes (1992) has pointed to two critical developments responsible for the success of the campaign towards same race placements, or in her terms 'racial matching'. The first, mentioned previously, was the New Black Families' Unit (see Arnold 1982; Arnold and James 1989), the second was the formation of the Association of Black Social Workers and Allied Professionals (ABSWAP 1983a) and its subsequent adoption of 'Black Children in Care' as its major theme for its inaugural conference in November 1983. ABSWAP drew heavily and explicitly on the example set by the National Association of Black Social Workers (NABSW) in America, which had expressed vehement opposition to transracial placements in the United States in the early 1970s, describing the practice 'as a form of genocide, in which the black community's most precious resource, its children, was being taken from it to satisfy the needs of childless white couples' (Rhodes 1992, p.20). In its submission to the House of Commons Social Services Select Committee's enquiry into children in care, ABSWAP stated its view unequivocally:

> Transracial placement as an aspect of current child care policy is in essence a microcosm of the oppression of black people in this society ... It is in essence a form of internal colonisation...a new form of slave trade (although) this time only black children are used. (ABSWAP 1983a, p.12)

The response of black workers associated with ABSWAP to the publication of Gill and Jackson's (1983) findings illustrates this link between political perspectives and professional practice. In this book, which formed the third report on the British Adoption Project, the authors found that the children placed with 36 white families were doing well at the age of 12 on measures of self-esteem, educational achievement and social skills, and there were no marked differences between them and the smaller number (8) who were placed with black families. However those placed transracially had little sense of a black identity and no contact with black communities. The authors concluded by arguing for black families for black children on the grounds that the black community needs to be given opportunities to preserve its dignity and promote its self-determination, rather than because black children need black families. Divine (1983) pointed out the danger that the measures of adoption success used in the study might lead to the conclusion that children did not need black families, since they were doing well on the measures cited:

> Having relegated ethnic identification to an irrelevance, which is the effect of not including it as one of the 'crucial' ingredients...in a 'successful' placement of a black child, one cannot turn around and argue, as an afterthought almost, about the 'dignity' and 'self-determination' of the black community and expect child care agencies and our communities to take it seriously. (Divine 1983, quoted in Rhodes 1992, p.18)

Indeed Divine describes the report as 'defective, hypocritical and patronising research'. The debate which followed was polemical and fierce, with proponents for transracial placements, such as Dale (1987), arguing that children were being psychologically damaged by being denied placements for political or ideological reasons. The proponents for same race placements argued that psychological and political concerns could not be separated either conceptually or in practice without damaging black children, hence the emphasis on the importance of a positive black identity (Maximé 1986, 1993; ABSWAP 1983a and b; Ahmed 1988), which is explored below. The pessimism of black writers was not borne out when the England and Wales Children Act 1989 concluded that a child's race, religion and culture should be given considerable weight when a decision was taken about placement and other services. This position has been slightly 'softened' but not changed by the most recent government circular on adoption (Department of Health 1998).

Apart from the British Adoption Project reports the only other major British research study specifically focusing on this issue comes from Bagley and Young (1979) and Bagley (1993a and b). Their work compares transracial placements for African-Caribbean children, including some of mixed race parentage, with a group of white children adopted by white families. At follow-up the children were 19 years of age. These studies report that in terms of developmental outcome the transracially placed children were doing as well as their white counterparts, with 90 per cent of the 19 year olds showing successful adjustment. In terms of identity, Bagley concluded that the transracially placed adoptees had no more identity problems than the white adoptees at the age of 19. However he did not report directly on ethnic identity. He noted that the transracially placed children had more black friends than their white counterparts but that both groups moved in predominantly white circles. His findings are thus similar to those of Gill and Jackson and also to those from the American literature on transracial placements (Simon and Altstein 1977, 1981, 1987; Ladner 1977; Silverman and Feigelman 1981; McRoy *et al.* 1982; Shireman and Johnson 1986; Barth and Berry 1988). Alexander and Curtis (1996) provide a comprehensive review of the American research for the special edition of *Journal of Black Psychology*. Their review is followed by critiques of researchers and practitioners taking a civil libertarian and anti-racist perspective.

McRoy *et al.* (1982) and Shireman and Johnson (1986) included a comparison group of black children placed in black families. McRoy *et al.* (1982) reported no differences in self-esteem between the two groups. They concluded that the racial identity of the transracially placed children was more positive for those children who were attending racially integrated schools and living in racially mixed communities. Shireman and Johnson (1986) reported that both transracially placed children and those in same race placements had similar rates of 'adequate adjustment' (78 per cent), but they noted that children in black families showed 'a rise in black preference' between four and eight years of age on the Clark Doll test. In their review of the transracial placement literature, Rushton and Minnis (1997) warn of the difficulties of interpreting the findings:

> Although the research appears to show convincingly that transracially placed children have similar developmental outcomes to other groups, there is a likelihood of selection bias. In several studies families were recruited at least partly through agencies specialising in transracial adoption. Also, in the prospective studies there has been a large loss to follow-up and it is possible that the outcomes of the 'lost' group are poorer than those followed up successfully. (Rushton and Minnis 1997, p.153)

It is striking that so far the bulk of the research has been about **transracially** placed black children, with little on black children in black families. This is particularly true of the British adoption literature in which, in all studies which do include black children placed with black families, the numbers are very small. In a study of long-term fostering outcomes for 166 children (which include 23 black children) Berridge and Cleaver (1987, p.67): 'would not conclude that the association between the racial characteristics of foster parents and children is paramount, although there was some tendency for mixed race children placed with white long-term foster parents to experience more breakdowns than one might expect'.

Barn (1993) noted, in a study of short as well as long-term placements in a single London Borough, that black children in black foster families were more likely to retain contact with their parents than those placed transracially, and that 'where there was no contact at all the majority of children and families were white'. This suggests that black families may be able to provide a more 'inclusive' style of parenting than white families (see Holman 1980 for an exploration of the concept of 'inclusive' and 'exclusive' foster care).

Rowe, Hundleby and Garnett (1989) include a chapter on over 1500 placements of children of minority ethnic origin in their survey of almost 10,000 placements of children in care. They found that adoption or long-term foster placement 'was planned for about ten per cent of mixed parentage children, but for hardly any children from the other black groups' (p.161). Although black children were over-represented in care, this difference was explained by the number of 'voluntary' short stay admissions of young African-Caribbean children. The authors found 'few differences in either placement patterns or outcomes for black children when compared with white children' (p.161). They did, however, note differences between the minority ethnic groups. African-Caribbean, African and Asian children were more likely to be placed with a sibling than was the case for white children or those of mixed race parentage. No data were collected on the foster parents so the authors are not able to contribute to the debate about the impact of the ethnicity of the carers on placement outcome.

In earlier reports of the outcomes for 1165 children placed from care which included 244 of the children on whom this book focuses (Thoburn 1991; Charles *et al.* 1992) (which we describe in more detail in Chapter 2), it was found that children born to two parents of minority ethnic origin were no more likely to experience placement breakdown than white children, but that those of mixed race parentage were more vulnerable to placement breakdown, a difference which was statistically significant when other variables were held constant. It was also noted that placement practice for children of mixed race parentage was more like that for white children in that both groups were less likely than those with two black parents to be placed with a sibling, to retain contact with birth parents, and to be placed as permanent foster children.

Butt and Mirza (1996), reviewing the research on social care and black communities, note that children of mixed race parentage are regularly placed with white families, and suggest that they have been regarded by placing agencies as 'white' rather than 'black'. Such a practice has been consistently attacked by advocates of 'black identity' (Maximé 1986, 1993; Banks 1992) on the grounds that children of mixed race parentage 'are regarded as black by society and eventually the majority of such children will identify with blacks, except in instances where reality and self-image have not merged' (Small 1986, pp.91–92). These authors therefore strongly argue that they should be placed with black families and that those children who fail to identify with black people are likely to encounter problems because of the disjuncture between (social) reality and (psychological) self-image. Maximé (1986) provides case studies of adolescents and young adults who experience such problems.

## Some important research questions

It can be seen from the review of the literature that the research on family placement for children leaves many gaps in our knowledge, and this is even more the case in respect of children of minority ethnic origin. All those who have undertaken research in this area have commented on the special ethical and methodological problems. The most comprehensive review of these difficulties of researching issues of race and ethnicity is an edited American volume (Stanfield and Dennis 1993). In an introductory chapter, Stanfield warns that:

> …the use of homogeneous and, I should add, reified terms such as *white*, and *black* buys into and indeed reproduces traditional racial stereotypes more than it facilitates adequate data collection and interpretation… Whether a social scientist examining racial and ethnic issues prefers quantitative or qualitative methodological approaches or a combination of both ('triangulation') there are daunting epistemological problems that he or she needs to think through. (Stanfield and Dennis 1993, pp.31–35)

He goes on to argue for the necessity of finding new ways of overcoming some of these problems by pouring 'new wine into new bottles through creating new ways of thinking and explaining a new world'.

In conducting this research we have encountered many problems and are only too aware of the gaps which remain in our understanding of the complexities of adoption and race. The modest aim of this book is to feed additional factual and subjective information into what must continue to be a crucially important debate about how best to meet the needs of this particularly vulnerable group of children who become separated from the families and communities into which they were born.

## Summary

In this chapter it has been noted that the literature on race, identity and child placement has been dominated by arguments surrounding transracial and same race placements and that empirical data, especially on same race placements are sparse. The opportunity was therefore taken to study in greater depth a group of children of minority ethnic origin who were part of a large cohort of children placed in permanent substitute families in the early 1980s.

The research and practice literature on the psychology of adoption was reviewed and the hypothesis introduced that adoptive parenting presents special challenges. The concepts of 'jeopardy' 'shared losses' and 'shared fate' are also explored since they provide analytical frameworks for this study.

There is a large and growing literature on race, identity and self esteem and the most relevant sources are noted. The concept of a homogeneous black identity has been called into question, most recently by a national survey of ethnic minorities in the UK. Of particular relevance to a study of children looked after by local authorities, amongst whom children of mixed race parentage appear to be over-represented, is the finding from the recent survey that there are increasing rates of intermarriage between the white majority and members of the ethnic minority communities.

The research on permanent family placement outcomes is briefly summarised. Around 20 per cent of all placements of children from local authority care disrupt within five years or before the young person reaches adulthood, and there is a strong association between age at placement and placement breakdown.

Most of the longer-term outcome research in the UK concerns children adopted transracially. On the most commonly used measure – breakdown rates – outcomes of permanent family placements of children with two parents of minority ethnic origin appear to be similar to those for white children, whether or not they are placed transracially or with families of the same race and culture. However, some studies find that children of mixed race parentage are more likely to experience placement breakdown. When measures of ethnic identity and racial pride are used, findings are more mixed, with a majority of the earlier studies finding that transracially placed children in their early to mid teens had little sense of their black identity and little contact with the communities into which they were born.

# CHAPTER 2

# The Background to the Study and the Methods Used

## The aims of the research

In the mid and late 1970s, influenced by the success of American adoption agencies in placing older children from care with permanent substitute families, several British voluntary adoption agencies changed the focus of their work. In part, this was a response to the dramatic fall in the numbers of babies placed 'voluntarily' for adoption. They had already started to place black infants who had earlier been regarded as unsuitable for adoption (Raynor 1970). The research by Rowe and Lambert (1973), which demonstrated that substantial numbers of older children (including disproportionate numbers of children of minority ethnic origin) were remaining for long periods in residential care, gave a further impetus to pioneering adoption workers to follow the example of their USA colleagues.

Twenty-four of the agencies who were most active in this work agreed in 1986 to provide basic information on all the 'special needs' children (a total of 1165) they had placed with adoptive or permanent foster families between 1980 and the end of 1984.

The aim of that study was to evaluate family placement for older children in care or for those considered 'hard-to-place' because of physical or learning disabilities or their particular complex biographies. The study is described by Thoburn (1991). At the start of that original study we debated whether to include infants of minority ethnic origin on the grounds that they were 'hard-to-place' because they needed a family of the same ethnic and cultural background, but were advised that local authorities and voluntary agencies were actively seeking to place these children with families of similar ethnic origin and that they should not be included in this 'special needs' cohort.

The research on which this book is based builds on the earlier survey of 1165 children in care who were older or had special needs as a result of early deprivation, abuse or disability.

Between October 1991 and May 1992 a file search was undertaken on the placements of the 244 children in the survey who were of minority ethnic origin. Since the focus of the new study was on race and culture (and not specifically on 'special needs' adoption), the sample was enlarged to 274 by the addition of 30 children who were under the age of three when placed by the same agencies during the same period. One or both parents of most of these young children were of African, African-Caribbean or South Asian ethnic origin but 15 children were included who were of other minority ethnic origin.

A study of the records on these 274 children undertaken in 1991–2 (Charles *et al.* 1992) provided descriptive material on the families with whom the children had been placed, and indicated that it was feasible to undertake a qualitative study involving interviews with some of the young people and their new parents some 10 to 15 years after they joined their new families.

The 24 agencies participating in the original survey who placed children of minority ethnic origin were contacted and 21 agreed to take part in a more detailed study by writing to those families whose addresses were still known to ask if they would be willing to be interviewed. Five agencies each placed more than 20 of the children (accounting for 149 placements – just over half of the cohort). At the other end of the spectrum three agencies placed fewer than five children of minority ethnic origin.

Using data from the file search and the intensive interview study, the aims of the research were:

- to provide a descriptive account of the children's lives in their new families, including information about being brought up in families of the same or a different race, culture, or religion

- to set this in the context of the earlier experiences of the children

- to offer an account of the experiences of the new parents and other members of their family

- to pay particular attention to the experience of the black parents and mixed partnerships, since these were under-represented in the studies of permanent new families available at the start of this project

- to learn about the parenting strategies adopted by the substitute parents of similar or different ethnic origin

- to describe the social work and other support services offered to the families
- to evaluate the placements using a range of outcome measures.

## The placement process

Before describing the children and families on whose stories this book is based, a brief account of the placement process is in order. The voluntary adoption agencies who, in the early 1980s, arranged the placement of the children in our study were, along with a small number of local authorities, the pioneers in the field of permanent family placement for children in care in the UK. They were greatly influenced by similar agencies in the USA, and met regularly to discuss the methods for recruiting and supporting new parents and preparing the children for placement. It was no surprise to find that the methods used by the agencies to place these particular children had much in common. The nature of the social work and placement practice is described in an earlier detailed study of one of the agencies (Thoburn *et al.* 1986). The methods used today have changed very little and have been taken on board by most local authority and voluntary agency adoption or 'permanence' teams (Lowe *et al.* 1999; Thomas and Beckford 1999; DH 1999).

Briefly, children who cannot return home to their birth families are identified through the system for reviewing plans for children in care as children for whom adoption or permanent fostering may be appropriate. An adoption or permanence panel reviews the plan in the light of information provided by the social worker, and, since the implementation of the Children Act 1989, must be given information about the wishes and feelings of the birth parents, children and anyone else who is close to the children such as grandparents or siblings, and must 'give due consideration' to them. This information is usually all provided on *Form E,* a schedule for collecting the required information about the child, the family and the reasons why adoption or permanent foster placement is considered appropriate. The panel also considers whether the needs of the child are such that an Adoption Allowance should be payable. The recommendations of the Panel are almost always accepted by the head of the local authority adoption agency. In a minority of cases the parents will have requested a placement for adoption, or will be in agreement with the plan, but most frequently one or both parents opposes the plan and the court is asked to dispense with parental consent, either before placement using 'freeing' procedures (Lowe *et al.* 1993) or in the course of a 'freeing' or adoption hearing after the child has been placed.

Once the plan for placement has been accepted by the agency and, if necessary, approved by the Court (in the post-1989 Act situation by the acceptance of a care plan which states that a permanent substitute family placement will be sought) the local authority social worker will start to prepare the child for placement. From this process, and from discussions with the birth parents, a profile will emerge about the sort of family which can best meet the child's long-term needs. Most often an adoptive family not previously known to the child is sought but sometimes it is decided that the child's needs can best be met by the placement with the short-term foster parents becoming an adoptive placement. Our present study does not include any of these adoptions by foster parents, which, not surprisingly since parents and children have already got to know each other, have a higher success rate than 'stranger' adoptions. In some cases the decision is taken that a permanent fostering placement rather than an adoptive placement should be sought or that the short-term foster parents with whom the child is already settled should be confirmed as 'permanent' foster parents (five of the placements in our study). (The picture is further complicated by the fact that, as we know from looking backwards, some placed for adoption are never adopted but remain with the family as permanent foster children and some children are adopted by foster parents even though the original plan was permanent fostering. In some cases the child leaves care because the foster parents successfully apply to the courts for a Residence Order (Custodianship Order in pre-Children Act 1989 language).

The profile of the family to be sought will also include information about whether it is proposed that there will be continuing contact (face-to-face or indirect) between the child and birth parents, birth relatives, siblings or previous foster carers. The preparation work with the child usually also results in a *life story book* which is often used to tell prospective new families more about the child before a meeting is arranged. The scene is then set for the matching of the child with new parents.

A range of methods is used to bring to the attention of potential adopters that there are children in care who need a new family. Individual children are also profiled on television, in newspaper features and special 'families needed' columns in the advertisements section, and in window displays of those agencies who have high street premises. The adoptive parents' group *Adoption UK* (then called *Parent to Parent Information on Adoption Services*) started to produce their newspaper giving details of adoptable children in the late 1970s and the *Be My Parent* book and the *Adoption Resource Exchange* were set up by the British Agencies for Adoption and Fostering (BAAF). After contacting the local authority or voluntary agency, those expressing an interest are usually invited to an 'information' meeting where they learn more about the sorts of children needing placement and about the process for approving families and matching them with children. Some approach the agency with a particular child in mind, perhaps one they read about in one of the photo-listing services or saw featured on a television programme. Most have a particular age group and type of child in mind. At this stage, those who say they wish to proceed complete a form giving basic information and checks are made with the police and health services. During the following period the prospective new parents will usually attend a series of group meetings at which they learn more from professionals and from adoptive or foster parents about the needs of the children for whom families are sought; a 'home study' will be undertaken by one or two of the agency's workers; a medical report will be obtained and two referees will be interviewed. The home study will involve a series of discussions with all members of the family, including any children already in the home and close relatives. The resulting report (usually on a form referred to as the *BAAF Form F*) will go to the adoption panel and a recommendation will be made to the head of the agency as to whether they should be approved as adopters or permanent foster parents. Very occasionally a family is approved to take a particular child only, who is already known to them, but most often the approval is linked with information about the age range, sex and needs of children who would best fit into their home. Once approved, the potential adopters are usually asked to prepare an album or video about their own family which can be shown to social workers looking for homes for children.

The matching process involves discussions between the child's worker and the workers for any families who appear, on paper, to be suitable, and visits by the child's worker to tell potential families more about the child and form their own impression on the less tangible aspects of the potential 'fit' or 'chemistry' of the proposed matching. The recommendations of the child's and the new parents' workers are taken to the adoption or permanence panel which recommends the match to the head of the adoption agency.

It is only at that stage that arrangements are made for the adopters and children to meet, though in some of the cases in our study a 'blind viewing' was arranged so that adopters could gain more information for themselves as to whether the child would fit into their family. (The use of video recordings has, in the main, replaced this practice.) It was then, and still is, very unusual for the adopters to meet the birth parents before a decision about matching is made, even when it is proposed that there will be continuing face-to-face contact. After a placement has been agreed and usually after the adopters have met the child, in the majority of cases now but a large minority at the time of our study, the adopters will meet the birth parents. Sometimes, if there is to be no further contact, a 'goodbye visit' will be arranged between the parent and the child.

From then on, the new parents gradually take over, a plan of introductory visits is arranged which will vary according to the age and any special needs of the child, and the child will move into his or her new home. Supervisory and supportive visits by the family placement team worker and the child's worker will continue until the adoption order is made. The child's progress is reviewed by the agency and finally by the courts. When children remain 'looked after' the social work and review process continues, although a different model of practice from that which applies in short-term foster care is usually followed, which delegates to the substitute parents as much parental responsibility as legislation allows. In all the cases in this research, the foster parents, or those adopters whose children were initially placed under foster care arrangements, were firmly 'in the driving seat', seeking social work assistance when needed and answerable for the child's welfare through the reviewing system.

## Research methods

### The extensive and interview samples

In the first phase (1991–1992) more detailed information was collected from the records than was available for the full cohort. We specifically focused on issues of race, ethnicity and culture which were identified at the time of placement and on any recorded accounts of the work undertaken after placement. Some families were known to have moved, and new addresses were not known. There was further loss from the sample because, in consultation with agency workers, it was decided that no attempt would be made to contact some of the families. These included cases in which, for example, it was known that the child had died, or the child had left the home within two years of the placement. Unless it was considered inappropriate, placements which lasted for at least two years but subsequently disrupted were included. A small number of letters was returned 'Not known at this address', and it is not clear how many of the letters actually reached the families.

Thirty-six responded in some way – just under a quarter of those who were written to. Seven of the 12 who responded but did not wish to be interviewed gave reasons for this, and also gave more recent information about the outcome for the children. Their responses included some very sad as well as some more encouraging information. Of those who responded 24 parents of 29 children from the original cohort agreed to take part.

The research design sought to include in the interview sample roughly equal numbers in four groups:

*GROUP 1* – CHILDREN BOTH OF WHOSE PARENTS WERE OF MINORITY ETHNIC ORIGIN PLACED WITH PARENTS AT LEAST ONE OF WHOM WAS OF MINORITY ETHNIC ORIGIN.

*GROUP 2* – CHILDREN OF MIXED RACE PARENTAGE PLACED WITH PARENTS AT LEAST ONE OF WHOM WAS OF MINORITY ETHNIC ORIGIN.

*GROUP 3* – CHILDREN BOTH OF WHOSE PARENTS WERE OF MINORITY ETHNIC ORIGIN PLACED WITH WHITE FAMILIES.

*GROUP 4* – CHILDREN WITH ONE WHITE PARENT AND ONE PARENT OF OTHER ETHNIC ORIGIN PLACED WITH FAMILIES WHERE BOTH PARENTS WERE WHITE.

(New families where the single parent or both parents were black, and mixed partnerships, were grouped together because there were too few cases for separate analysis where a child, both of whose parents were black, was placed with a mixed partnership, or children of mixed parentage placed with two black parents).

There was a larger response from Groups 3 and 4, and a decision was taken to leave out some of the children with severe learning disabilities who would be unable to give their views. However, some children with severe disabilities **were** included so that the views of the families of these children with very special needs could be represented.

It soon became apparent that children in Groups 1 and 2 would be under-represented unless the sample were broadened. The original agencies were asked if they would approach black families with whom children had been placed just before or just after the 1980–1984 initial period, and this resulted in a further seven children from four families being included. These children were included in the statistical analysis, to give a sample of 281 placements made by agencies taking part in the earlier survey.

It was also decided to ask a London borough which was known to have made 'same race' placements in the early 1980s to contact families on behalf of the researchers. As a result of this approach 16 children from 10 families where at least one of the adoptive or foster parents was of African, African–Caribbean or Asian origin were recruited to the intensive interview sample. Thus the full sample is of 297 placements. Figure 2.1 gives the ethnic origin of the children and show that the majority were of mixed race parentage.

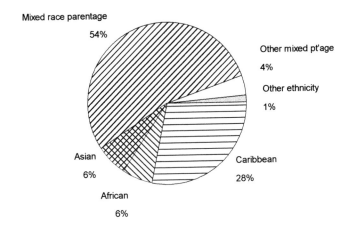

n = 297

*Figure 2.1 Ethnic origin of children*

Tables 2.1 and 2.2 give details of the background cohort and the intensive sample.

| Table 2.1 Background cohort | |
|---|---|
| Number of voluntary adoption agencies | 21 |
| Number of placements of white children* | 922 |
| Number of placements of children of minority ethnic origin* | 281 |
| Number of additional placements made by local authority | 16 |
| *Total placements* | *1,219* |

*There were slightly more **placements** than **children** since a small number of children was re-placed after a disrupted placement during the data collection phase of the original study (see Thoburn 1991 for more detailed information).

### Table 2.2 The intensive interview sample

|  | Children | Families* | Children interviewed |
|---|---|---|---|
| From original cohort | 27 | 21 | 15 |
| Added for this study from same agencies | 8 | 7 | 6 |
| London borough | 16 | 10 | 3 |
| Total | 51 | 38 | 24 |

* There were 8 families with whom 2 children were placed (not necessarily birth siblings) and 2 families with whom 3 children were placed.

This cohort of 297 placements is unusual in that all the families were approached by the researchers rather than volunteering in response to an advertisement or using a post-adoption service. Also it comprises a fairly large group of children of minority ethnic origin placed with substitute families from across the UK. Its weaknesses are that, for the full cohort, data were drawn from a file search only and on some important variables were not available for some cases. Further, it must be acknowledged that practice has moved on since the early 1980s when the children were placed, especially in respect of birth family contact, and the more consistent, knowledgeable and skilled attempt to place children with families of similar ethnic, cultural and religious backgrounds.

The interview study was undertaken in order to learn more from the adoptive and foster parents and the young people about their experiences of substitute family placement, and also, albeit for a smaller number of cases in a non-random, stratified sample, to come to more broadly-based conclusions about outcome than was possible with the original survey, which relied solely on whether the placement lasted or broke down.

Although still not entirely 'self-selected' in that **all** families in the original survey were **invited** to take part, it cannot be claimed that those in the intensive interview sample are representative of the full cohort. In particular, cases where the placement broke down are under-represented.

*The interview sample in more detail*

The data from the files of the 297 children were supplemented and enriched by information from interviews concerning 51 children placed with 38 families. At the time of interview, 14 of the young people were aged between 11 and 17; 18 were between 18 and 22 and 19 were between 23 and 30. At least one adoptive or foster parent in each family was interviewed, as were 24 of the young people. Over half were aged 21 or over. Researchers also met some of the young people whose disabilities were too severe for them to be interviewed, or who still lived at home but declined the invitation to be interviewed separately. Sixteen of the 51 were young people, both of whose parents were of minority ethnic origin who were placed with 11 families with at least one parent of a similar racial background (Group 1). Thirteen were children of mixed race parentage placed with nine families where at least one parent was black (Group 2). Eleven children with two black parents and 11 children of mixed ethnicity were placed with 18 families where both parents were white, (Groups 3 and 4).

A guided interview schedule was used which included checklists compiled from findings and hypotheses taken from earlier studies. Where checklists were used, an open question was first asked to elicit the opinions of the interviewees without prompting from the researchers. The checklists were then introduced as a way of ensuring that a possible response had not been omitted merely as an oversight. Areas covered by checklists included reasons for adopting and fostering; attitudes towards the birth family and types of contact; attitudes towards other members of the new family; attitudes towards social workers and other services.

Standardised scales were used with the young people. The Coopersmith Self-esteem inventories (Coopersmith 1981) were completed by 21 of the young people and responses checked and a commentary provided by a clinical psychologist. For the teenagers the Kovacs and Beck depression inventory (Kovacs and Beck 1977) was used and the young adults completed a 'malaise' check list devised by Rutter and colleagues (Rutter, Tizard and Whitmore 1981). The small number who had already established their own families also completed Gibbons' family problem checklist (Gibbons, Thorpe and Wilkinson 1990). The Rutter 'A' children's behaviour scale (Rutter *et al.* 1981) was used with the parents of the younger children, and also as a guide when talking to those whose sons or daughters were now adults about behaviour problems encountered as the children grew up. These scales contributed to the 'research ratings' of the different outcome measures.

All interviews were tape recorded, listened to again by the researcher, and partially transcribed and coded using themes and issues identified after listening to the interviews. A check on researcher reliability on interview data selection for transcription was made by a second researcher listening to a random sample of a quarter of the tapes.

## An overview of 297 placements

Most of the children were placed with adoptive families, but 29 per cent were placed as foster children, though in all except five of the placements made by the London borough (with three families), the clear intention was that this was to be a 'family for life' placement.

The majority of the children (71 per cent) were placed with white families, and this applied especially to those of mixed race parentage – this difference being statistically significant. A total of 19 per cent were placed with a single parent or two parents of minority ethnic origin and 9 per cent joined mixed partnership families in which one parent was white (Figure 2.2). It was more likely that the younger children would be placed transracially, or with mixed partnerships – an important point when we consider breakdown rates and other outcome measures since it is now well established (see especially Fratter *et al.* 1991) that children who are placed when older are likely to have less positive outcomes (Table 2.3).

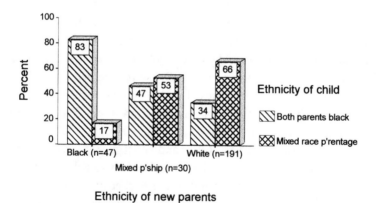

$\chi^2$: 32.76; df: 2; p<0.0001

n = 268  missing data = 29

*Figure 2.2 Ethnicity of new family by ethnicity of child*

### Table 2.3 Age of child at placement by ethnicity of new parents

| Ethnicity of new parents | Age of child | | | | | | | |
|---|---|---|---|---|---|---|---|---|
| | 0–4 | | 5–8 | | 9+ | | Total | |
| | n | per cent | n | per cent | n | per cent | n | per cent |
| Both parents of minority ethnic origin | 7 | 15 | 14 | 30 | 26 | 55 | 47 | 100 |
| Mixed partnership | 14 | 47 | 10 | 33 | 6 | 20 | 30 | 100 |
| Both parents white | 78 | 41 | 48 | 25 | 64 | 34 | 190 | 100 |
| Total | 99 | 37 | 72 | 27 | 96 | 36 | 267 | 100 |

missing = 30
not significant $\chi^2$ 15.8    df:4    p . < .07

This table shows that in the early to mid-1980s the majority of black children were placed with white families, although some agencies were making concerted efforts to recruit black families. We concluded in an earlier article (Charles *et al.* 1992) that the division of placements into 'trans-racial' and 'same-race' was unhelpful in that it implied a better 'matching' of children to families than was in fact the case. For subsequent analysis each placement was allocated to one of the categories in Table 2.4.

### Table 2.4 'Matching' of child with new family

| | n | per cent |
|---|---|---|
| Ethnically and culturally similar family | 52 | 19 |
| Ethnically similar/culturally different | 8 | 3 |
| Culturally similar/ethnically different | 1 | 0.5 |
| One of new parents of similar ethnic and cultural background | 13 | 5 |
| Both parents white British or Irish | 141 | 52 |
| Ethnically and culturally dissimilar but with good contact with child's culture* | 4 | 2 |
| Ethnically and culturally dissimilar but with other children already in placement of same ethnicity as child* | 50 | 19 |
| Total | 269 | 100 |

missing = 28
* Includes 5 families in which at least one parent was of minority ethnic origin but ethnically and culturally different from the child's.

It was more likely that children both of whose parents were of South Asian, African or Caribbean descent would be placed with families of similar racial and cultural origin than was the case for the other groups. This was especially so for those of South Asian origin. However, 6 of the 13 children of African descent were placed with a family where the mother was of African-Caribbean origin and in only one case was she of African origin. None of the new fathers of the African children was of African origin, 2 being Caribbean and 11 white.

Children both of whose parents were of minority ethnic origin were more likely to be placed in permanent foster homes; to be placed with a sibling; and to retain contact with a birth parent, relative or sibling than was the case with the white children. In these respects the pattern of placements for children with one white and one black parent was more like that for the white children. Table 2.5 gives some comparisons between the white children in the cohort of 1165 placements and the children of minority ethnic origin.

| Table 2.5 Some comparisons between the white children and those of minority ethnic origin in the total cohort | | | | |
|---|---|---|---|---|
| | *White children* | *Children with one black parent* | *Children with two black parents* | *Significance* |
| | *per cent* | *per cent* | *per cent* | |
| Aged 11 + at placement | 24 | 18 | 32 | p<0.001 |
| Aged <4 at placement | 14 | 29 | 12 | p.<0.0001 |
| Placed with sibling | 40 | 27 | 46 | p<0.01 |
| Had contact after placement with birth parent | 15 | 16 | 37 | p<0.0001 |
| Had contact after placement with a relative or sibling but not birth parent | 13 | 10 | 8 | ns |
| Placed as a permanent foster child | 16 | 17 | 42 | p.<0.0001 |
| Placed child was a boy | 59 | 64 | 64 | ns |

ns = not significant

The amount of factual detail on the files varied considerably, but information about wishes, feelings and attitudes (for example on ethnicity, racism, the nature of adoptive parenting, parental maltreatment and contact between children and members of the birth family after placement) was extremely sketchy or missing on the majority of these forms. A minority gave a detailed picture including information about attitudes and aspirations, but most were inadequate for our purposes as researchers and even more so as the basis for judgements about such crucial questions as whether a family should have a vulnerable child placed with them; or whether particular birth parents and children should have their links with each other permanently severed. No doubt other information was contained on social workers' records of interviews and verbal accounts to the adoption panels would have supplemented what was on the forms. However, this was a surprising and disturbing find, since both research and practice wisdom have stressed that the attitude of the child to placement, and the values and attitudes of the substitute parents (especially towards child maltreatment and the nature of adoptive parenthood) are of crucial importance if the placement is to meet the child's long-term needs.

## Summary

The study builds on an earlier survey of 1165 children in care who were aged three or over at placement or had special needs as a result of early privation, deprivation or maltreatment and were placed with substitute foster or adoptive families. In order to increase the number of children in the intensive interview sample placed with families of minority ethnic origin, eight children who were placed by the same agencies with seven black families in 1979 or 1985–86 were added, as were 16 children placed with 10 black families during the same period by a London borough.

The total cohort is therefore 297 placements made with 268 families by 21 voluntary agencies and one London borough between 1979 and 1987. All the children would have been placed at least ten years before the outcomes were considered, and for a substantial proportion information is available 15 years after placement.

- At the time of the study the young people were aged between 10 and 30, with around three quarters being over the age of 18.
- Just under a third of the 297 children were placed as foster children though, in all except five of these (placements with three families made by the London borough initially as 'temporary'

foster placements), the hope at the time of placement was that these would be 'families for life'.

- Most of the children (71 per cent) were placed with white families. Children of mixed race parentage were more likely to be placed transracially (84 per cent compared with 55 per cent with two black parents – a difference which is statistically significant).

- Important differences between the white children in the full survey, those with both parents of minority ethnic origin and those of mixed race parentage were noted. More of those with two black parents were aged 11 or over at placement; had continuing contact with a birth parent after placement and were placed as permanent foster children. Those with two black or two white parents were more likely, than those of mixed race parentage, to be placed with a full or half sibling. Those of mixed race parentage were more likely, than those with two black or two white parents, to be placed when under the age of four.

# CHAPTER 3

# The Stories Behind
# the Placements

## The birth parents

The information on file about the birth mothers, and even more so about the birth fathers, was limited. For the 51 interview sample cases we were able to supplement the information gleaned from the file search from parents and young people. Information about birth fathers was also limited by the fact that 61 were said to be unaware of the child's birth, and six denied paternity. Just under half (95) were recorded as being aware of the children's existence but were said to play little or no part in their lives and only 49 (just under a quarter of those about whom this information was available) had played an active part or taken an active interest in the children's lives.

The major sources of information about the birth parents were the reports prepared by the social workers for the adoption panel or the court. Both of these are written by social workers whose aim is to convey to the adoption panel or the court the reasons why the writer considers that adoption is in the child's best interests. It is therefore hardly surprising, though nonetheless disturbing, that these documents contained little that was positive and much that was negative or even offensive about the birth parents. If the reports read were representative of the generality of such reports (and there is no reason to believe that they were not) this is especially problematic since these documents are often shown to the adopters (often without the consent of the birth parents, especially if they are opposing the placement and without them having the opportunity of checking their accuracy).

An adoptive parent commented:

> I don't think the father had much of a say [about placement]

and was critical of the way in which fathers living away from the family home tended to be left out of planning for the child. Others regretted the lack of information about the birth father. This led to difficulties when they wanted to help the child with issues of racial identity, especially if, as was most often the case, the father of a child of mixed parentage was black. In other cases the birth mother had refused to give information about the birth father. In one case even his ethnic origin was not known, although it was assumed he was of South Asian descent.

> We know nothing about the birth father. She [Asian birth mother] wouldn't say anything at all about him to the social worker.

There was a tendency, in these circumstances, for the young person to invent a father who was most often imagined in a positive light.

> There is a statement in my file where my mother says social services would be better carers for the children as she has certain things to do with her life. With regard to my father, I have the notion that when I meet him I will get on with him very well.

There were indications from the interviews that, for some birth mothers, the child's mixed ethnicity was one reason for placing him or her for adoption. It was not clear whether this was the result of pressure from relatives or racism, but it was interpreted as racism by some African-Caribbean adoptive of foster parents.

> From what we know, it seems that if Darren had been white, she probably would have kept him, but he was black and that was unacceptable.

Half of the birth mothers and (in the 65 per cent of cases where this information was recorded) 45 per cent of the fathers were unmarried. About one in five of the mothers and the fathers were separated or divorced and two mothers were widowed. Just over a quarter of the mothers and a third of the fathers were married or cohabiting. Only 40 per cent of the mothers were employed. Most were in unskilled occupations but ten held professional posts. Of the cases where this information was recorded, one in five of the fathers was in a professional occupation; two in five were unemployed and two in five in unskilled manual occupations.

Table 3.1 shows the ethnic origin of the birth and new parents of the whole group and the children.

In most statistical and population data it is not possible to know whether those recorded as 'mixed parentage' are of South Asian, African-Caribbean or other descent. There were 97 cases where we did not have data on the ethnic origin of either parent or (most often) where we had data on one parent but not on the other. Table 3.2 therefore gives the information on only 203 children but shows that 67 of the children of mixed race parentage were of Caribbean descent, 12 of African descent, and 22 of South Asian descent.

Although most mixed partnerships involved one white parent (most often the mother) the parents of 12 of the children were of different ethnic origin, most frequently with one or both parents being of mixed race parentage (10 children). One child had one mixed parentage and one African parent, and one child had a Caribbean mother and South Asian father. This complexity lends weight to our note of caution about the inappropriateness of reducing the issue of placement to a simple same race/transracial dichotomy.

## Table 3.1 Ethnic origin of birth parents, child and new families

| | Birth mother | | Birth father | | Child | | Adoptive mother | | Adoptive father | |
|---|---|---|---|---|---|---|---|---|---|---|
| | n | per cent | n | per cent | n | per cent | n | per cent | n | per cent |
| Caribbean | 94 | 36 | 136 | 55 | 84 | 28 | 51 | 19 | 31 | 12 |
| African | 7 | 6.5 | 29 | 12 | 18 | 6 | 2 | 1 | 0 | 0 |
| South Asian | 16 | 6 | 39 | 16 | 19 | 7 | 8 | 3 | 9 | 4 |
| Other ethnic group | 6 | 2 | 11 | 4 | 4 | 1 | 2 | 1 | 2 | 1 |
| Mixed race parentage | 20 | 8 | 10 | 4 | 160 | 54 | 4 | 1.5 | 5 | 2 |
| Other mixed parentage | 1 | 0.5 | 0 | 0 | 12 | 4 | 1 | 0.5 | 1 | 0.5 |
| White European | 108 | 41 | 21 | 9 | 0 | 0 | 199 | 74 | 199 | 80.5 |
| Total | 262 | 100 | 246 | 100 | 297 | 100 | 267 | 100 | 247 | 100 |
| Missing | 35 | | 51 | | 0 | | 30 | | 40 | |

The religion of the birth parents is given in Table 3.3. There was no information on file as to the wishes of the birth mother in respect of religious upbringing for the child in half of the cases and this was so in respect of three quarters of the birth fathers. In most cases it was stated that the parents had expressed no wish about religious upbringing. Only 14 mothers and 4 fathers are recorded as having expressed a wish that the child should be brought up in their own religion, with 9 mothers and 2 fathers wishing the child to have a religious upbringing of any faith and 6 mothers specifically requesting that the child be not brought up in their own faith. The discrepancy between the religious affiliations of the birth parents and the adopters indicates that a significant minority of the children will have been brought up in a faith other than that of their parents.

| Table 3.2 Ethnicity of family of origin | | |
|---|---|---|
| | *n* | *per cent* |
| Both parents Caribbean | 84 | 35 |
| Both parents South Asian | 19 | 8 |
| Both parents African | 18 | 7 |
| Caribbean father/mother mixed race parentage | 4 | 2 |
| African father/mother mixed race parentage | 1 | 0.5 |
| South Asian father/Caribbean mother | 1 | 0.5 |
| South Asian father/mother of mixed race parentage | 2 | 1 |
| Father of mixed race parentage/Caribbean mother | 2 | 1 |
| Father and mother of mixed race parentage | 2 | 1 |
| Father white/mother Caribbean | 9 | 4 |
| Father white/mother African | 1 | 0.5 |
| Father white/mother mixed race parentage | 7 | 3 |
| Father Caribbean/mother white | 51 | 21 |
| Father African/mother white | 10 | 4 |
| Father Asian/mother white | 20 | 8 |
| Father of mixed race parentage/mother white | 7 | 3 |
| Father white/mother other ethnicity | 3 | 1 |
| *Total* | *241* | *100* |

This total is lower than for other tables since full data on ethnicity was not available for a substantial number of the parents

| | Birth mother | | Birth father | | Adoptive mother | | Adoptive father | |
|---|---|---|---|---|---|---|---|---|
| | n | per cent | n | per cent | n | per cent | n | per cent |
| Roman Catholic | 48 | 26 | 9 | 7 | 31 | 14 | 34 | 17 |
| Anglican | 48 | 26 | 11 | 8 | 109 | 50 | 98 | 48 |
| Jewish | 1 | 0.5 | 1 | 0.5 | 3 | 1 | 2 | 1 |
| Hindu | 3 | 2 | 6 | 4.5 | 0 | 0 | 0 | 0 |
| Moslem | 10 | 5 | 20 | 15 | 6 | 3 | 6 | 3 |
| Sikh | 3 | 2 | 6 | 4.5 | 0 | 0 | 1 | 0.5 |
| Rastafarian | 2 | 1 | 3 | 2 | 0 | 0 | 0 | 0 |
| Other Christian | 18 | 9.5 | 6 | 5 | 48 | 22 | 39 | 19 |
| Other | 2 | 1 | 1 | 0.5 | 8 | 4 | 6 | 3 |
| None | 53 | 28 | 70 | 53 | 14 | 6 | 17 | 8 |
| Total | 188 | 100 | 133 | 100 | 219 | 100 | 203 | 100 |
| Missing | 109 | | 164 | | 78 | | 94 | |

Table 3.3 Religion

## Attitudes to placement

Surprisingly, information was not available on the attitude of the birth mother to the placement plan in respect of half of the placements. Where it was available, just over half the mothers were said to be in agreement with the placement plan; a third to oppose it, and ten were unaware of it. Information on the attitudes of the birth fathers was rarely available. When it was, 30 per cent supported the plan; 40 per cent opposed it and 30 per cent were unaware or said to have expressed no opinion. Thirty-one birth mothers and 19 birth fathers were recorded as wanting the child to return to their care.

Where their attitudes to the placements were known, seven of the eight birth mothers who were of South Asian origin were in agreement with the long-term plan compared with only 18 of the 40 African-Caribbean mothers, three of the seven African mothers, four of the eight mothers of mixed race parentage and six of the 27 white birth mothers.

Whilst some adoptive or foster parents had a generally negative view of birth parents, or knew little about them, others had a more realistic picture of their strengths and difficulties. Delroy was placed with foster parents at the age of 14, initially as a temporary placement but with a decision subsequently taken that the placement should last for as long as it met his needs. His foster mother said:

> Delroy loved his mother and his half sister. They got on very well. And I think his behaviour was a result of the life he had with his natural mother. I don't think she did this deliberately, it was because of his step father. It was because of his attitude that she had to put him in care. He never said he wanted to return to his mother. However, he talked a lot about his grandmother who lived in Jamaica. Delroy was born here but he was sent to Jamaica with a brother to live with his grandmother for several years. He returned to England when he was about twelve.

### Birth parents' expressed wishes on the ethnicity of new parents

Information was also sought from the file about the birth parents' wishes as to the ethnic background of the family with whom the child was to be placed. This information was not available in respect of almost two-thirds of the mothers and over three-quarters of the fathers. A quarter of the mothers whose wishes were recorded were said to have no preference as to ethnicity of the new family; 24 wanted the new parents to be of a similar ethnic origin and four specifically asked that the child should not be placed in a family of the same or similar ethnic background. We learned very little from the new families or the young people themselves about the wishes of their birth parents in respect of the ethnic background of the new parents

Here again the views expressed tended to be negative unless there was actual contact with the birth family.

> I was told because I did not meet his biological parents, that his mother did not want him to be adopted because she thought he would go to a white family. However, when she found out that we were from Jamaica, she didn't want that either. But I think that was an excuse.

Paulette was of Caribbean descent and was placed at the age of eight with a single mother who worked in one of the caring professions. She was insistent that contact with the birth family should be retained even though at times Paulette was less than thrilled at this idea.

> I think she [the birth mother] felt a lot better because she thought I was rich. Paulette found it difficult to cope with sometimes. As a child she needed us to be enemies and couldn't cope with us as friends. I met her

father after she was placed. He was relieved that she was settled and that she had been placed with a fellow Barbadian.

## Difficulties leading to placement

There was considerable detail in the records about the problems which had led to the children being placed with substitute parents, and we gained additional information from some of the adoptive or foster parents and the young people. At one extreme, the foster mother told us that her foster son had no contact with his biological father because, as she later learned, he had killed somebody in a fight some years before the young person joined her family. She maintained that her foster son would not have known about this incident because it happened before he was born. Learning disability and mental health problems figured in the lives of many of the birth families. The adoptive parents were mostly sympathetic towards families with difficulties.

> If he didn't have the problems he had [mental health] he would have been a good father. The children spoke well of him.

Others were less sympathetic

> I actually don't feel anything in particular towards her birth mother. I don't feel anything towards her not unless the issue is physically brought up, she does not cross my mind, and when I do there is a feeling of dislike, because I feel that she did not protect her daughter. The feelings are of negative indifference rather than anything else.

The reasons why the young people had first entered the care system did not figure greatly in our research interviews. One teenager spoke sadly of his memories:

> My brother and I were picked up by the police. I only saw my mother once more after that. She must have been very upset. I know very little about it all, but I do realise that my real mum was not coping very well with life. I only saw my brother a couple of times after that because we went to different foster homes.

Finally, we looked in the records for specific information as to whether the birth mother and birth father had expressed a wish to retain contact with their child after placement with a new family. This information was not recorded in respect of 46 per cent of the mothers and 78 per cent of the fathers. Where it was recorded, two thirds of the mothers wished to have contact with the child after placement. Five mothers wanted the child to keep in contact with siblings placed elsewhere but not themselves. Sixty-four per cent of the 63 fathers about whom this information was recorded wished to retain contact with their children after placement. Although contact had been formally terminated in less than 10 per cent of cases, there was good contact for only 12 per cent of the mothers and 8 per cent of the fathers during the period leading to the placement decision. Figure 3.1 shows that the mothers of children of mixed race parentage were less likely than those of the children with two parents of minority ethnic origin to be in touch with their children immediately prior to placement.

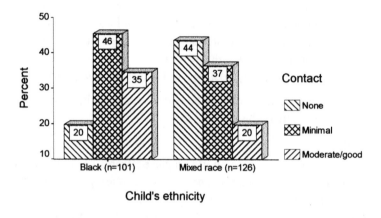

$\chi^2$: 15.43; df: 2; p<0.0001

n = 227  missing data = 70

*Figure 3.1 Child's ethnicity by pre-placement contact with birth mother*

One or both parents were known to have had face-to-face contact with the child in the early years after placement in 34 per cent of the placements. As we have already shown in Table 2.5, children with two black parents were far more likely to retain contact with parents than was the case for white children or those of mixed ethnicity. Those who had contact with parents usually had contact with siblings either still at home or placed elsewhere, and with other relatives. It seems likely that the extent of contact with birth parents at any time after placement is underestimated. A substantial number of the children in the interview sample restarted contact with members of the birth family in the later stages of their placements or when they moved into independent living as teenagers, and it is likely that this happened in other cases in the full cohort about which we had less information.

## The characteristics of the children

Sixty-two per cent of the 297 placements were of boys and 38 per cent were of girls. However, there were differences within the different ethnic groups, with only 40 per cent of the South Asian children being boys.

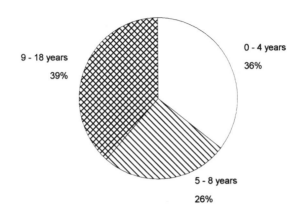

n= 297

*Figure 3.2 Age of children at time of placement*

Figure 3.2 gives the ages of the children at the time of placement and shows a very broad spread of ages. The age bands (0–4; 5–8 and 9 and over) are chosen because, from earlier studies, they include children who present similar ranges of difficulties or rewards to the substitute parents, and breakdown rates within these groups are broadly similar. It has been established by several studies (including the larger study from which this cohort is taken) that around one in five placements of children with special needs will break down within a five year period, and that break-down rates increase with age at placement, with the average break-down rate of one in five being found for children placed at the age of eight. Thirty-five per cent were in the under five's group and 39 percent were placed when aged nine or older.

Figure 3.3 shows that children of mixed race parentage were significantly more likely to be in the youngest age group.

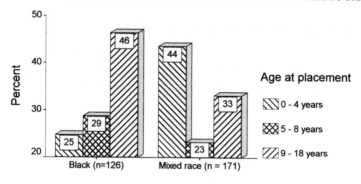

$\chi^2$: 7.38; df: 1; p<0.01

n = 297

*Figure 3.3 Ethnicity of child by age at placement*

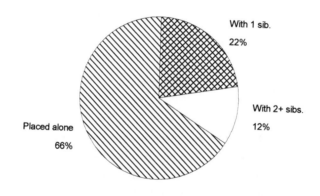

n = 297

*Figure 3.4 Placement with siblings*

Figure 3.4 gives details on the placement of siblings. In the original cohort of 1165 placements (Thoburn 1991), it did not prove possible to ascertain whether the children being placed alone did or did not have siblings from whom they had been separated. This weakness is unfortunately carried through into this study, although it has been estimated that around 80 per cent of children who are looked after within the care system will have siblings. They may not have had any contact with some of these (more usually half-siblings) who were born after they were placed or who left the family home before they were born. Several of the children in our intensive sample did, as young adults, come to know these younger or older siblings. It is clear from the fact that 66 per cent were placed alone that a not inconsiderable proportion will have been separated from one or more siblings along the way. This was something about which the young people in our interview sample commented, usually with regret. Children placed alone were over- represented in the interview sample with three quarters of them being placed alone in the adoptive or foster family, although their new siblings within this family may well themselves have been adopted or fostered. Children both of whose parents were of minority ethnic origin were significantly more likely to be placed with a sibling (43 per cent) than those of mixed race parentage, only 27 per cent of whom were placed with a sibling (p<0.01).

Turning to culture and religion, the files recorded that in some cases religion at the time of birth had changed by the time the child was placed. For 123 children at the time of birth and 114 at the time of placement the child was said to have no religion or, if an infant, no religion specified by a parent. Whilst there was no change in the numbers where 'Roman Catholic' was recorded as the religion of the child, the number where 'Hindu' was recorded had gone down from three to one; 'Moslem' from ten to four; 'Sikh' from four to one, whilst the 'Anglican' and 'other Christian' groups had increased. (It should be noted that no information on the child's religion was recorded on a third of the files even though this information is specifically asked for on several adoption service forms. The most frequently recorded religion was 'none'.) Least information was available about the religion of the birth fathers but it appears from the data available that children of Moslem, Sikh or Hindu fathers were least likely to be brought up by parents who were of the same religion as their birth fathers. This was perhaps not unexpected since several of the children of mixed parentage were living with their white mothers at the time they came into care and some had never lived with their fathers nor had contact with them.

With the older children it might be anticipated that there would be information on file about their own attitudes to their culture and ethnic background. Although in some cases such details were well documented, these were a small minority, and there was no information in 61 per cent of cases (excluding 74 cases where the child was too young or too severely disabled to be consulted). In 12 cases it was recorded that the children were aware of and generally positive about their ethnic and cultural heritage; in 28 cases that they denied or were negative about it and in seven cases that they were ambivalent. On only 19 files was there reference to the possibility of the child needing help to gain a greater understanding of his or her ethnic or cultural identity, in 11 cases such work being said to be needed and in eight cases not needed. In only one case was the child's first language noted as other than English and ten children spoke English and also the language of their parents.

Information on file was also sparse in respect of the child's wishes about placement. It was noted that nine did not wish to move from their current placements; that 11 wanted to go back to their parents or relatives and that six had mixed feelings about being placed with a new family. Eighteen were said to want to move to a new foster family; seven to a new adoptive family and 28 to a new family but were not specific as to whether it should be for adoption or fostering. Fourteen were said to want to move to an ethnically similar family; 13 to a white family and 24 were said to be unsure or have mixed feelings. This lack of data in so many cases means that little can be inferred from these small numbers. It may nonetheless be worth noting that four of the nine who were said to be reluctant to move from their current placements in care, but only one of the 11 who wished to return to natural parents, experienced disruption when they moved to new families. (In a more recent study involving interviews with children recently placed for adoption Thomas and Beckford (1999) describe the distress of some children at being moved from their foster carers to join adoptive families). There was even less information on the child's attitude towards continuing contact with birth parents. It was recorded that 49 wished to retain contact and 24 did not wish to retain contact, with one being described as ambivalent.

No child was said **not** to want contact to continue with siblings placed elsewhere and 59 were recorded as wanting continuing contact with siblings placed elsewhere or remaining with birth parents. The recent study by Thomas and Beckford (1999) confirms that there is still a tendency not to listen carefully to children's expressed wishes about continuing contact with birth parents and siblings.

Prior to placement, half of the children were on care orders, and 28 were Wards of Court. Parental Rights Resolutions had been passed in respect of 58 of the children (Table 3.4). Only 13 were in 'voluntary care' and 24 were placed directly for adoption without ever being in the care of the local authority. Table 3.5 shows that just under half were in foster homes prior to joining the new family (including 13 who were in specialist 'bridging' foster families. Just under half were in residential care, including 26 who were in specialist 'preparation for permanence' units.

| Table 3.4 Legal status at time of placement | | |
|---|---|---|
| *Status* | *n* | *per cent* |
| Care Order | 141 | 53 |
| Parental Rights Resolution | 58 | 22 |
| Ward of Court | 28 | 11 |
| Voluntary Care | 13 | 5 |
| Placed directly for adoption | 24 | 9 |
| *Total* | *264* | *100* |

missing data = 33

| Table 3.5 Placement of child before joining new family | | |
|---|---|---|
| *Placement* | *n* | *per cent* |
| Specialist pre-placement residential unit | 26 | 10 |
| Other residential care | 95 | 37 |
| 'Bridging' foster home | 13 | 5 |
| Other foster home | 104 | 41 |
| Other (e.g. hospital) | 19 | 7 |
| *Total* | *257* | *100* |

missing data = 40

Eighty-seven children (29 per cent) of the cohort were placed as long-term or 'permanent' foster children.

As has been noted in Chapter 2, it was significantly more likely that children with two parents of minority ethnic origin would be placd as permanent foster children than was the case for children with two white parents or of mixed race parentage.

## Table 3.6 The children at the time of placement* (percentages)

| Status | 2 black parents | Mixed race parentage | 2 white parents** | Significance ($\chi^2$ test) |
|---|---|---|---|---|
| Learning disability | 14 | 5 | 10 | ns |
| Physical disability | 7 | 4 | 12 | p <0.01 |
| Experienced multiple moves | 53 | 53 | 58 | ns |
| Described as 'institutionalised' | 40 | 27 | 28 | p <0.01 |
| Had a history of deprivation or abuse | 56 | 44 | 58 | ns |
| Already experienced a disrupted 'permanent' placement | 16 | 26 | 21 | p<0.05 |
| Behaviour difficulties | 57 | 43 | 50 | ns |
| Emotional difficulties | 49 | 51 | 64 | p <0.01 |

* Does not add up to 100 per cent since most children listed in several categories.
** The 922 placements of white children are those included in the original cohort of 1165 placements described by Thoburn (1991).

Table 3.6 gives additional background information on the children and compares them with the white children in the original cohort of 1165 placements. Whilst 11 per cent had no apparent difficulties or special needs, 31 per cent had six or more. In most respects those with one or both parents of minority ethnic origin were similar to the white children. However, a larger proportion of the children with two black parents was described as 'institutionalised' and fewer of those of mixed race parentage were described as having a history of deprivation or abuse, although they were more likely than the other two groups to have had a previous 'permanent' placement which had disrupted. More of the white children were described as having emotional difficulties but almost equal numbers in all the groups were described as having behavioural difficulties. More of the children of mixed race parentage had no, or only one special need or difficulty. This is in large part explained by the fact that as Figure 3.3 shows, a larger proportion of the children placed as infants was of mixed race parentage. Table 3.7 lists in more detail, for the children of minority ethnic origin, the problems and special needs noted on the files at the time of placement. For most of the characteristics listed in Tables 3.6 and 3.7 any differences represent trends and do not reach statistical significance. However, those with two parents of minority ethnic origin were more likely to have been described as 'institutionalised' at the time of placement (p <0.05) and were more likely to be said to need continuing contact with a birth parent (p <0.001).

| Table 3.7 Problems and special needs of children identified at time of placement (1297 children of minority ethnic origin) | | |
|---|---|---|
| *Problem or special need* | *n* | *per cent* |
| Child has Down's Syndrome | 5 | 2 |
| Child has learning disability | 21 | 7 |
| Child has serious physical disability | 16 | 5 |
| Child has acute or chronic ill-health | 15 | 5 |
| Child has already experienced multiple moves (defined as living in at least three homes with different main carers) | 162 | 55 |
| Child has history of neglect, or maltreatment | 153 | 52 |
| Child is described as 'institutionalised' | 106 | 36 |
| At least one previous 'permanent' placement has disrupted | 67 | 23 |
| Child has marked emotional problems | 152 | 51 |
| Child has marked behavioural difficulties | 136 | 46 |
| Child needs to retain contact with a parent | 73 | 25 |
| Child needs to retain contact with sibling placed elsewhere or a relative | 68 | 23 |
| There is likelihood of a contested adoption | 70 | 24 |

*Reasons for leaving home*

We learned something about the children's earlier histories from their foster or adoptive parents or the young people themselves and from the files. A small number of the children were placed for adoption at the request of their parents and others initially started their career under voluntary arrangements (28 per cent). However the fact that over half were in care on care orders and that 52 per cent were described as having a history of deprivation or abuse indicates that the early histories of the majority of the children were not conducive to positive psychological development. Despite the fact that life story work had been undertaken with most of the young people interviewed, a substantial minority of those interviewed were vague about why they had left home. A young woman placed with her present foster carers at the age of 12 together with two younger siblings said:

> Well I don't know what they got down on paper. All I know is that there was an argument between my mum and Social Services. The next thing I knew is that they took us away. I don't really know why we came into care; nobody has talked to us about it. I suppose my mum couldn't cope with three of us. Probably my mum couldn't cope and I don't think that was our fault. I don't know if my mum wanted us to come into care and be fostered. Maybe at the time she did.

A teenager placed at the age of five seemed even more confused, especially as her siblings remained at home. Unlike the young woman previously quoted, she seemed to blame herself to some extent.

> I think it was something to do with me entirely (why I left my birth family). Because I don't know the proper reason for this, I think its something to do with me why I left my family.

A young man of African descent placed with his foster parents at the age of 14 said:

> When I was born I was ill and I should have died. She was mad anyway. I'm not being funny, my dad says she is intelligent but I think she was an African woman, not very clever and superstitious. She thought I should have died that time and I didn't…and I think it gave her a different attitude towards me personally than to the other kids…I used to wish I had died when I was little.

The foster or adoptive parents had little to say about the reasons why their children left their birth families. Some were conscious that some of the children still worried about their first parents after they were placed.

> At that time, earlier on when she came here [aged five] she would show a lot of concern about the well being of her family. I remember on one occasion she thought that they may have had an accident and died in a car crash and then she said quite clearly over a period of time that she wanted to talk to somebody privately about her mum and dad as they kept popping into her head.

This comment gives an indication that the symptoms of 'post traumatic stress disorder' may be present in some young people who have suffered the trauma of precipitate removal from home, as well as those who have been sexually or physically maltreated. There was no indication in this case that the child had been maltreated and at the time of our interview she was a regular visitor to the home of her birth parents.

It appeared that most of the young people left home because of their parents' problems but some of those who were placed when older clearly had difficulties of their own, which in part contributed to their going into care. An adoptive father said:

> He truanted a lot from school and he stole things from local shops, for example, Evosticks and other kinds of glue. He cuts himself and that was for attention, because he would do that in my presence. He was just covered in cuts all over where he had tried to harm himself.

*Previous experiences in care*

We have already noted that most of the older children had experience of living both in residential care and in foster homes. They had more to say about these experiences than about their lives with their birth families. Because of the way in which the original data were collected, we cannot give exact details of the number of placements, although 53 per cent were described as having experienced multiple moves, and almost a quarter had experienced the breakdown of a previous placement which was intended to be permanent.

The long-term foster mother of a young man who joined the family at 14 said:

> Phil's emotional involvement is with the family who adopted him. He was with them for about two years, and he will still say he wonders how his adoptive sister is doing.

A teenager who had got on well with her previous foster family before she was placed at the age of five as an only child said:

> I missed my foster parents and their children. I missed having someone my own age that I could talk to.

A small number of the children moved from black foster parents to white adopters, but more frequently the move was in the opposite direction or from one white family to another. This Asian adopter spoke very warmly of the attempts of the white foster mother to keep cultural links alive.

> The previous foster mother had made tremendous efforts to keep her in touch with her Sikh Asian roots. She went to Punjabi classes; they tried to teach her how to make chapatis; they didn't cut her hair, and she wasn't allowed to eat beef. I was really touched about that.

A young woman placed initially with an Asian foster mother who then moved to a white adoptive family said:

> The lady [foster mother] tried to speak to me in my language, but I couldn't do it and now I can't even speak it. I have to pick it up all over again, and its really difficult. Now I'm left like getting the blame for not knowing it, and my family [she is now in touch with her birth family] are saying you have **got** to learn it.

Some children had many moves in their short lives. The adoptive father of Darren, placed at five, said:

> He had to be taught how to be a member of this family. For a long time he thought it didn't make any difference. He had lived in seven other families and wondered what being in a family actually meant.

In a similar vein, referring to a child placed at the age of three whose placement disrupted after several years, an adoptive parent said:

> I think he was always expecting to move on. He was so used to moving on and he never settled. He came with a lot of [emotional] baggage and he wasn't secure.

The children who were placed with their new families from residential care tended to have had the most disturbed backgrounds but a small number had found stability in residential care and had formed attachments with house parents and other children which they were sad to lose. Issues of race and ethnicity were particularly commented upon, sometimes positively, but more often negatively.

> When he came to us it was a little bit strange because he was not used to family life and with us being black he would say, 'What did you say?' [alluding to the fact that the young man, placed at the age of six, had had very little contact with African-Caribbean people and found the different accent and intonation difficult to understand].

In a small minority of cases young people had been physically maltreated by residential workers. Some of the negative comments made by the new parents about residential care were:

> I shall never forget the night I sat at the table at the home. It was worse than a pig sty; it was appalling the way they were expected to eat and behave.

> He was so withdrawn when he came that it was ages before he told me what happened to him at the home. And our daughter always felt that the people in the home never treated her properly so she was glad to be

here. Her brother told me that he had climbed the trees to get away from being beaten, and at another home, if they were naughty, they were put in a cupboard without any dinner. He was so scared when he came here that he would never close his door, never went to bed with his bedroom door closed.

A young woman said:

> When I was younger I had a lot of asthma attacks. The white people in the residential home were ignorant. They thought I was playing up. They would tell me to stop being silly, and I thought I was going to die. My condition was not diagnosed as asthma. If I stayed in the home, I probably would be dead by now. It [the asthma] was probably to do with all the stress with my mum. Its good that my aunty [adoptive mother] took me out. I feel anger towards them. I am mentally scarred. I think it stems from then – having to go into a home and everything. It made me feel that I'm nothing. Every time somebody came to pick up some of the other kids, you want them to pick you up as well. But I didn't know whether I was coming or going. I wished I had gone to my aunt's from a baby.

There were however positive comments about the children's homes from the foster carers and the young people. Tanya (aged 14 at placement) was described by her foster mother as:

> intelligent enough to know what was happening because she put herself into care. She was living in a large but very nice children's home which was closing down because the lady who ran it was selling up and going back to her own country. The two eldest saw the distinction between black and white, but not Mary (aged three at placement). The children had an aunt who used to visit them in the children's home and she would bring Caribbean food and oil for their hair to let them know they weren't totally forgotten. The house mother also knew about black hair care and if she was going to London she would bring some product back for the children. She didn't try to treat them like they were white, and did a lot of things to make them be happy.

Several of the black families we interviewed commented about the importance of the children being placed as quickly as possible so that they could feel comfortable within their own culture.

> Marvin (aged six at placement) did not have a problem about being black. Before he came to us he did not really see himself as black, but after he did not have a problem about being black. I feel that if he had

stayed in the children's home and been brought up there, he would have done, and he would feel obligated to white folks.

Support for this came from the white foster mother of three young people, two Asian brothers and a young man whose father was African-Caribbean and mother white, who said:

By the time the children came to live with us they were very damaged; they had been in a white environment for most of their lives. I think it damaged them in terms of their own self image and culture. At eleven and twelve when they came to us they were racist. They said they did not like black people, especially our foster son who was already here. This was bewildering. How do I cope with this because I don't have anybody in my house who is racist? But these two are boys who are black and are racist. So I was faced with the problem of how to teach black children not to be racist. They would actually shout racist things at black people in the street, so first of all I had to teach them not to do that and that I did not allow that kind of language. The second thing was to help them realise that they are black but we are miles and miles away from achieving this.

Comments were made about difficulties experienced when children of mixed race parentage had lived for several years with their white mother before being placed with black, Asian or mixed partnership new families.

At the age of six she had an identity problem. When she first came she felt she was white – she used to say 'how can I be black when I have a white mother with blonde hair?' It took her time but now she is more black than white.

Some adopters and young people spoke of racial abuse in the period before they were placed. One adoptive mother said:

He had been so used to it (racial abuse) that it probably would have been of no remark. He probably would have taken it as a matter of course.

A young woman placed at the age of eight from a children's home where most of the staff were white said of her adoptive mother who, in common with some of the other children, she referred to as aunt:

My aunt introduced me to a black culture and I realised that I wasn't white and I'm glad she did because some people stay that way. But I'm glad I was given the opportunity to change and be the colour that I am because its terrible acting white when you're black, and acting black when you're white. The children's home did not provide me with any help to adjust moving to a black family. But how would they help me anyway? They didn't know anything.

Another young woman placed with two younger siblings had previously lived in a children's home in an area where there were very few black people.

> At the children's home we were the only black children there. If you walked down the street you were the only black children. If you went to the market you were the only black children. So we had to build ourselves up and be strong because we were the only black children there. I hated it there. I'm not being wicked, but I hated being around white people because I knew that's not how it was supposed to be. I couldn't wait to come to London and get out of that place. I don't know why we were sent there because nobody knew about our culture. Nobody could do our hair; we had to say 'please can you do this?', 'please can you do that?' – otherwise we would be like little tramps. Being in that place did knock my confidence. But I showed my black more because I didn't want to be like them.

Another young man, placed at the age of 11 talked of his survival strategies and the important role of the school. He clearly gained from remaining within his home neighbourhood with a large proportion of people of a similar background and the school played a very important part in his overcoming some negative experiences in residential care before he joined his new family.

> The fact that I was in care, forget fostering, the fact that I was in care, I could use it as a weapon with the white people. You know, if I said I was in care they would give me a bit of leeway. When I was at school I loved it, I mean I loved that school, believe me. I had a great time.

## Summary

In this chapter we have provided information about the birth parents and about the children before they joined their new families. There are many gaps in our information abut the birth families, which reflects the generally poor standard of information about birth families in the adoption records. Birth families were not interviewed for the intensive study although the data from records is supplemented by what the new parents and young people told us about them. Information on *birth fathers* was particularly scanty.

- Nearly one-third of birth fathers were said to be unaware of the child's birth.
- Half of the birth mothers and nearly half of the birth fathers for whom information was recorded were unmarried.
- *Birth mothers:* 41 per cent of were white/European, 36 per cent were African-Caribbean, 8 per cent were described as being of

black mixed parentage, 7 per cent were African, 6 per cent were Asian and 2 per cent were of 'other ethnicity'.

- *Birth fathers:* 55 per cent of were African-Caribbean, 16 per cent were Asian, 12 per cent were African, 9 per cent were white/European, 4 per cent were of black mixed parentage and 4 per cent were of 'other ethnicity'.

- Attitudes of *birth mothers* to the placement plan were not recorded in respect of half the placements. Where they were recorded: 50 per cent were said to be in agreement with the placement plan; 33 per cent were said to oppose it; a small number (10) were said to be unaware of it. Attitudes of *birth fathers* to the placement plan were rarely recorded; 31 birth mothers and 19 birth fathers wanted the child returned to their care.

- Of the 297 children, 62 per cent were boys and 38 per cent were girls.

- The largest proportion (39 per cent) of the 297 cohort children was placed at the age of 9 or over; 26 per cent were aged between 5 and 8 at placement and 35 per cent were under 5 when they joined their new families.

- Of the 297 cohort children, 66 per cent were placed alone; 22 per cent with one sibling and 12 per cent with two siblings.

- Before placement, over 80 per cent of the 297 were on Care Orders, Wards of Court, or subjects of Parental Rights Resolutions. Some 6 per cent were in voluntary care and 9 per cent were placed directly for adoption without being looked after by the local authority.

- Of the 297 children, 29 per cent were placed with the intention that they would be 'permanent' foster children, though we know that some of these were subsequently adopted and that some of those placed with the intention of adoption remained as 'permanent' foster children.

- Around half were recorded as having a history of deprivation or abuse; had experienced multiple moves; were described as having emotional or behaviour problems. Over a third were described as showing some features of 'institutionalisation' and about a quarter had a previous placement which was intended to be permanent but which had broken down.

# CHAPTER 4

# The New Families

As with the young people, information on the new parents from the files was supplemented by detailed information and opinions gained during the interviews with the 38 adoptive or foster families.

## Material circumstances, family composition, and ethnicity

In all respects there are marked differences between the adoptive and the birth parents. At the time the 297 placements were made, 91 per cent of the new families was headed by a married couple and in a further four cases the parents had a long-standing relationship but were not married. There were no same sex partnerships. Five were single (never married) women and 14 were single women after divorce or separation. The interview sample was untypical in this respect in that 19 per cent of the placements was with single parents.

We know from the families interviewed that more were single parent families at the end of the study with the percentage for the 51 cases in the interview sample going up from 19 to 27 per cent. One adoptive mother who was single when the child was placed had a male partner at the end of the study. In a small number of cases a marriage had broken down and there was a new partner in the home. We shall return later in the Chapter to the impact of the arrival of an adoptive or foster child on the marriage.

Whether or not children went to live with families of a similar ethnic and religious background, they were highly likely to move to a different cultural and class environment. Forty per cent of the new mothers and 60 per cent of the new fathers were in managerial or professional occupations compared with 6 per cent of the birth mothers and 18 per cent of the birth fathers about whom this information is available. There was an interesting difference when the occupational status of the mothers and fathers in the new families is compared for the different ethnic groups. A larger proportion of the **mothers** in families where both parents or the single parent were of minority ethnic origin were in managerial or professional jobs (46 per cent) than was the case for those in mixed partnerships (25 per cent) or for white women with a white partner (39 per cent). However, the position is reversed when the **father's** occupation is considered and this difference is statistically significant. Twenty-nine per cent of the fathers in the families with two black parents were in professional or managerial occupations and 16 per cent were in unskilled manual jobs. In mixed partnerships 58 per cent of the fathers were in managerial or professional jobs and the proportion for white fathers with a white partner was 68 per cent. Thus, it appeared that the children who were placed with white families were more upwardly socially mobile as a group than those who went to live with black or Asian parents.

At the start of the placement, only six of the mothers in the interview sample and two of the fathers had no employment other than home duties. In no case was state benefit the main source of income. At the end of the study the pattern was similar but six families relied primarily on income support or retirement pensions. However, only three described themselves as well-off or comfortably off; half said they were 'managing OK' and a quarter said they were sometimes or often short of cash. At the end of the study over three-quarters were owner-occupiers. Several, however, were very cramped for space and one adoptive mother, whose daughter regularly visited her birth mother, confessed to twinges of envy at the higher material standards of the birth mother who had not had other children.

> They don't lead the same sort of life when they haven't got children. I would love a nice home.

There were 41 families where both parents (or the single parent) were of African-Caribbean descent; six where both parents (or the single parent) were of South Asian ethnic origin, and 30 mixed partnerships. Table 4.1 shows the wide range of partnerships represented in these mixed relationships. The parents in a large majority of the families (191; 71 per cent of the 268 about whom this information was available) were both white. However, 50 of these were already **families** of mixed ethnicity in that the child joined another adopted or foster child of minority ethnic origin.

It has already been noted (Figure 2.2) that it was far more likely that children with two black parents would be placed with families where at least one of the new parents was of Caribbean, Asian or African descent. Children of mixed race parentage were more likely than those with two black parents to be placed in mixed partnership families but the overwhelming majority were placed with white parents. However, eight children of mixed race parentage were placed in families with two black parents, and 14 children with two black parents were placed in mixed partnership families.

| Table 4.1 Ethnicity of new parents | | |
|---|---|---|
| | *n* | *per cent* |
| Both parents Caribbean | 41 | 15 |
| Both parents South Asian | 6 | 2 |
| Father mixed race parentage/mother Caribbean | 2 | 1 |
| Both parents of mixed race parentage | 2 | 1 |
| Father mixed race parentage/mother white | 3 | 1 |
| Father Caribbean/mother white | 1 | 0.5 |
| Father white/mother mixed race parentage | 5 | 2 |
| Father white/mother Caribbean | 9 | 3 |
| Father white/mother African | 2 | 1 |
| Father Asian/mother white | 4 | 1.5 |
| Father white/mother Asian | 2 | 1 |
| Father white/mother white | 191 | 71 |
| *Total* | *268* | *100* |

[missing data = 29]

Thirty-six children joined families where there were siblings still living at home as well as older siblings who had left home and for 15 all the siblings had already left home. Just over a quarter of the children went to families where there were no adult or younger children by birth, fostering or adoption. When children no longer living at home are included, almost half of them joined families where there were already two or more children. In 66 per cent of the families where there were other children, the child was placed as the youngest; in 19 per cent of placements he or she became the eldest child in the family and in 15 per cent there were both younger and older siblings. We know from the interview cases that there were new arrivals, either by birth, fostering, adoption or step family formation, so that children who started off as the youngest did not always remain so.

Thirty-six per cent joined families where the only new siblings in the household were birth or step children of the new parents. In almost one in five of the placements there were already fostered or adopted children and one in ten joined families where there were both 'own grown' and adopted or fostered children (Table 4.2).

| Status | Cohort | | Interview Sample | |
|---|---|---|---|---|
| | *n* | *per cent* | *n* | *per cent* |
| Birth or step-children only | 95 | 36 | 21 | 41 |
| Adopted/fostered children only | 49 | 19 | 5 | 10 |
| Birth and adopted/fostered | 35 | 14 | 14 | 27 |
| None | 82 | 31 | 11 | 22 |
| *Total* | *261* | *100* | *51* | *100* |

**Table 4.2 Status of children living in new family (full cohort and interview sample)**

[Missing cases = 36]

In the interview sample more of the new families had 'own grown' children in the household.

Over half (54 per cent) of the new parents planned from the start that it would be an adoptive placement and 32 (12 per cent) wished the placement

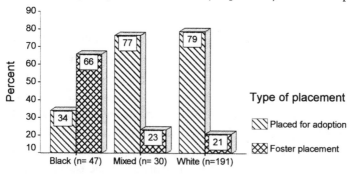

χ²: 37.59; df: 2; p<0.0001
n = 268; missing data = 29

*Figure 4.1 Ethnicity of new parents by type of placement*

to be on a 'permanent' fostering basis. Just under a quarter wished to foster before proceeding to adoption. Figure 4.1 shows a statistically significant difference between the ethnic groups, with a majority of the two black parent families being foster families. The position was reversed for white parents and mixed partnerships.

There was an even more significant difference when the age of the child placed is considered. Figure 4.2 shows that the majority of children placed with two black parents were aged nine or over; that mixed partnerships and white families were more likely to parent the under fives, and that a higher proportion of the children placed with mixed partnership families were in the five to eight age group.

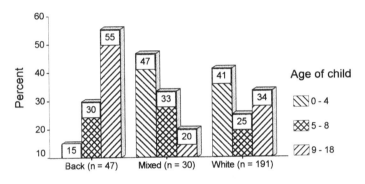

$\chi^2$: 16.07; df: 4; p<0.01

n = 268; missing data = 29

*Figure 4.2 Ethnicity of new parents by age of child at placement*

## Attitudes towards child placement

It has already been noted that information on the files about attitudes on important issues which might have an impact on the success of the placement was sparse. We sought information on:

- their understanding of the different challenges and rewards of parenting by adoption or permanent fostering and parenting a child born into the family
- the willingness and indications of the ability of the new family to parent a child of a different ethnic or cultural background

- the reasons why the parents decided to provide a long-term home to a child of minority ethnic origin

- their willingness and indications of their ability to parent a child with a disability

- their willingness, motivation and indications of ability to parent a child who had been maltreated, neglected or suffered the ill-effects of further separation and loss or institutionalisation within the care system

- their ability to understand and empathise with parents who had maltreated or neglected a child, as well as those who 'voluntarily' placed their child for adoption

- their attitudes towards meeting the birth parents either before or after placement and their ability to see the value of, and facilitate, appropriate post-placement contact between the child and parents, relatives, siblings placed elsewhere or former carers.

Since some writers and researchers have stressed the importance of the new parents being able to understand and feel positive about differences between birth and adoptive parenting, files were scrutinised to see whether this sort of information was made available to the adoption panel or described elsewhere in the reports. It was available in respect of only 74 of the 297 cohort placements, less than a quarter of the sample. Sixteen were noted as having an intellectual understanding of the difference and two had experienced substitute parenting and confirmed their understanding of the differences but also the rewards of this special sort of parenting. Forty-four parents who already had experience of adoption or fostering, and two who hadn't, gave indications during the approval process that they considered parenting by adoption not to be different from having a child by birth. Thirty per cent were said to be willing to have contact with a birth parent after placement. Information on their attitudes to contact with siblings placed elsewhere or relatives was very sparse.

Thirty per cent of the 257 sets of parents about whom this information was known specifically applied to take a child of minority ethnic origin (including a quarter of the white parents). There was detailed information about the motivation for wishing to foster or adopt a black child in respect of only 101 families. For eight families social conscience, and views about the nature of a multi-racial society or black consciousness were mentioned. Thirty-one of the white families wished to have a child placed with them who was of a similar ethnic origin to a child already living with them. Twelve

(11 white, 1 mixed partnership) applied because they had an affinity to a particular ethnic group, perhaps because of having worked overseas.

In the light of the information available, a rating was made of the ability and opportunity of the new family to meet the cultural needs of the child and help him or her to deal with the impact of racism. There was insufficient information in respect of half of the families and 74 were of similar ethnicity or culture to the child placed with them. Thirty-four white families were living in racially mixed areas where the peer group of the child would include many families of similar ethnic and cultural background. Thirty-eight were white and living in predominantly white areas but had black friends or a black child already living with them and were keen to take measures to ensure that the child had opportunities to explore racial and cultural issues. Seven of the white families were living in areas where the population was predominantly white British and where there were indications (such as a preference for a lighter-skinned child, or statements in the papers that they considered race and culture to be unimportant) to suggest that they may have difficulties in helping the child to have a positive sense of his or her ethnic and cultural heritage. The lack of information about this issue in the adoption papers which would be used for matching and approval purposes merits comment since, even in the early 1980s there were already suggestions in the professional literature that one of the factors which could help white parents to parent black children was living in an ethnically mixed community.

## The new families in more detail

Much of what follows is taken from the interviews with the 38 parents. Quantitative data from the full cohort is included where appropriate. Because the interview sample was non-random and was stratified to include larger proportions of ethnic minority families, it is important to note any differences between the two samples. It comes as no surprise that more of the families interviewed live in city areas since black families are over-represented within cities. Twenty per cent of the children in the interview sample joined single parent families compared with only 7 per cent in the full cohort. They were also more likely to join larger families. Thirty-one per cent of the children in the cohort joined their new families as the only child whereas this applied to only 21 per cent in the interview sample. In contrast, 17 per cent of the children in the cohort, but 27 per cent of those in the interview sample joined families where there were already three or more children. There were also more likely to be grown-up siblings who had moved out of the home.

The children in the interview sample were also more likely to be placed together with a sibling (35 per cent compared with 27 per cent in the larger cohort.) There were no obvious differences in the degree of difficulty presented by the children in the cohort and interview samples in that almost equal numbers were described as having five or more serious problems or handicaps at the time of placement (37 per cent and 35 per cent respectively).

Differences were noted in terms of the placement itself. Seventy-one per cent of the cohort children but only 59 per cent of the children in the interview sample were placed for adoption and more of the full cohort placements (48 per cent as compared with 27 per cent in the interview sample) were placed in a permanent new family with the consent of the birth mother. Perhaps related to the lower incidence of foster placements, 33 per cent in the full cohort, but only 17 per cent of the interview sample were no longer in contact with birth parents at the time the placement was made. However, almost equal numbers (26 per cent of the cohort and 29 per cent of the interview sample) had moderate or good contact with birth families at some stage after placement.

## Motivation for fostering or adopting

In earlier studies (Thoburn *et al.* 1986 and 1990) it was concluded that the art of child placement involved being clear both about what the parents had to offer but also about what they would expect to get back from taking a child with special needs into their home. The next stage was to place with them a child who needed what they had to give, and in return could provide the hoped for rewards. Motivation was grouped into broadly altruistic reasons and reasons concerned broadly with self-interest. It was, however, clear from earlier studies that motivation is complex and that most families who successfully take a child with special needs into their home have a range of motives which include both altruistic and self-directed ones. During the interviews the parents were first asked to say why they had decided to adopt or foster a child and whether, in the light of hindsight, they still thought that this was the major reason. Sometimes husbands and wives had slightly different views, but a discussion usually resulted in agreement. Having gained their unprompted opinions about this, each family was asked to complete a checklist which included the different motivations identified in earlier studies. They were asked to tick any which applied and then to identify the main reason. Table 4.3 shows that the reason most frequently given as the main one was 'to become a parent' (20 per cent) followed by 'to help a child of own race and culture' (14 per cent of the families where at least one parent was of a similar race or culture to the child).

### Table 4.3 Motivation for adopting or fostering this child (interview sample)

| Motivation | Main motivation | | per cent of cases in which mentioned |
|---|---|---|---|
| | n | per cent | |
| To become parents/could not have children | 10 | 20 | }47% |
| To enlarge family | 5 | 10 | |
| Sibling for child already in family | 3 | 6 | |
| To fill gap in lives now children grown up | 1 | 2 | |
| Enjoy a challenge and could help a child who has difficulties | 2 | 4 | 49% |
| Lots of love to give | 3 | 6 | }86% |
| Really enjoy children | 2 | 4 | |
| Good with children and something to offer | 3 | 6 | |
| To help child of own race or culture | 7 | 14 | 79%** |
| Religious duty | 2 | 4 | }21% |
| Other sense of duty, including 'racial harmony' | 1 | 2 | |
| To give child a better life | 4 | 8 | 86% |

\* There were 38 families but 43 responses since 5 families had different 'main motivations' for different children placed with them.
\*\* White families omitted.

Taking the first four as broadly self or family-focused and the others as broadly child or society-focused, it can be seen that for many of the families altruism or a sense of religious or other duty was the major driving force. The importance of altruism is even more marked since most of those whose major motivation was self-focused were additionally motivated by altruistic or child-focused reasons. The most frequently mentioned reasons were 'because we have lots of love to give', 'because we really enjoy being with children', and 'because we think we are good with children and have something to offer them.' All families ticked more than one reason, the range being from two to eight with an average of five.

Apart from a small number of both black and white families who were primarily motivated by a desire to have a child of a minority ethnic group join their family, there was little difference between the way in which black and white families talked about their motivation for adopting or fostering.

The interviewers did not specifically ask questions about infertility, but this was raised by some of the parents themselves who spoke of their sadness at being unable to have children by birth and their deep longing for a child.

> When we went initially to the adoption society it was so very formal and so very drab. We felt very uncomfortable and we sat on hard chairs and it really hit home to me on that day that I could not have a child. This is it. It was just so overwhelming that I remember crying during this interview.

A mother who had been unable to have children by birth and experienced many difficulties in parenting the disturbed 5-year-old who was placed with her said:

> If you are desperate to have children because you can't, you want to be a mummy to a child. Whatever anybody says you don't really hear it.

Single women also talked about their sadness at not having children by birth, and in some cases had sought infertility treatment. However, their pleasure at having a child by adoption or fostering seemed less tinged with sadness than was the case with some of the married couples.

> For me, it is part of the acceptance that I would not have natural children of my own. I did not have a particular child in mind. Secretly in my deepest heart, I would have loved a little girl.

However, this wish to have a child was accompanied in almost all cases by a strong altruistic motive.

> I was appalled by the number of black children that were in the home and what was going on in their lives. Once I knew her personally, I knew it was this one because I had actually met a child from my culture and wanted to give her a chance of a family of her own. In my wildest dreams I could not see how I could have had a child to be brought up unless I went back home [the Caribbean] and brought a child back. The agency made my dreams come true.

Some families already had children either by adoption or by birth and wished to enlarge their families. These included parents who specifically did not wish to have another child by birth.

> I had two children already and did not like the image this presented. I wanted another child but did not want to have one of my own. I had some experience of disadvantaged children through my work as a teacher. I felt that I could be more helpful in providing a whole environment rather than just a taste of it. I did not initially think about adopting a black child. I had been brought up in the Caribbean and felt totally at ease with black people.

Whilst those who already had a child were more willing to consider the placement of an older child, those who had been unable to have children by birth were more likely to want to have an infant placed with them. The researcher's notes on one interview state:

> The agency tried very hard to convince the couple to go ahead and see an older child of around 18 months, but the couple felt they really wanted a baby, and if they had gone to meet this child they would have felt duty-bound to go through with it, and they felt this would have been the wrong approach to take.

Several of the black families mentioned the importance to them of being able to help a child of a similar race, culture or religion. This mother who originally started as a short-term foster parent but eventually provided a permanent home for three siblings expressed her shock on realising that there were many black children in care.

> I was a bit naive. I didn't think that black children were fostered or put into homes or anything like that. I thought it was children that were born in England, white children. I thought that all black children were sort of cared for by the mother and grandmother or what have you. And that gave me the feeling that if I ever had the time, fostering would be something that I would like to do. We wanted to help our own – that is, black children. It doesn't matter how good it is in a children's home, its not like a family.

Although it seems to have been assumed by most of the Caribbean or Asian parents that a child of a similar ethnic background would be placed with them, this was not automatically the case with the London Borough foster parents.

> I was given a choice about the race of the child I could foster. I could have fostered a black or a white child, a boy or a girl. But I did ask about the race. I wanted a black child. This could have been an African-

Caribbean child, an African child or an Indian child, but not a child of mixed parentage. It had to be a child with two black parents.

Although many of the foster and adoptive parents spoke about their strong religious faith, this did not figure prominently when they talked specifically about their motivation to adopt. It was something which was in the background but became more important to them as the placement progressed and they gave thought to how to bring up the children. A Roman Catholic family who adopted three children, two of whom were of mixed race parentage, did so initially because of infertility. However, the adoptive mother was much involved with the local 'Life' group and felt very strongly that adoption rather than abortion was the appropriate response to an unplanned pregnancy.

Several of the adopters or foster parents were professionally involved with children in special circumstances and were aware of the harm which could be done to young children remaining for too long in residential care:

> We determined that whatever we could do to close children's homes down we would do it. You've got to put your money where your mouth is, and fostering was one of the ways in which we could achieve that. So first of all we took Matthew on in anger, but when he came to us as a foster child it was a great pleasure. We took on the system and beat it, and he was going to stay with us. [This was one of the placements which started on a temporary basis but became a 'family for life' for a child who had had numerous placements including a broken adoption.]

This single parent of Asian descent considered that she had something to offer children and enjoyed being with them, but, unlike some of the other single parents, did not appear to regret not having a child by birth:

> It took me a very long time to decide. I come from a very large family and I've always been used to being with lots of children. I think I always believed that my life would involve children. Personally, though, I was not very keen on producing my own children. So the main reason I wanted to adopt was because I really like being with children. I'm not fussed about being a mother.

As with self-directed motives, altruistic motives were not invariably associated with success. This young man, who left his family after two years, said:

> I presume, I can't remember what I was told, they were not poor, they felt they had more to offer. They'd already adopted their daughter. She told me they decided to foster me because of the poster. They might have been thinking about it or something before they saw the poster, and then

they must have walked by the shop or something and saw the poster. I remember one of them saying that fostering was like having a boat – get out of the harbour and take it out to sea, and it's not quite what you thought it would be. That's what she said to me. So, yes, they gave me a home and thought they could manage, and then found out that they couldn't, or whatever.

To conclude this section on motivation, it was of note that the majority of the parents in mixed partnerships described their motivation for adopting as being self- or family-focused, whereas the majority of the families where there was a single parent or two parents of minority ethnic origin, fostered or adopted for primarily altruistic motives. A slightly higher proportion of the white than the mixed partnership families also discussed their motivation primarily in terms of altruistic rather than self-directed motives. However, we again stress that whatever the prime motivation, in almost all cases, the reasons included a mixture of self-focused and child-focused reasons.

### Reflections on birth parenting and parenting by fostering or adoption

The adoptive or foster parents interviewed were asked if they thought that parenting a child in this way was similar or different from parenting a child by birth. Their comments were sought on the following statements which were drawn from the literature on the psychology of adoption (Kirk 1964; Brodzinsky and Schechter 1990) and the hypothesis that successful adopters tread a narrow path between accepting that adoptive or foster parenting is different from birth parenting but not over emphasising it.

> Some adoptive or permanent foster parents say the best strategy is to forget about the past and parent the adopted or foster child just like your own. Others say that parenting an adopted child is a different but special sort of parenting. Where would you put your own views in this respect? Have they changed over time? What influenced you in thinking this?

For the foster carers and adopters who had taken older children into their homes, there was no doubt that this was a very different and challenging sort of parenting which nevertheless brought special rewards. This position was also taken by some of the parents of the infants (all of whom were adopters). There was no obvious difference in this respect between the parents of minority ethnic origin and the white parents.

Responses were grouped into those who broadly considered that adoptive parenting was different from birth parenting (a large majority) and those who thought that in most essentials it was the same. However, there were elements of both in all the responses and no family was rated as considering that there were no differences between adoptive parenting and birth parenting (other than the fact of birth). This implies that most of the parents interviewed were very close in their attitude and adoptive or foster parenting styles to the approach suggested by writers on the psychology of adoption. They walked a delicate tight-rope between recognising that adoptive parenting is a different form of parenting but at the same time not emphasising the difference in their daily lives as a family.

ADOPTION AND BIRTH PARENTING BROADLY SIMILAR

This comment of a parent who had first had a child by birth and then two adopted children represents the views of those adopters of infants who thought that birth parenting and parenting by adoption were broadly similar.

> We knew, because our first daughter had fitted in, that he would too. A child is a child. We believe that nurture has more to do with it than nature. Having gone through the experience of having a child born to you, in most cases what pops out is what you instantly start loving. The process is very similar. We became attached straight away. Love – what is love? Once you have sorted out the hormones? It is a function of time, changing nappies, kicking a ball around, so long as the child is young enough.

It was unusual for adoptive or foster parents whose children had joined them when over the age of nine to feel that there was no difference. This white family, who took into their home an 11-year-old of mixed race parentage and who had lived for long periods in both foster and residential care, said:

> It was a good move him coming here. He came to the right family for him. It was made for him. He got three brothers straight away. It has been like that – apart from the usual scraps – from the time he came. It's been a pleasure. I look at him and I feel I've done the right thing here. I think if someone is genuine and they are doing it to do a job for the child, they will do it right anyway because they will do it like their own family. If you start singling them out and doing different things with them I don't think you will succeed.

Although the young man was placed at 11 and there were indications of behavioural disturbance, it was one of the most successful placements. At 29 he was doing well in life, buying his own home and with a rewarding relationship with a new partner, but firmly still in touch with his adoptive parents and also with his birth siblings. He, like his adoptive parents, felt that they were very much a family. However when asked during the research interview what his adoptive parent would have thought about how he had turned out, he responded:

They would be proud of me, I know they are. But perhaps a bit jealous – that I am doing better than their own children.

When the interviewer took up with him what he meant by 'own children' since he had just said that he felt like one of their 'own children' he said that adoption is always bound to be different. He did not however appear to be uncomfortable with this difference and to all intents and purposes he and his adoptive family, who had fostered him for the first six years of the placement, had assumed that he was fully part of the family.

ADOPTION AND BIRTH PARENTING DIFFERENCES

Even the majority of the adopters of infants thought that there were important differences. Their views are represented by the following comments although again they also refer to similarities:

> I don't think it is right to forget that the child is adopted because that would be a lack of respect for the natural mother of those children. All the four children we have adopted look like their natural parents. So how could you forget that when that is there. If you try to hide their past, someone else will tell them. [This was a placement where the children and adoptive parent were well matched in terms of ethnicity.]

This response was from the mixed partnership adoptive parents of a child of mixed race parentage.

> In a way you are parenting that child like your own child but at the same time you can't forget the child's past. Its a special parenting because you've actually chosen that child.

It was most likely that foster or adoptive parents of children placed when older would see that there were important differences.

> I think you have to stay in touch with the past and try to build on that. And that is a special task. Try to keep it alive – their past, their roots, and the good things about it. You should try to help the child make sense of unpleasant memories, and try to work towards resolving them, freeing the child from the trauma of separation that might have been felt. I think coming from a foreign country myself, it is best to help the child value and respect the systems of which they were born.

These adoptive parents linked their response to the attitude and responses of the social worker, or to continuing involvement with the adoption agency:

> The social workers have said to us, because you have adopted, we treat you like any other parents. But we don't know what ordinary parenting is like. We only know what adoptive parenting is like and it isn't like ordinary parenting. They say they treat us like any birth parents, and I

> think that's wrong. You don't have the bonding maybe because the genetic link is not there, that is the big flaw. We are not birth parents.

> I was lucky because I was doing some work for a post adoption centre for birth mothers so I was able to share some of their pain at giving up their children. So that was very useful. There is a difference between adoptive parenting and birth parenting, and you can make those differences special.

An adoptive mother made a point about adoption being different in the sense that it made it harder for the parents to seek help and support when problems arose.

> I think there is something about adoption and fostering. You go through the awful process of being approved, assessed, and its quite difficult after that to show any weaknesses.

Apart from the family of the 11-year-old cited earlier, the parents of the children aged nine or over at placement saw this form of parenting as very different from parenting a child by birth, although this did not necessarily mean that outwardly the child was treated differently. This white permanent foster mother said:

> I have to say, I've never seen myself as their mother ever and they don't call us mum and dad although they do describe us to other people as mum and dad. We have always made it clear to them that they come from other families, and we have never let them change their surname. I have always thought that I would want them to be who they are, but to live with us. I've never felt that I may want them to become my sons. [These three young men were placed as teenagers from a residential unit. All three were still closely attached to the foster family as young adults, one still living in the household and two having moved to independent living in their early twenties.]

This foster mother had grown-up children of her own and could explain the difference.

> I think being a foster parent involves a different but special kind of parenting. Its different because in a sense the children were chosen. With your own children you grow together. However, with foster children, relationships develop over time. You grow into a family. It's not something that instantaneously you wake up one morning and say you are going to be a foster parent and everything fits into a packet, and everything is going to be sweet and smooth for the rest of your life; it doesn't happen like that, its something you have to learn.

As most of these comments show, in talking about differences, many of the adoptive and foster parents of the children who were placed past infancy talked about the child's earlier life. Almost all talked about birth parents, a point to which we return in the next section.

> There is no magic wand. You can't go back and change the experiences they have had. Whatever happens they are going to be a product of all their experiences.

*Attitude of the new parents to the birth parents*

| Table 4.4 Attitudes of adoptive/foster parents towards birth parents (interview sample) | | | | |
|---|---|---|---|---|
| Attitudes | *Birth mother* | | *Birth father* | |
| | *n* | *per cent* | *n* | *per cent* |
| Generally negative | 4 | 8 | 13 | 28 |
| Sorry for | 12 | 25 | 2 | 4 |
| Empathise with | 13 | 27 | 6 | 13 |
| Grateful to | 3 | 6 | 1 | 2 |
| Generally positive | 3 | 6 | 4 | 9 |
| Don't think about | 13 | 27 | 20 | 44 |
| *Total* | 48* | | 46* | *100* |

* Information not available in respect of 3 birth mothers and 5 birth fathers. Figures do not necessarily sum to 100% as some had more than one attitude.

At various times in the interview the adoptive or foster parents referred back to their attitudes towards the birth parents (see Table 4.4) and the child's earlier life in order to explain and illustrate particular points. Whether or not they had ever met them obviously made a difference to the way they spoke about them as did the extent of any post placement contact between the child and members of the birth family. Table 4.5 shows that the new parents met a birth parent before, or in the early stages of well over half of the placements, with a further four meeting a birth parent at some time before the child was 18. We have already noted that some of the adopters of infants talked about their gratitude to the birth family and understood the sadness of having to give up a baby.

Those who were not in contact with the birth families often talked about the amount of information, or lack of it, they had received from the children's workers and adoption agencies. Some of those who subsequently met the birth parents felt that they had been given misleading information about the attitudes of the birth parents towards permanent family placement. For the adoptive parents of infants where there was no face to face contact, the discussion about the birth parents was often related to the question of how the child was told about the meaning of adoption and the reasons for it.

### Table 4.5 Adoptive/foster parents met a birth parent (interview sample)

| Birth parent met | Number of cases | |
|---|---|---|
| | n | per cent |
| Never, or not until child grew up | 18 | 35 |
| Before placement, not after | 7 | 14 |
| Briefly after/not before | 7 | 14 |
| More than two meetings after placement, but not continuous | 10 | 20 |
| Gaps and then contact while still a child | 3 | 6 |
| Continuing contact on a regular basis | 6 | 12 |
| Total | 51 | 100 |

Some of the parents who were not in direct contact with birth relatives referred to the contents of 'life story books'. Generally these were seen as a helpful source of information for talking to the child about his or her past. However, at least two parents objected strongly in retrospect to the sanitised and, as one of them put it, 'fairy tale like nature' of these accounts.

This added to the difficulties when, as teenagers, some of the young people re-established contact with birth relatives.

The way in which the new parents integrated their knowledge of, or continuing contact with, the birth relatives will be returned to in Chapters 5 and 6.

## Summary

This chapter describes the families involved in the 297 cohort placements. It illustrates the quantitative data with comments from the interview sample and note is therefore made of differences between the full cohort placements and the 51 placements in the stratified interview sample.

- there were marked differences between the material circumstances of the birth parents and the new parents, mostly in the direction of higher standards of living for the new parents

- forty per cent of the new mothers and 60 per cent of the new fathers were in managerial or professional occupations

- ninety-one per cent of the new families comprised a married couple

- there were 41 families where both parents were of African-Caribbean descent, six where both were of South Asian descent and 191 (71 per cent) where both new parents were white

- there were 30 mixed partnership families, including four where the parents were of different minority ethnic origins

- more of the families with two black or Asian parents were permanent foster carers and more of white and mixed partnership families were adopters

- the motivation of most of the new parents interviewed involved combinations of altruism and self-directed motives. Only a small number were motivated only by the desire to have a child, or to increase the size of their family, though 50 per cent of the full sample (32 per cent of the intensive sample) did not have children by birth. The wish to give a home to a black child in care was prominent amongst the reasons given by the black or Asian parents interviewed.

- most of the parents inverviewed expressed the opinion that adoptive or foster parenting was different from parenting by birth, but that, in day-to-day family life, it was important not to stress the difference.

# CHAPTER 5

# The Children: Settling in and 'Negotiating' Two Families

## Settling in and the early years

The memories of the parents and the children who were already in the household, as well as the young people who were older when they moved in, still appeared very vivid even after ten or more years. The descriptions of the parents ranged from totally positive to extremely negative with more being at the positive end of the continuum. The young people interviewed tended to express more positive views. A few were generally negative, but philosophical about the difficulties they encountered. The adults spoke both of their own reactions and of the reactions and behaviour of the children. The reactions of parents of different ethnic backgrounds were broadly similar.

Early reactions tended to be related to the experiences of the children prior to placement and, in particular, whether they wanted to move or were happy where they were. When her daughter was placed at the age of seven this adoptive mother found that she was having to compete, initially unsuccessfully, with the child's attachment to her previous foster parent. Her comment is echoed by those of some of the adoptive parents interviewed more recently by Thomas and Beckford (1999).

> It was often very frustrating. I had to match her foster mother. When she arrived, we felt second best. But although she was sad to leave her foster family, she wanted to let us know that she was here for better or worse, so she called us mum and dad from fairly early on, so on her part she was quite welcoming. She was nice, she tried, she was a complex personality, so I'm not sure whether one word is adequate enough to describe her. She was not meek, she was not subdued. On the other hand she wanted to please but at the same time she wanted to remind us where she came from. She wasn't belligerent, but she wasn't going to let go easily of her foster parent.

Some of the children wanted to be placed, particularly those moving from children's homes:

> I wouldn't have gone to any family, just because they lived in London. I would want to make sure they treated us right. But I wanted to come and live with my mum and dad now after I had met them. I would not have gone to a white family because I knew it wasn't right that we were living in a white home anyway. They didn't really talk to us about the sort of foster family we wanted.

Another foster mother already knew the 14 year old who joined her family as a foster child since she had been her teacher.

> It was a joy when Theresa came because I knew her so well. I had taught her, although I didn't see a lot of her at secondary school. We were both happy to be with each other.

Parents whose children were placed when younger tended to have a more positive early reaction. However, in a few cases, particularly on the rare occasions when introductions were not well handled, the adopters described their new son or daughter as being withdrawn and watchful for the early weeks. They sometimes described them as 'too good' and wondered what distressing thoughts or images were going through their minds as they came to terms with the loss of foster parents with whom they might have lived for several of those crucially important months after leaving their parents' care.

Using a wide range of words to describe their growing sense of attachment, or dismay that feelings remained distant, parents and children tried to help us to understand how their relationships developed.

> It is difficult to say whether Nazreen became attached to me as quickly as I did to her. I remember she was very concerned about me and very protective from the start. I remember she made my bed for me when we had visitors saying that she thought I looked very tired and I was very touched by this.

Whilst most children in the early weeks were 'on their best behaviour' some expressed their anxiety or their sense of loss in more negative behaviour. The adoptive parent of a six-year-old boy said:

> He didn't like himself so much when he first came. There was a part of him which was badly hurt, and I think that's the part that brings out that viciousness. However he did like himself eventually.

In a similar vein an adoptive parent said of another boy placed at the age of four:

> Pete came with a lot of baggage and he wasn't secure to start with. He was very angry towards his birth mother and we actually told him that he was attacking the wrong person – me. That's only because he can't reach the real target, and I just had to be substitute.

Moving in was easiest for the young people who had already got to know their new parents, in one case because the single adoptive mother had played a befriending role in the children's home before deciding that Paulette was the child who would fit in best.

> Paulette would leave things behind after an introductory visit. And I used to think she didn't want them. If I bought her anything, I'd think she didn't want it because she left it. However I was able to discuss with her worker what was happening and she explained that this was a good sign.

Most often the description was of uncertainty and ambivalence.

> It was an odd experience. I remember very clearly that it was like a visitor who didn't go home. She was meant to become part of our family but she was a stranger, she was strange to us and we were strange to her [despite a very careful introductory process]. It wasn't love at first sight. We soon began to see what some of the difficulties were. The honeymoon lasted days rather than weeks.

The young people had more to say than their parents about these early stages and generally spoke of this period as a difficult one for them. Ruth, who was nine when she joined her adoptive parents said:

> It was hard growing up, but things got easier. When I was first adopted I thought I was happy, but really and truly I wasn't happy because it was harder to adapt to a family life. I didn't really have any conversation with my parents when I was first adopted – it was 'yes', 'no', 'I don't know' – but when I went out of the house I was a totally different person, but that's how I managed to cope with it.

A young man, placed at the age of seven, said:

> I was confused and unhappy. I cried a lot of the time at night because I was trying to think what was going on with my life. I wouldn't eat a thing that my mum cooked for me. Everything was just so different for me.

Some of the young people recalled a turning point when they suddenly started to feel that they belonged and interestingly this often came after a period of turmoil or difficult behaviour. This was especially so for the boys. Ben, who was still living at home at 18, said:

> There was a time when I was going to go when I was about 13. My mum said I was going on Sunday. I either had to do what they said or something like that or I'd be going.

The parents talked with much feeling about the extent to which the young people eventually became attached to them and about their own feelings towards their children.

> I cannot remember not feeling attached to her (placed at the age of eight). But I wonder even now if she is attached to me. Sometimes I think she is, but other times there are periods when she isn't. I first realised that I loved her when she had a severe asthma attack. I had taken her to the hospital and they admitted her, and I thought she was going to die. My knees went weak and if I hadn't been holding on to the hospital trolley, I was a wreck. I had pains in my tummy at night. This is the time I realised you didn't have to give birth to a child to have these intense feelings.

Some foster parents or adopters were able to compare differences in attachment with different children.

> I cared for her a lot but I did not really have the chance to become really attached to her. She was 14 when she came here. With her I don't think she ever became attached to anyone. She was that type of person. She knew I was here for her and that she could call on me at any time. But that attachment – I don't know. Now her sister [placed at six] became attached to me very early even though she had her tantrums.

For some the early positive feelings continued to consolidate in an unproblematic way and although this normally was more likely to happen with the younger children, young people as old as 11 or 12 at placement sometimes also settled in very quickly and became fully attached to their new parents.

> You don't know really when it happens – you wake up one morning and they are your family. If they are late coming home from school you have the same gut feeling you would have as if they were yours.

The young person referred to in the above quotation, who was placed at the age of 14 together with her younger brother and sister said;

> I suppose it didn't take long for me to feel a full member of this family. We just sort of clicked. I was happy to be there.

More frequently the attachment process was slower. This adoptive mother of a youngster placed at eight told us ten years later:

> The thing is there are moments of it (love) now. Its just that sometimes I find that the difficulties get in the way of the whole picture. She knows that she belongs and as far as I am concerned she belongs with us. That doesn't fluctuate. She is here and she is ours. What fluctuates is how well I can get that over to her sometimes. It's a today thing, not the underlying things that change. There is attachment. There's no question at all about that. Its difficult to describe love. I love my own son – there's no question at all and that's because there's a two way relationship. In terms of Nicola, a lot of the relationship is one way.

Several of the young people and parents described how attachments grew in an unequal way with mothers and fathers, and in some cases one or other parent (usually the father) did not bond with the child. Growing attachment was often, but not always, linked with improved behaviour on the part of the children. On the other hand the behaviour of some of the children deteriorated and in some cases this led to the placement breaking down.

Attachment and behaviour difficulties were rarely reported for the children placed as infants. Those placed past infancy, including three placed when under three, displayed a wide range of behavioural and emotional difficulties. In broad terms it appeared that if attachments started to grow, the new parents were willing to tolerate difficult behaviours but lack of mutual affection was associated with a lesser degree of tolerance.

Sometimes adopters found it hard to put their finger on precisely what it was which bothered them during the early days. Often they would say that the child was 'too good'. This was often coupled with the child being described as keeping an emotional distance or a negativism which was hard to pin point.

> She couldn't say 'yes', she couldn't say 'please'. The issue of the 'yes' has been solved to a certain extent; it comes and goes. But still now her attitude is that given the choice between two options she will choose the one that has more negative issues attached to it. Its still very difficult for her to ask for things. She would always try and phrase things in such a way that people will have to offer.

Ricky, placed as a permanent foster child at the age of four, attended a psychiatric hospital because of the very serious soiling problems which persisted for some years. However his foster mother took it in her stride because of the warmth in their relationship.

> With Ricky, I loved him from straight away. They tried to match a child up with the family and he was a perfect match. There was something about him which I took to straight away. I think we both sort of gelled with each other. He took to me and I took to him. I see him as my own

child. He was brother to the others, my son, nephew, grandchild. That's how he was seen in the family, but he is still quiet. He found it difficult to relate to people.

Some parents described how the children themselves found ways of dealing with their difficulties in these early stages. The adoptive mother of Sandra, placed at the age of four when she was already attending the family psychiatry department because of serious behaviour problems, said:

> She went straight into regression. She had a baby's bottle. Also a bit later she used to wear a wig and talked to herself in the mirror. That was one of her salvations. She would slag everybody else off into the mirror.

The adoptive mother of another young woman placed at the age of four said:

> I knew from the start what she was like – that she had personality problems. My husband couldn't see that. She screamed and screamed when she arrived. We were perplexed and bewildered and de-skilled. We just felt she didn't want to be here. We were very naive. We had this view of children, love will conquer all.

For the older children, school was sometimes a help but sometimes added to their difficulties. The parents of children who had learning disabilities sometimes spoke with great warmth and gratitude about the schools, but in other cases described considerable frustration. With the older children who had behaviour difficulties, more of the comments about the school were negative.

However, some parents described very positively the way in which the schools tried to help the young people to deal with the curiosity of their class mates about why they had moved into the neighbourhood. Some ran projects about fostering or adoption which made the young people think more positively about themselves.

This young man placed at the age of 11 whose placement broke down two years later said:

> During my life I have not had many black male role models. I couldn't call my foster father a role model. But the head master at the school took me to his house a couple of times and did try to talk to me. I liked the way he approached me and I do remember him as a positive role model. He showed me that he cared.

## Attitudes to birth parents after placement

The comments of both the new parents and the young people about their birth parents differed considerably depending on whether there had been any contact after placement. Twenty children who had moderately frequent or good contact during the months leading up to placement no longer saw the parent after they moved in with their new family. Not surprisingly (since legislation and guidance at the time, as now, required contact to be facilitated between children in care and their parents unless it had been legally terminated), it was significantly more likely that those in permanent foster placements or placed in foster care with a view to adoption had continuing contact with a parent than those placed directly for adoption (59 per cent and 7 per cent respectively).

In those cases where there was no actual contact this was often a sensitive part of the interview and some of the young people either told us directly or made it clear by their monosyllabic responses that they did not wish to dwell on the topic. There was also a difference between those who were placed as infants and had no contact and those who were placed when older. The majority of the older placed children had had some contact by the time of our interviews, most often when they became young adults or when the placement broke down. It has already been noted that the children with two parents of minority ethnic origin were more likely than those of mixed race parentage or white children to have continuing contact with a birth family member. This was in part because they were, on average, older at placement and was also associated with the fact that they were more likely to be placed with black adoptive or foster parents, who from our interview data, appeared to be more welcoming of birth family contact.

For the baby adopters, discussions about the birth parents and their attitudes towards them were linked with the question of how they told their children about their origins. As well as feeling gratitude, most of the adopters of the infants tended to speak warmly or with empathy about the birth mother and, though less frequently mentioned, the birth father.

> Jill, the birth mother, has told me it was the hardest thing she did in her life. The father wanted to marry her. He was a disc jockey, out-going and a lovely person. He and Jill were a very handsome couple.

Particular sympathy was expressed by Asian adopters for the young Asian women who had to give up their babies.

> I was very sympathetic to her parents. I tried to understand that this was a young Asian mother new to this country, who was very unsupported and that perhaps her husband hadn't been that responsible in his attitude towards keeping the family together. There had been some problem with him because he had been unemployed, so there were a lot of issues. So I had a lot of sympathy with her mother from the start. I liked her enormously. I was just so sad for her. She was so isolated and did not have the capacity to be a parent. I remember thanking her for giving us two

children, you know, her loss was our gain, and this feeling stayed with me for a long time. I do not see her as a threat. If the children wanted to search for her, I would support them. She is part of their identity, and it is their choice.

When older children joined new families there was a greater awareness of their origins and earlier life and the question of 'telling' was replaced by one of repeating the information in an age-appropriate way.

We have always been very positive about her mother. We didn't see it as our job to rubbish her mother.

An adoptive mother, who met the birth mother early in the placement to set up contact arrangements, told how the birth mother had kissed her and asked her to look after her daughter. This mother was aware throughout the placement that she had to help her adoptive daughter to sort out her changing and ambivalent feelings towards her birth mother.

She found it difficult to cope with. As a child, she needed us to be enemies and couldn't cope with us as friends. [The 'us' here refers to the adoptive mother and the birth mother]

This foster parent had such strong feelings of empathy towards the birth father that she would not apply to adopt his son.

They asked me about adopting Clive and I said 'no'. Clive's Daddy loved him in his own way, and he had that link with his Dad, and it would have meant a lot of changes, and I don't think it would have been fair to rob him [the birth father] of someone that he had loved in his own way.

Some of the new parents linked discussing their attitudes towards the first family with how they talked to the young people about why they couldn't live with them. One foster mother had taken the children to the funeral of the birth father.

Some of the adopters talked more about contact with **relatives** and again they were generally positive in their attitudes and the way they talked about them.

The aunt was very helpful. She came and visited and she was like the one stable and constant relative. We fell out after a while because I think she thought the affection that she should have been getting, I was getting, and she became a little bit cool. Their mother and father didn't really give me any hassle. They didn't interfere.

This next comment was made by one of the small number who expressed more negative feelings about the birth parents or relatives.

I actually don't feel anything in particular towards her birth mother. Unless the issue is physically brought up, she does not cross my mind, and when I do think about it there is a feeling of dislike because I feel that she did not protect her daughter. The feelings are of negative indifference rather than anything else.

Table 5.1 shows that 34 per cent of the children had some contact with one or both parents in the early stages after placement, and that nine per cent had contact with relatives and possibly siblings but not parents. (These figures are for continuing contact at the time of placement and do not include cases where contact was resumed at a much later stage.) The figures for the interview sample are 39 per cent having contact with parents; 27 per cent with siblings placed elsewhere and 7 per cent with relatives. Even more of the young people actually interviewed (10 out of 23) had contact with a birth parent after placement, although in some cases it was resumed after a long gap. Only five had had no contact with any member of the birth family after placement.

| | | Child had contact | |
| --- | --- | --- | --- |
| | | n | per cent |
| With one or both parents (and possibly also siblings and relatives) | | 89 | 34 [n = 262] |
| With siblings placed elsewhere but not parents or relatives | | 53 | 32 [ n = 164]* |
| With adult relatives and possibly siblings but not parents | | 21 | 9 [n = 219]* |

**Table 5.1 Contact between birth relatives and child after placement**

* These data were not available for a substantial minority of the children

## Patterns of birth family contact

There were four patterns of contact with birth relatives after placement.

- Some children and adopters had **no contact**, although some of these, as young adults, decided to 'search' and re-establish contact, sometimes with the help of the adopters and also the placement agency. In a minority of these cases adopters met one or both birth parents shortly before placement, sometimes for a 'goodbye visit' which they had invariably found stressful and upsetting. Occasionally there was also 'indirect contact' such as the exchange of letters and photographs. In none of the cases in the small sample did this prove to be a successful way of helping the adoptive family and the young person. This contact was in no case maintained as was initially intended, usually because the birth parents failed to continue with it. It should be remembered that in the early eighties little serious thought had been given to how to make such indirect contact successful.

- **The second group** comprised those who had **no contact** initially but where, **after several years had elapsed, contact was re-started**. In some of these cases the adoptive parents and the adoption agency played positive roles, sometimes picking up on hints dropped by the young person.

- The **third group** consisted of those where there was **no contact until the young person initiated** it **as a teenager**, often after a serious row in the adoptive family which led them to 'burst out' and go in search of the first family.

- The **fourth group** comprised those where **contact was maintained** with at least one birth parent (and often also with relatives and siblings), at varying levels throughout the placement. In a small number of cases the contact was only with siblings placed elsewhere. Figure 5.1 shows that it was more likely that children placed with black or Asian parents would have continuing contact with a birth parent.

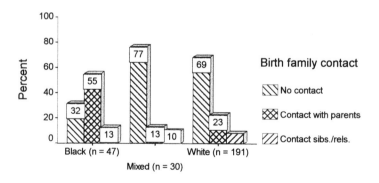

$\chi^2$: 26.56; df: 4; p<0.001
n = 268; missing data = 29

*Figure 5.1 Ethnicity of new parents by birth family contact*

*Those without contact*

New parents who did not have face to face contact with birth parents or relatives after placement were fairly evenly divided between those who would have wanted it; those who were fairly neutral, and those who definitely did not. Some would have liked contact, but found that it could not happen either because of the severe difficulties of the birth parent, including serious mental illness and hospitalisation and frequent moves of address; because the birth parent refused to have any contact, or because his or her whereabouts were not known.

> We would really want to find her and our son went through a period of wanting to find her when he was about eight. The social worker had left and the mother kept changing her name. Assuming the children would like to, we think that it is not only best for the children but it is also best for us because you are dealing with not a fantasy but also flesh and blood, and that has got to be better for the child. We don't have that. Once the social worker had left, that was it. I think we are at the stage now when we need to sit down with both of the children and talk about trying to find their birth parents. That is why we kept in touch with his half sister.

A family who adopted two unrelated children made a point of checking from time to time whether they would want them to take steps to contact the birth parent. In this case there had been 'letter box' contact which had died away very soon after the placement and the mother's whereabouts were unknown. The young man when interviewed by the researcher at the age of 14 said that he thought that this was about right. Although at the moment he was clear that he did not wish to see her, he thought he might want to in the future.

A young woman placed at the age of nine said:

> Personally I'm not too bothered about finding my birth mum because I'm happy now. Years ago when I was younger I used to cry for her. But now its more curiosity than anything. She might accept me, she might not accept me. I do love her because I've got memories of her but I don't know her.

A young man with no contact said:

> I had more of an urge when I was younger to meet my dad but it's not a big thing to me now. At the end of the day I'm not looking for a father figure. I've been looking after myself since I was 15 years old, but at the end of the day he could be a friend.

It was harder for those who did not have contact to resolve their feelings about their birth families and some spoke very movingly about their mixed feelings.

> If I wanted to know more about my mum and dad I used to go to my mum now, but she doesn't know much. I really don't want to go to my mum and say 'hey, why did you adopt me'? I don't really want to do that. They tried to explain to me when I was a child but I was only five years old and was I meant to understand? I didn't understand at all. I still don't understand why I was adopted. Apparently it was just because I was unhappy, but I get unhappy now and I'm not taken away from my mum. Its not a good enough excuse and I think Social Services didn't explain it to me properly. I have asked my mum here but she doesn't understand. She says, 'you were unhappy and your mum couldn't cope' and its like it's all my fault. You know, I wasn't happy, mum couldn't cope with me because I was being a pain. I don't think she really knows because she hasn't had anything explained to her properly either. I doubt she is trying to hide anything from me.

When interviewed at the age of 15, she described her birth parents whom she had subsequently met as follows:

> Mum has already told me, she said they fought for me. I don't think my parents had a choice about placing me for adoption. I didn't have a choice either. They thought they could do anything they liked with me. So they just picked me up and shoved me somewhere. That's what it feels like at the moment. When I was younger I hated them. My feelings towards them started to change when I started to have contact. Before I'd write letters to them and say 'why didn't you do this' or 'why did you let this happen' but I never posted them because they didn't know her address. I wanted to run away many times but then I thought where am I going to go. There was a time when I thought about hitch hiking all the way back there, but I didn't realise how far away it was. I was about eight or nine then and I've never attempted to run away since.

This comment was made about Jamie, who also had no contact with his birth family when he was placed at three with his infant brother.

> He never asked to see his mum, but as he got older he used to throw in my face 'Don't touch me. You're not my mum', and I got that quite a lot. I reminded him that as he got older we would support him seeing his mother but we can't do anything about it for the minute because the law says no. Get to 17, and if that is what you still want we will help you with that. But he never actually said that he wanted to see her.

Either this adoptive mother was being 'economical with the truth' or she had not been informed that, if the adults thought it appropriate, it was not necessary to wait until 18 before initiating contact. In many respects this young man was doing badly as a teenager but no help appeared to have been given to him to resolve the issues around his early life and his separation from his mother.

Adoptive parents who had no contact with birth family members tended to leave it to the young person to take the initiative, although some brought up the question of contact if relationships were not going too well.

> It was always us who brought the subject up. She expressed a lot of bitterness. I used to sometimes sit her down and ask her if there were any problems. 'Let's talk, you know, anything you want to talk about, just tell me. You know, is anything bothering you? Are you happy here? Just tell me. Would you like to see your mother? Would you like me to find your mum for you if you are not happy? or would you like me to find your dad?' and we used to get it out of her that – no, she didn't want to.

This was one of the 'letterbox' cases where there had been an agreement to exchange photographs and cards with the birth mother. Letters had been sent by Nicola but she had received no response and eventually stopped writing.

> The mum was pestering us to meet her, and she got in touch with Social Services. This was last year when Nicola was 18. So we said to her 'look, your mum has written to the adoption agency looking for you, and would you like to meet her?' and she said no, not until she meets her dad. When she met her dad she was even more angry with her mum because she found out that she'd always been in touch with her dad although she had previously said that she never knew where he was. But meeting her mum was good because she got to see who she looked like, and learned about her life history and where she came from.

This young woman was representative of the group who left their adoptive or foster families in some turmoil in their mid-teens. Contact had been terminated, as was the usual practice in the early 80s when she joined the family at the age of five, and she herself initiated further contact in her late teens.

Tanya's mother, in retrospect, thought that contact would have been helpful. In this case there had been an emotional and very upsetting 'goodbye visit'. With hindsight, both the young person and the foster parents, thought that more should have been done to help her mother to care for her.

Her mother really fought for her. Actually smashed the nursery. She should have been given more help. We met the mother. It was very difficult. She was crying, she didn't want Tanya to go, she cuddled her. We found that difficult and she always said she didn't want her adopted. The child had been in care for three years so we didn't think we were taking her away from her mother. They didn't offer any contact or ask us about it. They said they thought it would be disruptive for Tanya, but she had this rosy picture of her mother. When she was first placed I don't think it would have helped for her to see her mother. She would have played one up against the other. But in retrospect I think its helpful for children to see their birth parents because they do have fantasies. In retrospect, its easier to do the parenting; at the time I thought it would take her longer to bond, but in retrospect it would have helped us because of the fantasy. She always asks the question 'Why is it that she is looking after her other two children and she sent me and my brother away?'

### Contact re-started some years after placement

In some of these cases it was not at all clear why contact had initially been terminated, sometimes without the adoptive parents having met the birth parents. The adoptive parents were expressing positive views about the birth parents, and it was they themselves who initiated contact five or six years after placement when the children were aged anywhere between eight and 15.

For other young people for whom contact had been terminated at placement, the relationship was re-started only after the placement disrupted, as was the case with this young man placed at the age of six whose placement broke down when he was 12.

He was moving away from us. Deep down I think he wanted to find his real mother, which he did.

Young people who had been perplexed as to why other siblings remained at home seemed particularly driven to re-establish contact, as was the case with a young woman placed at five. When she was 10, contact was reestablished with the help of the adoption agency at a frequency of once a year.

More recently, when the young woman was in her mid-teens, she started to visit the birth family in their own home with the adoptive family and the birth parents making the arrangements themselves.

I think she feels better about herself than she did before, although this is a more difficult time because she is in the teenage phase. I have not really had much opportunity to talk with her about what she feels about being adopted. I think she is comfortable talking about her birth family openly, and in a way she can say that she has got two mums, but being here has an added point to it. Sometimes she will say, 'I wish I was with my family'. But she usually says that when she has chores to do.

The young woman herself, when interviewed, talked freely about her relationship with both families. It was not at all clear to the researchers why she had been unable to remain with her birth family since other children in the family had not been removed. Since there was a Care Order there must have been evidence of some form of maltreatment or neglect. When she was not in touch with her birth family she said that she 'hated them'. But having resumed contact she had been able to reassure herself that they had fought to keep her with them. It was clear from the interview that she regretted the long gap. When asked whether there was a difference between adoption and fostering, she said:

> Adoption is more for life, and you have to be prepared for it. With fostering, at least you would get to see your parents. I mean, with adoption, you do get to see your parents, but it's usually after a very long gap. With me, it was like when I was about nine or ten when I saw them, so that is five years. That's quite a lot to be away from your parents. But I really feel part of this family. They do not treat me like an outsider. They treat me like I was born into this family. I think they even treat me better than the other kids in our family – they treat me with respect and love.

Her adoptive mother said:

> Since coming to live with me she talked of her family as being kind to her, particularly her brother to whom she was very close. It is really uncomfortable to see the good things she has lost from her family. Then I think she very much missed her dad and she would keep making up some lovely stories explaining her situation. I remembered people coming up to me and saying how sorry they were that my husband had died. I then had to explain that her father was very much alive and that I was her adoptive mother. She particularly wanted to meet her dad and she started to write to him and this was something I encouraged although she never posted them. Also she didn't have any photos of her dad. I felt she wanted to have contact with her birth family and I took it up with the adoption agency.

Her daughter, along with some of the others who re-established contact in their mid-teens, seemed to have found a way of having generally positive relationships with both families despite her mixed feelings.

> I know my mum and dad still love me, but I'm not sure whether they want me back. I think they are happy with the way things are and may be they would feel I would muck up everything. I know I'll never return. I know that this is a full-time thing. Mum's explained to me that I will be here until I am 18. By the time I'm 18 I'm not going to move back and live with mum and dad. I'll probably move out by then, do my own thing. But I would give everything to go and live with them. I'm not saying I hate it here, I really love it, I'm really lucky but if I had the chance I would go and live with them. I love my brothers and sisters, we get on so well.

In one case it was the birth mother who restarted contact 'out of the blue'.

> Our adopted daughter's mother turned up when she was about 16. It was a shock. I suggested she take her up to the bedroom and have a chat with her. After 40 minutes I went up and I saw the anxiety on our daughter's face and I said, 'I'm sorry but you will have to leave now.' Our daughter said she did not want to see her again. She should have phoned us. She had our phone number. The adoption agency asked her not to come again.

The following two comments are about cases where contact was not re-established until the young person was 18 or older. In one case it was the older birth daughter of the adopters who made the arrangements.

> We had no contact with the birth father until she was 18. I traced her birth father because I became aware of his whereabouts through a classmate who happened to be her first aunt. This aunt had seen her at school when she came to meet me and later came up to me and revealed that she was her niece and had not seen her for several years. It was meant to be a surprise for her 18th birthday. It was something that we did so that we knew where he was when she asked. We were going to say, 'Do you want to know now?' We always felt it was important that we had this information to hand, and it was always left open for Nina to ask us whether or not she wanted to see her mum or dad.

There was often a sense of unease as the adoptive family members spoke to us of the way in which the adopted young people contacted their birth relatives as young adults.

> She still sees us as family. We have left her to deal with her own mother, and we hope in time she will get a more realistic picture of her.

Several adoptive parents spoke about their distress that the reunion with the birth families was painful and often, after an early period of excitement, resulted in a further disappointment or rejection for their adopted son or daughter. This was, indeed, the most common pattern for the young people whose contact was totally severed, and who went in search of their birth parents when the relationship with their adoptive parents became difficult in their teenage years.

> Any child would have the idealised 'let me go back to my own lovely family' thinking. But I think that now she has gone back and found out how chaotic and wild her family is – I mean the children all left home because they couldn't stand her [the birth mother] – she now has a more realistic picture of what her family is like.

It should be noted that, because of the structure of the research, none of those placed as babies with the more traditional 'closed' adoptive families was yet old enough to seek information or 'Section 51' counselling on reaching the age of 18. Our interview data are therefore weighted towards the more complex situations of the older placed children.

Young people who remained as foster children were more protected from launching out into the unknown, since, even if there was no face to face contact, the review system usually meant that there had been some updating of family information.

For some of the children this return back home in early teens was followed by a spell in a children's home, followed by an early move into independent living and considerable vulnerability as they moved into adult life. Those who had been adopted and thus left care before the age of 16 could not benefit from leaving care schemes and grants. Although such assistance could have been made available to them as young people 'in need' (Section 17, Children Act 1989) or as a post-adoption service, it appeared that those who left adoptive homes as teenagers had less assistance from Social Services Departments or Adoption Agencies than those who left foster homes.

> I gave him the emotional permission to contact his birth mother and father. If I had said no, he would have been relieved because basically it would have been much too much for him. But obviously he had to go ahead with it. It was obviously very painful for me because you have given 13 years of your life and you loved this kid and he is suddenly going off and finding another family. His family now are none of my business. He has to sort out his family. You know, I don't have to worry about them. He is now living with them.

*Contact maintained*

Whilst it is most often the children placed past infancy who retained contact, this was not invariably the case. There were no cases where continuing contact with birth parents was imposed against the wishes of the adoptive or foster parents. Consequently they had been determined to make it work in the interest of the children, and, from their comments, appear to have succeeded. In some cases they did so by incorporating a birth parent (usually a birth father) into their extended family.

Those who remained in contact with one or both parents throughout the placement made both negative and positive comments about them, but they dealt in reality rather than fantasy. This young man, who remained in his foster home for two years before returning to his mother and then going to live independently said:

> I feel angry at my birth mother. You see if you make one mistake with one child, that's OK but with a second one you could say OK again but if you make the same mistake with the third or fourth one, then that's rubbish really, isn't it? You ain't no good mother, simple as that. But you can't choose your parents, you can't choose your relatives and what you're stuck with you're stuck with.

He was however clear that he did want to go on seeing his birth mother when he was with his foster family:

> It would have made a difference if I hadn't seen my birth mother because I knew that I wanted to see her. I think you should either have regular contact with your birth parents or no contact. Contact should not be taken as a joke. The mother should become part of the extended family like a grandmother or whatever.

This young woman was placed at 12 with her 9-year-old brother and three-year-old sister. The placement was originally intended to be short-term, but was confirmed as a 'permanent' placement and was one of the more successful placements we studied in detail.

> Mum says there were times when I used to say I'm going back home to my mum. But I can't remember this. Nothing was set up by Social Services. Mum would just turn up at the house. I think this worked out all right for me but my foster mum would probably have preferred if these visits had been arranged. My foster dad didn't mind, he just sat and watched television. Mum thought it was OK, she got looked after, she got dinner. Sometimes my brother didn't even bother to stay in when she came; he just went out to play. If they [foster parents] had said that mum

wasn't allowed to come to the house it would have bothered me. I would want to know why.

Painful feelings about the experiences which had led to them having to leave their first families never went away, but they could be talked about and worked through with both sets of parents. One young woman had since had a child of her own and this brought back earlier feeling of anger. Her adoptive mother said:

> She was very angry with her birth mother after the birth of her own first child. She couldn't understand how her first mother could be so dismissive. Her feelings for her little son, she can't imagine leaving him or giving him up without a fight. As she was growing up her mum was very much an idealised figure. She used to miss her mother a lot and this was something I had to talk to somebody about. She still feels this way now because there is a role for her mum. There are things she'd like to ring her mum up about and talk about.

For some, the contact helped the young people to feel less badly about their early lives and to understand the predicament of their parents. For others its re-enforced the reason why they could not be at home.

> The contact with my mum has helped me to see what she is really like. She used to be nice in the beginning, but she's not nice any more. If I hadn't seen my mum and dad I would have been wondering what they were like.

> I don't hate my mum. I suppose I love her because she is my mum. We used to get on sometimes, and sometimes we never used to. I'm glad that we didn't stay with her.

Some other comments about continued contact were more negative or ambivalent. This young woman was still working out her feelings as a young adult:

> I used to take out my anger and how I used to feel with my mum on aunt [adoptive mother]. I think I still do that now sometimes. I can't seem to bring myself to tell my mum how I feel. We don't get on very well. I know that if I hadn't left my mum I'd be dead by now because she used to batter me. My mum never really liked me. Even now if I go up to see her, she can be really horrible. On one occasion she went to hit me and my brother was there and he intervened. When I was younger I used to like them [birth mum and dad]. I didn't know much then. I was living in a fantasy world.

A young man of African descent who was placed at the age of 14 and whose placement disrupted two years later, shortly before his foster parents' marriage broke up, said about his birth father:

> We do get on but he's a bit African – the way he thinks is not like me. I only met my mum once after I was nine, then I met her again when I was 18 when I went to Africa where she was living. I was really scared. She was still mad; she didn't recognise me at first. I like my dad now but, you know, I'm older – he is my dad and I haven't got one if you see what I mean.

### Contact with siblings

It was a matter of concern that information on the records about continuing contact between separated siblings was often not available. It was recorded that 53 (22 per cent) of the children had contact with a birth sibling and that 34 per cent were placed with at least one sibling. Figure 5.2 shows that there was a trend (which did not reach statistical significance) towards families in which both parents were of minority ethnic origin, being more likely to have sibling groups placed with them.

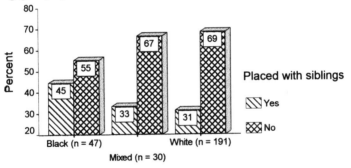

not significant

n = 268;  missing data = 29

*Figure 5.2 Ethnicity of new parents by placement of siblings*

Some of the young people had significant links with brothers and sisters who had been in care but were placed elsewhere. One young man was particularly upset that he had been separated from his sister, and that his sister had been placed with a white adoptive family. The parents of both had tried to keep links going but both spoke of their regret that they had become emotionally distant from each other.

> I think the foster parents wanted to help a black child and they saw my advert in the newspaper or something. But they should have taken me and my sister. I remember that one of my social workers took me up to see my sister, but I don't rate them highly. The biggest mistake they made was to separate me and my sister. They play God with people. Me and my sister had been together so many years and then they went and separated us just like that.

A 15-year-old told the researcher that he would like to see a sister who was born to his mother after he had gone into care, and his adoptive mother was aware that he sometimes worried about his birth mother and the sister.

> He talked more about his sister. He said, 'I would like to see my sister. But one day I will see my mum, but not now, later. I'd like to see my sister now.' But no-one seemed to push it. He started to stay away from school and had a violent temper. He pushed our grandchild down the stairs. He could have had his own reasons for not wanting to stay. Being adopted is a big burden. He went looking in the part of the town where she lives. I started to think why he kept going away from the house and travelling around might be to see if he could see her.

Another young man, placed as an infant and well-settled, told the researcher he would like to see a sister born after he had been placed. He did not want at that point to see his mother but thought he would like to see her some time. When asked to tell the researcher his three wishes, he said that one of them was to have his sister come and live with him in his present family. There was no contact between the birth family and the adoptive family other than indirect up-dating through the adoption agency.

## Decisions about adoption or fostering

Attitudes towards birth parents and contact were often linked, though not invariably, with whether the children were in foster care or were adopted. Indeed in some cases the contact issue determined the question of legal status, sometimes because of the views of the Social Services Department or Adoption Agency, but sometimes because of strongly held views of the children or the new parents. Ricky was placed at four and had a good relationship with his father. He was the only child under five placed as a foster child (though others placed under five were not, in the event, adopted) and was still in close contact with foster parents and birth relatives in his twenties.

> They asked me about adopting Ricky and I said no. Ricky's daddy loved him in his own way and Ricky had that link with his dad.

The time between placement and adoption could be long for those who were placed for adoption and during this time social work visits continued. Attempts had therefore to be made, usually successfully, to ensure that children and new parents had a 'sense of permanence' whether the plan was for adoption or fostering. Fifty-six of the children in the full cohort of 297 were adopted within 12 months of placement. However 20 children were adopted three or more years after placement. Some of the children placed originally as permanent foster children were adopted, often as they moved towards their 18th birthdays and because it was the young person who wanted this to happen. Others who were placed with the intention that they would move quickly to adoption remained in the placement, either as permanent foster children or under a custodianship or residence order. Sometimes the position differed within families. A residence order was made in respect of the youngest of three siblings (placed at the age of three) but her older siblings were 9 and 12 when placed and remained in care as foster children. Table 5.2 gives the intentions at the time the placement was made and shows that in 71 per cent of cases the child was either placed directly for adoption under the Adoption Agencies' Regulations, or there was a clear intention that adoption papers would be lodged after a short period in foster care. Fostering with a view to adoption in the longer term was less frequently the placement choice than 'permanent fostering'.

| Table 5.2 Legal status anticipated at time of placement | | |
|---|---|---|
| Legal status | n | per cent |
| Adoption | 175 | 59 |
| Fostering with a view to adoption | 35 | 12 |
| Permanent fostering | *87 | 29 |
| Total | 297 | 100 |

* Includes five children where a temporary foster placement was confirmed as 'permanent' after placement.

As far as we could tell from the information on the files, 55 per cent of the 297 children were adopted and 38 per cent remained as fostered children. Another outcome was recorded for 20 children, including return to the birth parents with the agreement of all concerned. There were disrupted placements in both of the main groupings as we shall see in Chapter 9. Eighteen of the adoptive placements did not result in adoption and three of the foster placements did lead to adoption together with the two already mentioned which resulted in custodianship orders being made.

The young people were asked whether they told their friends that they were adopted or fostered and it was in this context that they tended to express their views about whether they themselves, and their friends and acquaintances, perceived either the foster care or adoptive status to be a positive or negative aspect of their identities.

> I don't really tell anybody that I am fostered. When I talk to people about Annie, it's easier to refer to her as my aunty. They know she is not my mum. When I was little I was teased about being fostered at school. We used to tell them that we were fostered and they used to think that we were adopted. They didn't really understand. They treated us like we had some sort of disease. They wanted to know where we had come from, how we got there, why we were there. They said stuff that was hurtful, like: 'Where is your real mum? Are you an orphan?' – stuff like that. I was happy to come to a black family because if you saw us in the street together you wouldn't know we were fostered. It was more natural. I didn't want people to think that they were our real mum and dad, but at the same time I wanted people to think that we were just family instead of being fostered. At one time they wanted to adopt my younger sister and give her their name. And I was opposed to that. They could adopt but they couldn't change her name. I was really strong about that. She was our sister and I didn't see why she had to change her name. [A residence order was subsequently granted in respect of the younger sister.]

Comments were often linked with the issue of names they used for themselves, their new families and their birth families. As can be seen from some of the earlier quotations, children and young people appeared, contrary to views frequently expressed by the adults who made decisions about them, not to find it difficult to have two mums and dads. In the course of the research interviews, young people in both foster and adoptive families used 'mum' and 'mum' and 'dad' and 'dad' interchangeably to refer to either birth parents or new parents and there was clearly no confusion in their own minds as to which person they were talking about. Occasionally they used the given name of one or other of their parents and sometimes this changed within the same interview. They did not particularly seem to adopt the convention preferred by some substitute parents and social workers of referring to their birth mother as 'mummy Pat'. It was almost always 'my mum', 'my birth mum', or 'Pat'. Some of the children placed with African-Caribbean adoptive or foster parents referred to them as 'my nan' or aunty and uncle and found this a particularly satisfactory way of avoiding prying questions in the street or at school.

## Summary

- *For the settling in period and the early years of placement* descriptions ranged from totally positive to extremely negative. Some parents were able to describe a growing sense of attachment, others recalled their growing sense of dismay that feelings and relationships remained distant.

- The young people interviewed spoke more about this period than did their parents and they regarded it as difficult for them. Some recognised that they had not been easy to manage, others recalled a turning point when they started to feel that they belonged often after a period of particular difficulty.

- Behaviour difficulties appeared to be related to age at placement. They were rarely reported for children placed as infants.

- Older children found school an important influence, for good or for ill.

- Thirty-four per cent of the children had some continuing contact with one or both parents after placement; 22 per cent had contact with siblings placed elsewhere but with no other birth relatives; 9 per cent had contact with relatives and possibly siblings but not birth parents.

- For the cohort as a whole, it was significantly more likely for children with two black parents to have post-placement contact with a member of the birth family than for those of mixed race parentage (45 per cent and 28 per cent respectively).

# CHAPTER 6

# Parenting, Family Relationships, and Parental Satisfaction

## Parenting

In this chapter we consider what the new parents had to say about the day-to-day parenting tasks. In asking about their parenting methods, we used the seven headings identified for the 'Looking after children' project (Ward 1996): education; health; identity; family and social relationships; emotional and behavioural development; social presentation; and self-care skills. These dimensions are considered in more detail in our chapter on outcomes. We consider here some of the children's behaviour patterns as they grew up and the way in which their adoptive or foster parents sought to help them through any difficulties and encourage and nurture any strengths and special aptitudes. Whilst some of the parents placed more emphasis than others on the nature of attachments and bonding, all considered that providing good parenting in all aspects of daily living was of vital importance to the children. The young people themselves concurred with this view and, in retrospect, expressed considerable gratitude to their adopters, even though they might have resented some aspects of parenting and discipline whilst they were living in the family.

There were two broad patterns in terms of the children's behaviour. Those who were placed early and a minority of those placed when over the age of three experienced few behavioural problems, although they may have had some emotional difficulties around the area of adoption and identity in their teenage years. Those placed when older, including some of the pre-schoolers, were more likely to experience behavioural and emotional difficulties as well as problems in school. At the time of placement 51 per cent of the cohort of 297 were described as having emotional problems; 46 per cent as having behavioural difficulties, and 36 per cent as showing some signs of having been 'institutionalised' as a result of long stays in residential care or hospital.

It has been noted in Chapter 3 that some of the older children entered care because of their own behaviour difficulties. However, by the time they came to be placed, some of the younger children were also showing worrying disturbances of mood and behaviour. Two children placed at the age of four were already having psychotherapy.

For most families, behaviour difficulties were not so apparent at the start but later behaviour made them realise that the children had already been harmed by earlier experiences.

For the youngest children in the interview sample, the Rutter (parents) scale (Rutter *et al.* 1981) was used during the interview. For those who were older it was used as a prompt to help parents to recall any problems they had experienced as the child grew up. Twenty-three per cent of the interview sample were said by their parents to have experienced no emotional or behavioural difficulties as they grew up; 40 per cent had only slight difficulties. Twelve per cent had moderate difficulties and just over a quarter (26 per cent) had serious difficulties.

The adoptive or foster parents tended to concentrate on the ways in which they sought to help the young people to overcome these difficulties. They also spoke about day-to-day parenting, particularly talking about discipline and about ways in which they helped the young people to acquire social and life skills.

### Reactions to behavioural and emotional difficulties

Attitudes towards behavioural difficulties depended very much on the perceptions of the parents. Whilst some took apparently seriously disturbed behaviour in their stride, others would be put out by fairly minor misdemeanours. Parents became particularly concerned when other children in the family were threatened, whilst they tolerated extreme difficulties if the impact was only upon themselves.

> He was threatening my grandchild. He would tell her things – tell her that he would stick a knife in her, you know, really violent things. I saw the knife he had. I don't know where he got it and we took it away from him. I always took him with me. I saw him as my responsibility, but I also wanted him for my company too. We talked a lot in the car.

At the other end of the scale some of the children who had adverse early backgrounds thrived in their new families and showed few problems.

> I have always had compliments about Jane. Her enthusiasm is second to none.

New parents made very considerable efforts to help children recover from the effects of trauma and separation, but as time went on and if they saw little or no improvement, their ability to tolerate these difficulties and to deal positively with them diminished.

> It was sheer bloody-mindedness that kept me going. Sometimes I thought I might kill him, or he might kill me. And then he would come and sit on my knee. His one aim in life is to survive for himself. He is totally selfish. He knew exactly what to say to put the needle in. I spent half my life protecting the other children and my husband from him. I don't think he ever settled in some ways. He was always wanting to be thrown out.

In some cases the young people left home to go to boarding schools or had respite care built into the placement. Those families who had regular respite care considered this to be highly appropriate and others considered that social workers should have insisted on building it into the placement in view of the difficulties which they should have anticipated. Several of the parents spoke of the fight they had had to get children 'statemented' so that special education on a day basis or in boarding-schools could be provided. As in some American studies, we found that out-of-home placement could save the adoptive or foster family placement from total disruption. The longer the child hung on in the placement, if necessary supported by periodic out-of-home care, the more likely was it that the adoptive or foster family would continue to provide practical and emotional support as they moved, perhaps too early, into independent living. However, only two of the children in the intensive sample were provided with planned care or schooling away from home, rather than emergency arrangements with friends or relatives.

Whilst some children placed as young as three or four experienced difficulties from the start of the placement, in other cases children described as very well behaved early on started to experience difficulties around the age of ten.

In some cases the difficulties were so great that new parents who had initially intended to adopt the children felt unable to do so.

> One thing I was adamant about. I could never adopt her because of all the problems. I could be forced to be her parent but I couldn't be forced to adopt her.

Some of the young people settled initially but then earlier problems from before they were placed began to emerge.

> I had quite a lot of problems with him. He had been in trouble with the
> police and arrested several times. One was with drugs. Another time he
> was stopped with offensive weapons.

Darren, a young man of white/African-Caribbean descent was placed with
African-Caribbean parents at the age of six. The placement was confirmed as
a long-term one after six months. His foster mother said:

> He started giving me trouble and we thought 'My God, we have made a
> mistake'. I told him off and he went upstairs and I could smell matches. I
> had a new quilt on my bed and Darren gashed it and he lit it in about
> three places with the matches and set fire to it. We decided that, well,
> maybe we will have to give him up. When I came home from work I said
> to my husband 'You know, when I was at work I was thinking, maybe we
> will give him another chance' and he says 'Seems we were thinking the
> same thing'. So we decided to carry on. We had to watch him all the time
> with matches.

Some of the children who had serious behaviour difficulties when placed
around the ages of three or four had left their new families in difficult
circumstances by the time of the interview, though most remained in touch.

Having described the range of children's emotional and behavioural
problems, we consider the ways in which the new parents sought to help
them. Often they went back to the question of similarities and differences
between adoptive and birth parenting and compared the way they treated
their adopted children with the way they thought parents treat children born
to them.

Generally they worked hard to settle the child into their family and at that
stage all those who had children born to them said that they had to treat the
children joining the family differently because of their very different early
histories.

> It was something that just fell into place. I think having my own children
> helped, because they got to know them for a while first and it wasn't as
> difficult as I thought, apart from the fact that I think we were doing
> something every minute of the day (three siblings were placed in this
> family). When I scolded them they used to say, Bea never said that to us'
> (house parent), and I would say: 'Bea is not here. This is me and we have
> to get used to each other. You are not going back there.'

Others, however, thought they lacked the skills to help children over their
behavioural difficulties as was the case with this child placed at eight.

> We would have liked to have helped her more but we did not have the
> necessary skills which would help her enhance the image of herself. The

other problem was in terms of schooling where I do not have the skills and where specialist skills would be more effective.

The most frequent reaction, once the children had settled in, was to get on with parenting as best they could, seeking advice where appropriate, if any difficulties arose. Several parents commented on the importance of being very explicit with the children about what was the appropriate way to behave in this household. This was particularly so if the children had behavioural or learning disabilities.

Some of the parents related the anxieties of the children to the frequent moves they had had in the past. One young woman placed at fourteen had had fifteen moves before the age of ten, including a broken adoption and total rejection by her adoptive parents.

> To help her settle in, I had to say you are here and nothing you can do will make me take you back. I had to say this constantly. But I think what clinched it was a trip to Jamaica to my family and she then saw me not in isolation but as part of a family unit myself. It helped her to be accepted as part of a family unit. Here in England it was just me in isolation.

This return to the Caribbean was experienced as a turning-point for several of the families.

For a variety of reasons several of the children who were placed with the intention of adoption were not formally adopted for periods of six or seven years. It was, therefore, important for a 'sense of permanence' to be reinforced for those in adoptive placements as well as those in foster placements. A foster mother who did not proceed to adoption until seven years after the placement, told us that a visit to relatives in the Caribbean had an important part to play in the developing sense of belonging. The mother thought very carefully about ways in which she could give her daughter a 'sense of permanence', always talking about a point in the distant future when they would do something together – when you are doing your GCEs – when you are having driving lessons – we will do this or that – were topics of conversation with her 11-year-old.

The final stage at which adoptive parents had to work especially hard was the stage when the young people left the family. This was particularly the case if they left in stressful circumstances. Whilst some of the foster or adoptive parents insisted on the young people leaving, often because of real fears of violence or disruption to other children in the family, they nevertheless pulled out all the stops to make sure that they had somewhere to go.

> His leaving was not planned. He wasn't working with his social worker and he wasn't co-operating with me. Because there was no vacancy on

the Independent Living Scheme, I had to go and find him accommodation and I found him a lovely bed-sit and he went there. But after a while he began stealing things from other people and he wasn't paying his rent, which resulted in him hiding from the landlords so he couldn't go there any more. He comes round when he wants a bob or two to borrow from me. I felt it was the right thing for him to leave because I was knocking my head against a brick wall – both for his sake and for our younger [adopted] son's sake because he was frightened of him.

A family whose very disturbed son went to boarding-school where he made good progress felt compelled to insist on him leaving the family home when he became violent at the age of 17.

> Year in year out I fought for him. But I had to say 'you have to stand on your own two feet.' Sometimes it would be something dramatic like setting a fire, but most often it was just total undermining the whole time. It was exhausting for us and for him. We lived on the edge of disaster the whole time so he lived on the edge also. I found him a place in a homeless hostel. He has good social skills and knows how to look after himself.

All the parents spoke briefly about their links with the school. Generally schools were helpful although several of the children were excluded at some stage. There was no indication in any of these interviews that the children were pushed to perform above their ability by their adoptive or foster parents, a complaint which has sometimes been made in other studies. However, all the parents were determined to make sure that the children did as well as possible. Whether they were foster or adoptive parents appeared to make little difference in this respect, a finding which differs from other studies (Triseliotis 1983; Triseliotis and Russell 1984). Several of the parents talked about their children being of above average intelligence and ability at school. This and their 'street-wise' apparent confidence meant that older children often dominated or even bullied others in their class.

> Right through her school life she never had friends. She has always been a loner. She never brought friends home. I think other people at school were afraid of her because she was so bright. They used to call her names because she was bright, and because of that, she stopped excelling. She was always trying to be part of the gang, and she followed the wrong crowd, basically.

Few of the foster or adoptive parents of the children placed when older described them as having good peer relationships. However, most of those placed as infants had few problems in school or with their peers and this applied also to some of the more resilient older-placed children.

Appearance was seen by the parents as being very important to the children's self-esteem and this applied especially to the African-Caribbean children who were placed from children's homes or foster homes in predominantly white areas. Their new parents found that time spent together on skin and hair care brought them closer.

### Discipline

Most of the families used telling-off, 'serious talking to' or withdrawal of privileges, especially refusal to let the children watch favourite television programmes, as a way of teaching them about appropriate behaviour. However, a substantial minority used physical punishment. This applied particularly to the adoptive parents since foster parents were aware that physical punishment was not permitted by social services guidance and regulations. However, some foster parents thought that it was appropriate to smack and others were inappropriately heavy-handed.

> I did not treat him [placed at the age of four] in a different way from my own children. The only difference I see is that I didn't spank him as much as I did my own children, although I did spank him occasionally because I could see that he was mine. I feel it was more of a punishment to deny him watching the television or sending him to his bedroom.

The young people gave us their version of parental punishment. A young man placed at nine said:

> Dad would punish me. He would pull my ears. Yes, I hated him. I remember once he hit me with a wooden ruler and it snapped in half, and I had a big gash at the back of my leg. My mum couldn't believe that my dad would do such a thing, but neither her or me said anything to him. My mum would just shout at me, tell me off. It was usually dad that gave me the punishment. I think the best thing to do is to sit down and just talk to them. I really hated being smacked, it just built up into a hate thing. I always hated my dad more than I did my mum. I would listen more to my mum than what I did with my dad. There is a fine line between beating and punishing a child and I think that my foster father crossed the line several times. Way over the line. In my opinion, looking back, I would say that man was enjoying himself. He terrorised my life for the whole two years that I was there.

In most families the father was the disciplinarian. Sometimes there was inconsistency of discipline which did not involve actual physical punishment. The adoptive mother of a boy whose placement subsequently broke down, said:

> Initially it worked out well. They would go out jogging and ride their bikes together, but there was always the discipline problem that our son was expected to jump when he was told to do things, and I think that started to be a problem.

The above comments about discipline were, however, unrepresentative of the more common approaches which were based on reasoning and withdrawal of privileges.

> If anything happened that I didn't like I shouted. I didn't hit them. Like any other mother, I suppose, I did the same things to them that I did with mine.

The expression 'tough love' characterised the way in which several of the African-Caribbean parents encouraged the young people to fit in with the family's behaviour codes.

> I'm strict. I'm sort of an affectionate type of person. I like touching and I think, once I get to know them and I find they can relax with me, I begin to cuddle them. I think that gives them the bond of security, continuously saying that I care. Continually saying, even if things go wrong, and I'm talking to them, I will put that in. 'I care about you, that is why I am doing x, y, z.' I'd be continually doing that.

Some noted that different forms of discipline were necessary with different children.

> Peter did not seem to be bothered if he was punished. If I withdrew his pocket money, he knew he would get it next week. But Andy would cry if he wasn't able to watch television.

## The impact on family and friends

### Marriages and partnerships

It is not surprising, given the degree of pressure which the arrival of a child with special needs placed on the family members, that some of the marriages or long term partnerships collapsed under the strain. This information is not available for the full cohort but, of the 38 families interviewed, five had experienced separation or divorce during the ten or so years following the placement, and the marriages of several others came under severe strain. This was not always as a direct result of the arrival of the adopted or fostered child, and indeed there were indications that at least two of the marriages were in difficulties before the child was placed.

At the start of the placement seven of the children in the interview sample were placed with five single women, one of whom had a long-standing partner at the time of the research interview. Thus 34 of the families with whom 45 of the children were living had marital or partner relationships. In one case a father died and the mother subsequently remarried.

| Table 6.1 Marital problems after placement | | |
|---|---|---|
| Problems | Number of families | |
| | n | per cent |
| No significant problems | 22 | 71 |
| Problems not related to placement | 2 | 6.5 |
| Problems related partly or wholly to placement | 2 | 6.5 |
| Marriage breakdown linked wholly or partly to placement | 5 | 16 |
| Total | 31 | 100 |

[n = 31 families with whom 41 children were placed; seven single parents are excluded. Six children were affected by the five marriage breakdowns, and five others by serious marital problems.]

Table 6.1 shows that there were serious marital or partner problems in 29 per cent of the families which were not single parent families. In all except one of the seven cases where there was serious partner conflict (involving eight children), the relationship subsequently broke down. In the one case where it did not break down, problems were very clearly associated with the difficulties and stresses encountered when the child joined the family. In three of the marital breakdown cases, problems appeared not to be related to the child placed, but in the other two, the difficulties of the child exacerbated existing difficulties. In four other families, although problems were not so serious, marriages were put under stress at some time as a result of the placement. In these cases the difficulties were surmounted and, in some cases, the marriage was strengthened.

> Billy's stay had a positive effect on our family. It wasn't negative in any way. For Delroy's stay, I would say it affected me and my husband. Delroy would stay out and never come home when he should. My husband couldn't bear to see the effect this was having on me. He

became protective towards me because I started having headaches and he thought that this was because of the worry.

The stresses on the marriage only disappeared when the older child left the home as a teenager. Parents whose marriages were strengthened or supportive in caring for the child tended to mention this to the researchers and say little more about it. However, it was the families whose marriages had broken down who had most to say, sometimes in very sad and emotional ways as they remembered the strains of that period in their lives. This mother did not consider that the marriage breakdown was directly the result of the child's placement:

> I don't want to say that his behaviour had anything to do with my marriage break-up. Certainly the environment at home was not a good environment. I felt unsupported and by this time I was working full-time so it was just four years of sheer hell with little support.

In another case the growing fondness of the adoptive mother for the child, placed at the age of 14, and her willingness to spend time to help him with his problems, caused marital difficulties which were exacerbated by different views about discipline. The adoptive father's attitude could, as reported here, be described as racist:

> I think that as I got fonder of Martin that also became a problem. I probably made the mistake of being over-protective towards him and this created tensions between myself and my husband. It's really hard to say if there is an attachment between Martin and his adoptive father because at the end, I think it became him or me. To be fair to my husband, he is six years older than me and he said he did not want to go back to the teenage thing, and he also said things like – which really shocked me – 'What if Martin leaves school and we have this black teenager hanging around the home without a job?', and what he really was saying was that he saw Martin as some sort of rival – another male in the house. I think personally that was it. He would never admit it and I don't think he'd know it consciously, but I think that's what was going on. This sort of male rivalry business. But the problem lies with my ex-husband and me rather than with Martin. I remember our social worker saying that if there are any cracks in the marriage, this will find them and that is true.

The young man left the placement before adoption was finalised when the prospective adoptive mother was given an ultimatum to choose. He was placed in a bridge foster home with the mother hoping that this would relieve pressure.

But, of course, I was devastated. I was so cut up about it because I thought that Martin hadn't really had anybody say he was the most important thing in their life, so I said to my husband, perhaps he and I could part for a couple of years and I could see Martin through school. It was unrealistic but that's how I felt at the time. But my husband was, of course, devastated that I could say this – that somebody who'd only been in the house for a year could have this effect on me.

Not surprisingly the marriage ultimately broke down.

Several examples were given where children from the age of three onwards came between the parents and marriages were temporarily destabilised. It was not unusual for the child of the opposite sex to make a strong bid for the affections of the mother or father and attempt to exclude the other. This father said about the period shortly after their four-year-old daughter joined them with a view to adoption:

If I am honest, she did become a daddy's girl. I felt warmer to her than my wife did. She was lively, she had a lot of personality. I like lively children and I responded to that. She enjoyed that but what she was not prepared to do was to share.

His wife said:

My husband said, 'How can you reject a child?' and I said, 'If she stays I am going'.

The father concluded the discussion on this point by saying:

It was the shock to me because of what it did to our marriage in the first year. At one point I thought the only way we were surviving as a family was to stay in our own little boxes.

With time and with the listening ear of the adoption agency worker, the parents were able to understand the nature of the stress which this little girl, who was very deeply disturbed and already in therapy at the age of five, was placing on their marriage. When interviewed they were very much older, sadder, and wiser and looking forward to growing close as a couple now that their children were moving away from home and into independence.

You now realise the complexities of things that go wrong for people. It's a minefield. For me, I've experienced feelings I never thought I could experience.

The white adoptive mother of a young man of Caribbean descent who was placed from a children's home at the age of seven, and who made excellent progress after surmounting emotional difficulties, made some very thoughtful points about her ex-husband's relationship with their adopted son. She wondered aloud whether their son's very different appearance was a continuing public reminder to her husband of his infertility. She remarked that, when speaking of him, her husband always spoke of him as 'that lad of ours' rather than 'my son', and contrasted his behaviour with his newly acquired (white) step sons. The strong attachment in this family was clearly between mother and son, although the father had played an important social parenting role in the early years.

Ruth, in her early 20s, gave her perspective on the marital problems of her adoptive parents. Her adoptive mother later remarried and was in a more stable relationship to which Ruth returned (emotionally if not physically) after a period of living on her own.

> When I was first adopted I went out of the house a lot. I was a totally different person, but that is how I managed to cope with it. If I got told off by my mum, she would go and tell my dad. It felt as if it was like a war. I felt as if I couldn't win anything or do anything right. I used to lie, steal, throw tantrums. I went away and still was not really close to my mum or dad, but when my parents separated that's when I became close to my mum. I'm happy now and very close to my mum. I'm doing OK.

This young man was aware that he came into a situation where the marriage was already under strain:

> He didn't want me there. They were going to break up their marriage before I came. They were in a crisis and then they put me in that kind of situation. Those people in the adoption agency should be held accountable for their actions because they put me into a troubled situation. Simple as that.

### Other children in the family

In the cohort as a whole a hundred children were placed as part of a sibling group; there were 'own grown' children in 50 per cent of the households and adopted or foster children in 33 per cent of the households. Because these were not mutually exclusive, there were other children in 69 per cent of the households. In 43 per cent of the new families where both parents were black there were no other children in the family, and this was the case for 27 per cent of the mixed partnership families and 30 per cent of the white families.

A third of the children in the interview sample were placed together with a full or half sibling. Generally those placed with a sibling were positive in a 'matter-of-fact' sort of way. Some of the placements did not work out but none of the adopters thought that initially the children should have been separated. None of the sibling breakdowns occurred within a five year period of placement apart from one of a young man placed at 14 whose younger half-brother, then aged four, was said by his adoptive mother to be afraid of his increasingly violent and abusive brother.

In only 11 interview sample cases were there no children in the household at the time the young person joined the family. In several cases one or more children joined the family later, by birth, adoption or fostering.

An earlier study of the outcomes for 21 children five years after they were placed, Thoburn (1990) found that 50 per cent of the birth children of the adoptive or foster families were dissatisfied with the placement in their home of a child with special needs, and that this applied to all the siblings of children over the age of ten at placement. In our present study more time had elapsed and it appears that some of the earlier dissatisfaction of birth siblings may diminish as they come to see, as time passes, that they have not lost out.

At the time of the research interviews, most of the 'own grown' children had now left home and were in higher education or pursuing their careers. In only two cases did parents report that one of their own children was dissatisfied by the experience. However, in the earlier study the siblings themselves had been interviewed, whereas in this study, although occasionally joining in the interview, most often we only had the reports of their parents as to whether they had found the situation to be a generally positive experience. Caution therefore needs to be exercised in interpreting these answers. Several of the parents did talk of occasions when the children born to them had been under stress. One eight-year-old, the youngest of a family of boys, had found it very difficult when a boisterous 11-year-old brother arrived. He initially withdrew and started to pull out his hair; he then regressed and wanted to climb on his mother's knee alongside the new brother. Her determination to persist was rewarded and at the end of the study her husband said:

> It has worked very well. He has got three brothers. They are in and out of each others' houses the whole time and will always help each other out if there is a job to be done.

Older siblings of the family often played an important part in helping the youngsters to settle in.

> He spent a lot of time in the early days with my daughter, who was a trainee nurse. She is that kind of person, children stick to her. He saw that in her, and the two of them were always good friends.

Sometimes older siblings played a more parental role.

> Even my daughter had to discipline them sometimes. I used to call her the second Mummy.

Some of the more neutral comments were:

> My other two children are quite independent and I think they will probably be alright, but the eldest child was clinically depressed for a year due to the child. However it wasn't that simple. In the end they probably gained something. [This placement broke down after several years when the young person moved into independent accommodation and subsequently back to his birth family.]

The young people who were interviewed were asked whether they got on well with the adoptive or foster siblings, as well as their own siblings in the placement. A third said they got on very well and 45 per cent said they got on quite well. Twelve per cent said that it varied and only two out of the 24 interviewed said that they got on badly with the brothers and sisters they joined in the new family.

### Relatives and friends

Relatives were described by black families and by white families as both sources of emotional support, and of disappointment if they disapproved of the decision of the family to adopt or foster, as they occasionally did. Some recognised that large extended families were not always easy for the young children to settle into.

> It was hard, so hard for her to get used to the extended members of our family because they are so rumbustious. They are really quite frightening in a way to some people. But she learnt to give as good as she got. She developed a relationship with some members but not all. She still doesn't have a proper relationship with my mum.

A more straightforwardly positive comment was:

> I don't think we ever needed support from the Social Services because we had so much support from our family and friends.

On the negative side, both adoptive and foster families received critical comments from relatives.

> Everyone seemed to think that I had enough to do with my own children and I didn't really get a lot of support from relatives. Relatives would say things like, "You didn't cope well with your own children, so how come you are taking on these?" I got the feeling that we weren't invited as often as we were invited before as we had these children who, as far as the older relatives were concerned, black people didn't do that sort of thing. I think they thought that I had these children and was treating them too good – at first it was like something you did not do. It developed better later.

Friends also were on the receiving end of positive and negative comments. As one foster parent, who lost some of her friends but made new ones amongst those who also fostered, put it:

> By the time you become a foster carer you know who your friends are because those that aren't don't want your two foster children along with your own two running and ruining their house. You find that they don't invite you as much as before but then you give up on them and make friends with people who are doing the same things.

On the more negative side, some adoptive families of children who had behavioural difficulties found that legal adoption led to even greater isolation, and indeed in some cases women lost their marital partners as well as their friends and relatives.

> My husband's parents were useless. They thought we were too old to adopt and said they weren't going to support us. They were honest but it made me very angry. The thing with friends is that you lose most of your friends and the ones that give you most support are the ones you least expect it from.

Some of the foster carers or adoptive parents, especially those who were single parents, found that friends could take the place of relatives still living in the country of origin.

> What I would call my family here are my friends. I have built my own family unit here. My inner circle of friends see her as my daughter. My other friends, such as work colleagues, still see her as that girl I adopted and will often ask how is "the girl".

Several commented on the importance of contact with families who belonged to other less usual family forms, mostly other adoptive or foster families.

> The most helpful thing is having a shared experience. Actually probably the most help are the people who have shared experiences which are outside the parameters of normal social life.

## Attitudes towards fostering or adoption

Parents and young people commented in general terms on the merits of adoption and fostering, and also made comparisons between the two. Although more of the fostering placements broke down than was the case with the placements for adoption, this difference is not significant when the age at placement is allowed for, since more of the older children experienced breakdown and more of the older children were fostered. It has already been noted in Chapter 3 that more of the children placed with two or a single parent of minority ethnic origin were older and were placed as foster children.

Generally those who adopted did so because they wanted to and the same applied to those who fostered. The study differed from some earlier ones (for example, Rowe *et al.* 1984) in that there were no examples of foster parents who would really have liked to have adopted but were prevented from doing so by lack of parental consent or social services agreement. The two main reasons for wanting to adopt were to secure the child's legal status, and also to be free to parent in the way they wished without having to be on the receiving end of social work advice or as some saw it, interference. When relationships were not working out as hoped, some parents thought it appropriate to remain as foster parents. Others in a similar position took a different view.

> Yes, it was right to adopt. She couldn't go on with the fostering because it wouldn't be fair on her. I said to her: 'It's not only that you will belong, be a proper A… But it's the birth certificate. Being able to go abroad – not need permission to go to Brownie camp.'

Her daughter, who was placed at two and adopted at 11 said that she never thought she would be taken away but

> there was a time when I didn't want to stay – all the time – not when I was really small – after I was about seven or eight.

When asked if, when she was adopted, that was what she wanted to happen she said 'no' in a sad tone, but did not elaborate.

In contrast, an African-Caribbean single parent, who originally intended to adopt but did not proceed quickly because she knew that the birth parent was strongly opposed to this, was pushed into making an application by her daughter.

> One day she rang me at work, asking me what did she need to do to become adopted. So I contacted the social worker. She knew I wanted to adopt her, but I felt adoption was a two way thing. It wasn't something I wanted to do to her. I got our social worker to come round and she spent some time talking with her on her own about it. Initially her mum refused to sign the adoption papers and then she agreed to sign in the end. I think it was the right thing for me to adopt – not only for her – but also for me. I would not like it if I died tomorrow or anybody to come and challenge her about anything as my daughter.

Where there were difficulties, in some cases the adoption application was proceeded with, and the order made, but this did not lead to any diminution of problems. In other cases, parents who had initially intended to adopt decided to remain as long-term foster parents.

> The social worker said it was drift – she should be adopted. The mother wanted her fostered still. She never wanted to take our name. She always wanted her own name. We had to fight the mother and the local authority on the custodianship.

The young people who were placed as long-term foster children tended to argue strongly in favour of this particular legal status for them. They made it clear that, although they may not be particularly comfortable in talking to their friends about being fostered, they did not wish to be adopted.

These two comments were made by young people who had felt comfortable with their foster care status.

> People know that I'm fostered. It's nothing I'm ashamed of. Questions tend to come up when I'm out with Stewart and Mary [white foster parents]. For me, fostering was the best thing that ever happened. It might not be the best thing for another child.

This African-Caribbean single parent foster mother who had first got to know one of the children when she was a teacher had a similar view to that expressed by the young people.

> They didn't talk much about being fostered. I find that some foster children don't like talking about it. It didn't seem to bother Justine, she would tell anybody that she was fostered. She would say 'It's not my fault. I didn't put myself in it. I just happen to be here'.

These African-Caribbean foster parents initially had a sibling group placed with them on an interim basis. The eldest foster daughter said:

> We were only supposed to be here for six months in the beginning, and when the six months was up, I asked her whether we would be staying or whether we would be going. I told her that we were happy here. That was the only time I can remember talking about fostering. It wasn't discussed on a daily basis.

Her foster mother said:

> I think we helped them to feel comfortable about being fostered by treating them like our own children. They treated us from the beginning like parents, and I suppose we did the same thing. We didn't set out to do anything special; we just wanted to give them a home and do the best for them we could as a family. There was some discussion about adoption, but we didn't really want to commit ourselves. We had had six children of our own and we didn't want to take on another three. Of course,

financially, it would have been a disaster. Its OK loving them, but when they want something that you know you can't afford, there's no point in doing something which you know you wouldn't be able to do.

It does not appear that the possibility of an adoption allowance or a residence order allowance had been discussed with them. The foster mother of a young man placed at four said:

I see him as my own child. He was brother to the others, my son, nephew, grandchild – that's how he was seen by other family members. He called me aunty. I don't know whether the pupils at his school knew that I was his foster mother. He feels good about himself for the simple reason that I sit him down and explain to him that 'You are in a foster home with people who love you very much. You are not my natural child, and I am not your natural mother. I am only giving you the love that your mother should have given to you. And my children are not your natural sisters and brothers, but they love you just the same.'

This young man was one of the minority who expressed strongly negative views about being a foster child.

When I was at the other school, being fostered was like a blight – was like a mark on your record. It was held against you, it was more like it was something bad if you were fostered. I called the foster parents mum and dad but I was always the foster kid. I never felt as if I belonged. The reason I say this is that at the end of the day, they didn't treat me like they treated their own son. They treated him better without a doubt.

The conclusion to be drawn from this section is that choice of foster care or adoption should depend on the needs and wishes of the individuals concerned, especially those of the young person, but also those of the birth parents and the new parents.

## The parents' verdicts on the placements

The parents were asked at the start of the interview to give a very brief account of their reactions to the experience of being adoptive or foster parents and then were asked if they could give two or three words which summarised what they had just told us. A check list was then used which included words taken from previous studies. They can be grouped into four categories. Straightforwardly positive words such as great, a good experience (in 28 per cent of cases); more complex but still positive descriptions of the experience and process including rewarding, enriching, exciting (35 per cent of cases); more ambiguous statements but still broadly positive including challenging, stretching (14 per cent); more negative descriptions of the process including hard work, exhausting, disturbing (18 per cent); and then negative expressions which included 'sheer hell', 'traumatic', 'disappointing', 'unrewarding', 'saddening', 'awful' (6 per cent). Often, alongside these reactions about the impact which the placement had had upon them, other words were used which expressed feelings towards other people. Most frequently used were 'gratitude' and 'anger'.

> I will always be grateful to her, the birth mother. We were just very very lucky.

Anger was more likely to be expressed towards previous carers or social workers who had failed to plan sufficiently quickly for the child to join a new family. Less frequently, anger was expressed towards the birth parent who had maltreated a child.

An African-Caribbean foster mother felt pride in the way in which she had helped a young man of mixed race parentage to feel more comfortable with his African-Caribbean appearance and culture. Although he left at 17, his foster family was still providing him with support in his mid-20s.

> They were in a children's home in a mainly white area. He was very damaged. He had lost his identity. He would talk about 'Bournville Selection'. I said, 'Hold on a minute. You are either black or you are white, and you are black.' 'I'm not', he said, 'I'm a light darkie'. I got really worried because I didn't realise that there were black children who had got sold down the line like that. He wanted to go back to the children's home. He didn't want to stay. That was very hard work. He was with me quite a while [nearly three years until the age of 17]. But he didn't want to get close to anyone in case he got hurt. He had got hurt so many times so whenever he thought he was getting close, he would do something. He was wanting to be chucked out and rejected and go back to the children's home. But I am the sort of person that will stick out as long as possible. I could weight up all the good bits and let them cover the bad bits no matter how bad they were.

These two mothers had very disturbed five-year-olds placed with them and, whilst the children remained with them until mid-adolescence, they experienced a range of negative but sometimes positive feelings which they described in very strong terms.

> Total extremes of experience, way outside the norm of having naturally born children. No tranquil periods. Total stress for 12 years. The emotions plumbed the primeval depths of one's being.

> Sheer hell. Its hard to tell you how awful it can be. One of the sadnesses is it's made me a sadder person. I made myself disgusted with myself. I

found myself hating a little girl. She was bringing such awful violent emotional feeling up in me. I never expected that. I couldn't believe that a child had the capacity at five to do this to someone.

Table 6.2 gives the responses of the parents interviewed to the question about whether they felt satisfied with the placement and whether they had achieved what they set out to achieve. The table gives the numbers of children rather than families since satisfaction sometimes differed with different children placed. The main response for each set of parents in respect of each child is given. Usually both parents were in general agreement although there might have been shades of difference. We did not, however, interview some of the fathers, and others had left the family following marriage breakdown. Sixty-three per cent were unambiguously satisfied; 25 per cent had more mixed feelings and six (12 per cent) were satisfied in some respects and only one was totally dissatisfied, disappointed or negative about the experience. However when the detailed comments are analysed, it can be seen that some of the families were experts at looking on the positive side, or 'making the best of a bad job'.

| Table 6.2 Overall reaction to experience of adoption or fostering this child | | |
|---|---|---|
| *Reaction* | *Number of cases* | |
| | *n* | *per cent* |
| Generally positive | 32 | 63 |
| Emotionally neutral/descriptive comments | 13 | 25 |
| Generally negative | 6 | 12 |
| *Total* | *51* | *100* |

The language in which people expressed their satisfaction was often couched in terms of their original reason for applying to adopt or foster. A typically positive comment was from a childless couple who had adopted a baby of mixed race parentage. They were a white couple who had kept the baby in touch with her white mother and her black father.

Am I glad? I shall start crying in a minute. She has given us such an awful lot. A little while back when I asked her something about Ann (the birth mother) she said "she didn't bring me up. You are my Mum and I love

> you. I love Ann, but she's not my Mum." I was upset that she was so harsh about Ann but it brought a lump to my throat.

Those whose motives were essentially altruistic were satisfied if they had been able to give the children what they had wanted to give them.

The white father in a mixed partnership with whom two children of mixed ethnicity were placed said:

> I have been able to share my knowledge and skills with them. It has brought us together as a family. Because we are a family we are respected by our church. We are called upon to help others.

There were no entirely negative responses from the adopters of infants, although it must be remembered that the oldest of this group of children was only 16 and the youngest was only ten and still had a few hurdles to surmount. This slightly more negative or ambiguous statement came from the African-Caribbean mother in a mixed partnership who adopted a baby of mixed race parentage.

> It's obvious that we have achieved what we set out to achieve. The only thing is that it didn't live up to expectations – that's a different thing. I can't think of any disappointments.

Not surprisingly there were more expressions of mixed feelings and satisfaction mixed with disappointment when we talked to the parents of the children who were older when placed.

The positive comments were again associated with having achieved what the parents set out to achieve. A foster father commented:

> Most of it I think I enjoyed. The thing is you can sit and chat with them; there is a lot of intercommunication that you can have.

A single woman who had surmounted many difficulties in parenting a very disturbed and institutionalised eight-year-old said:

> I feel fulfilled. I heard a psychologist talk about your 'fantasy child'; not to make your adopted child into your 'fantasy child', and I was aware that I was in danger of doing that. And I had to back off from the academic side and reading with her, because I supposed my child would be bright and like reading – my fantasy.

Those who were motivated by a desire specifically to help a young person or by a sense of duty could find satisfaction even when the placement had more than its fair share of problems, and even in some cases where the child had to leave earlier than anticipated. About an 18-year-old who left the home at 16 but was still in touch, an adoptive mother said:

> It's too early to say – it's up to her now. We have just done everything we can do. There is still a lot about our daughter which is very good. She is very protective towards us, the whole family. She still sees us as family.

The African–Caribbean long-term foster mother of two young women who had joined the family as troubled and troublesome teenagers said:

> I'm really proud of them. They haven't got a big education or done important jobs, but they never get into trouble with the police. They have their own flats and they are getting on with their lives. Christmas time they are here. You know it's a family get-together and they are part of it.

Some interspersed their comments about satisfaction with a wish that they had done some things differently.

> To some extent we got some satisfaction out of fostering but we think the children had more. It has been good most of the time, but we have had our moments. In a way you wish you could change things or put the clock back. I have no regrets. I know that I can look back and say that I have given my all. We have given them security and a way forward.

Some parents expressed satisfaction although there was still a sense of 'unfinished business', and, under the surface, disappointment.

> We have matched our experiences to that of other adoptive parents and in those terms it has been terribly easy. Christina has come all the way we have wanted her to come; she has done all the things we have wanted her to do; it's been absolutely perfect because if you see the disasters which have happened to other people, we have had it good, we have had it easy. I am attached to her, but I am actually still learning to love her. I find it really, really difficult.

Others who had a less positive experience still found something to say which allowed them to retrieve a sense of achievement.

> If things had not been so difficult with Peter, I think I would have been completely positive about the experience. There are times when I say to anybody who wishes to hear that I gave that child 12 years of my life, and I could not do any more. I think that for all the children who have been moved around, it really should not be a negative thing at the end of the day when we say maybe these children have got problems with intimate family relationships. I actually think that he suffered by being in a family. It was too close for him, too intense and he could not handle it.

A small number of families who described the experience in very negative terms were beginning, having had a breathing space when the young person had left home, to see that all was not as bad as it might have been, a finding similar to that of Howe (1996). However one could see that, in the light of the enormous investment of time and emotional energy they had made, they had to search hard to retrieve something positive from all those years. This mother described how their daughter was, after a period of living with her birth mother and then in difficult circumstances on her own, at 19 and pregnant, beginning to show them some affection.

> I have given and given and given and not got anything back. But I enjoyed seeing her earlier this year. She asked me how I was, and said I didn't look well. That is the first time she has said anything about *me*, otherwise it's been me, me, me the whole time. We have achieved our aim of being a family, but we are a dysfunctional family. We have been told so many times that we are a dysfunctional family. Would we do it again? It's hard to throw away 15 years of your life and say you have wasted them. You have learned from it. One of the sadnesses is it has made me a sadder person. I have lost my religion - but I have become more tolerant.

## Summary

In this chapter we consider the behaviour of the children, and the way in which their parents tried to help them with any emotional or behaviour difficulties.

- At the time of placement 51 per cent of the 297 children were described as having emotional problems, 46 per cent behavioural problems and 36 per cent as showing signs of institutionalisation.

- Fifty-one per cent of those in the full cohort and 57 per cent of those in the interview sample were described as having a history of deprivation or abuse.

- *The children's behaviour* varied widely and whilst growing attachment was often linked with improved behaviour, some children's behaviour deteriorated so that in some instances the placement broke down.

- Behaviour difficulties appeared to be related to age at placement and were rarely reported for children placed as infants. Those placed when over the age of five displayed a range of behavioural and emotional difficulties the frequency of which tended to increase with age at placement. There were, however, exceptions, with some placed when under the age of five displaying a range of difficult emotional reactions and behaviours. When children and parents became emotionally close, a wide range of difficult behaviours was tolerated within the new family, but lack of mutual affection was associated with markedly less tolerance.

- Difficulties could take the form of physical aggression, from girls as well as from boys. In other instances parents found children emotionally distant or negative. Being seen as 'too good' brought its own problems.

- Older children found school an important influence, for good or for ill. Children who had behavioural difficulties were more negative in their comments about school. Some parents described the school's response to the arrival of the new child very positively.

- In 63 per cent of the interview sample, parents were generally satisfied with the experience of adopting or fostering; 25 per cent had more mixed feelings and 12 per cent were dissatisfied, disappointed or negative.

CHAPTER 7

# Issues of Ethnicity and Racism
# in the Lives of the Children
# and their New Families

Details are not available about the environment and racial characteristics of the areas in which the children in the full cohort grew up. However, the researchers were able to gain an impression of the ethnic mix in the areas in which the young people in the interview sample grew up. The young people were asked whether they thought that there were enough teachers and potential friends of the same ethnic group, and about whether their friends were mainly black, mainly white or a mixture. Over half lived in areas where there were significant numbers of families of a similar background and for six it varied over time, usually because of a change of job for the adoptive father. Eleven of these 51 young people (22 per cent) lived in areas and went to schools where almost all the other children were white.

A high proportion of the white families as well as those of minority ethnic origin had strong religious beliefs and gained much support from church, mosque or temple communities. Few of the young people brought the questions of either religion or language into the conversation, although some of the parents did.

> Because we celebrate a couple of the Asian customs through the year, she is really proud of that and she tells her friends. Sometimes I say to her, 'Well, you know, don't tell them because they don't really understand'. But she is so proud of her religion and what we do that she has to tell them. Her grandmother is a very free thinking elderly Indian lady. She is not sari-bound every day of the week and she is not overtly religious, although she is religious, and I think that Ghita being at her house quite often, where she has satellised Indian films on and has Indian friends visit, and she also cooks Indian meals – have also influenced her.

## The young people's experience of 'race' and racism

The comments of the young people about growing up as a member of a minority ethnic group in Britain were often linked with comments about racism. They were also linked with views about how their parents or teachers had helped them or failed to do so. In most cases they felt that their adoptive or foster parents, whether of the same or a different ethnic background had been helpful. Most described how both black and white parents did battle with teachers, employers or neighbours who racially abused them or failed to protect them from such abuse.

Responses were sometimes related to the ethnic background of their new families, but more often were about the racial and cultural characteristics of the area in which they lived. Some compared the experiences before and after placement.

Young people and parents talked about racist attitudes and behaviour of white people but also about what was referred to by one of the African-Caribbean parents as 'shadeism'.

> Over the years, my confidence has probably got better about being black. As a child I was very dark and I always felt like I was the outcast because I was darker that my brothers and sisters. And when I went to this house, there was a mixture there, and I never got teased about being dark.

The African-Caribbean adoptive father of a young woman said:

> When she first came she thought she was white because she was fair. She used to keep on and on about it until one day I said, 'you think you are white?' and so I showed her some photographs of my family from which she saw they were people fairer than her. At the beginning she had a superiority complex with us because she was lighter in colouring. She had it in her head that dark was negative.

Another young man arriving in his foster home at age 11 from a culturally 'white' children's home referred to himself as 'not black but a light darkie'.

### Children placed with families of similar ethnic origin

Most children and young people had some experience of racism as they grew up which they described to us. However they concentrated on telling us about how they had managed to handle racist behaviour and abuse and how their new parents had helped them. Some referred to earlier experiences (described in Chapter 3) of living in predominantly white areas and favourably contrasted their lives with their new families.

> Being a black person in this family is normal. It was not normal where we were in the children's home. I mean, to get stared at when you are walking down the street, and get called names and stuff, isn't normal. I remember once there were some skin heads who came up to us and said 'there ain't no black in the Union Jack', and we were only kids. You know it was just frightening and I wondered whether we were ever going to get away from the place.

These responses explain some of the difficulties as perceived by the young people.

> There are problems with being black – like getting jobs, or if you go into a shop the security guard will watch you because that's how they train them; or if you go into a lift with people they tend to get nervous, you can see it on their faces, although they are smiling. I just take it with a pinch of salt really, because that's their problem if they are scared of me because I haven't done anything.

> Going out with someone is also a problem. That's probably why I don't have much luck with boys. I never see one of my friend's (white friend's) boy friends say, 'Oh she's quite nice'. They always say it to their white friends but never say it to me. So I feel exceptionally ugly. There is one boy I fancied; he is white. There are hardly any Asian boys around here anyway.

Most of the young people spoke confidently about the way they had handled racism, and been helped by schools or parents to do so.

> It's more of a problem being black than white in this society because people just laugh at you. But I love being black. I think my aunt [adoptive mother] has helped me to feel proud about my colour. In the home I used to think I was white, everything around me was white. I was like a coconut – black on the outside but white on the inside. My aunt introduced me to a black culture and I realised that I wasn't white and I'm glad she did, because some people stay that way. My aunt made the difference. The change happened naturally. It wasn't really a big issue. It's like when you could go to live in another country and you naturally start speaking the language. I don't know how it happened but all of a sudden you'd come back thinking Jamaican or what ever.

Some were more ambivalent.

> Sometimes I wish I was white. People are racist and they think that white people are better, or something. But I like it. I'm different. I like my colour and I like my race, but sometimes I wish I were a white person

because they'd treat me differently. I mean you don't ever hear anybody saying, 'Hey you, white person, come over here'.

I do remember being racially abused at school on one occasion. I was called names by a particular girl. I retaliated and was told off by the headmaster and I do remember that the foster parents came up to the school to defend me.

Even the small minority of young people who made negative comments about the black families with whom they were placed praised their attitudes towards ethnicity and racism. This young man left the foster parents who had originally planned to adopt him at the age of 15, having been on the receiving end of harsh discipline. However, he was very positive about the way in which they had helped him to feel good about himself as a black person.

The foster parents introduced me to some books like Martin Luther King and Malcolm X. So they set me on the road to learning about my blackness. But the bigger picture came when I started to read books like Jonathan Jackson and Edward J. Cleaver. I'm kind of glad that I went to the foster home in a way because they set me on the way to that black whole, because I think I would have been made confused if I'd gone to a white foster family.

### Children placed with white families

The large majority of the transracially placed children expressed approval about the way in which their adoptive or foster parents had helped them to cope with racist behaviour.

Humour seemed to be one of the ways in which white adoptive or foster parents and the young people themselves sought to deal with racism. Sometimes the young people thought that this was an appropriate strategy and sometimes not.

As a black person living in this [mainly white] area, it depended much on what kind of person you were like. If you were good and came across as funny, you would get people who were nice to you, because they want to prove that they are not racist, that they can claim to be not racist by being nice to you.

Some took on the 'hard man' image.

Me, personally, I don't get a lot of trouble with that. I was sort of hard. I never got bullied or anything at school. I was Jack the lad, no one ever took liberties, not once.

Young people described in particular the importance of linking up with other black youngsters especially in clubs where black youth culture was to the fore.

> Some of the clubs I go to now are black and you can get picked on because you're half caste, and I go with my friends and it's not too bad. But I just didn't connect up with them because they were black; there's a bit more to it than that. But it is a bit safer, though, with someone of my own colour.

The essentially plural nature of identity is brought out in these quotations, where class as well as ethnic origin is seen as relevant.

> I only know what it's like to be black from what other people have told me, and this means like being 'a rude boy'. I don't see myself as fitting in with this. There are plenty of black people who are business people and are doing well.

This young man was particularly positive about the boarding school he went to at the age of 15, where he met young people of mainly African upper class origin.

> The people who have helped me with my blackness are my friends at school. They took me under their wing and said they would sort me out. Because they didn't think I was black enough. They didn't do anything in particular. They helped me to dress fashionably. It was good to be a black person at that school.

Two others had similarly positive experiences in their private day or boarding schools. The young people reminded us that there are many black identities rather than only one, and that membership of a particular social class or religious grouping; the impact of higher education; or belonging to a specific ethnic group, will play their parts in the construction of self concept and the development of self-esteem.

Several of the young people in white or mixed partnership households described how the racism directed towards them was also directed towards their white parent when they were out together.

## Parental attitudes to issues of race, culture and racial abuse

All the parents interviewed considered that they had an important role to play in helping their children to feel good about themselves as people of minority ethnic origin and culture, and to be able to deal with racism or racial abuse. Families who were themselves of minority ethnic origin had a clear advantage over the white families in this respect and this was acknowledged by white and black parents and the young people themselves.

All the parents interviewed were asked to comment on the following statement and a series of questions about ethnicity and parenting:

> *There are different views about ways of helping a child to value and feel comfortable with his or her racial or ethnic identity. Some people say it is important to make a special effort to help a child to be proud of his or her racial origins, and others think it is best not to emphasise racial differences. What do you think?*

This was followed by a more practical question asking the parents if they could tell us how they had helped the children to feel positive about their ethnic and cultural heritage. They were also asked if there had been any incidents of racial abuse either towards themselves or towards the young person, and about strategies for dealing with these. By far the largest proportion gave answers to this statement which indicated that they believed that it was important to help the young person to feel positive about differences from the white majority community. However, Table 7.1 shows that the responses of the white parents and those of other ethnic origin differed in respect of the way they sought to help the young people. More of the families where both parents were white took an 'assimilationist' approach, or one which was not easily categorised, whereas 79 per cent of the families where at least one parent was of minority ethnic origin but only 41 per cent of the white parents unequivocally stated that the children should be helped to understand racial differences and develop strategies to deal with racism.

| Table 7.1 Views of adoptive/foster parents about best way to parent a child of minority ethnic origin | | | | |
|---|---|---|---|---|
| | *White parents* | | *Parents of minority ethnic origin* | |
| | *n* | *per cent* | *n* | *per cent* |
| Ignore differences | 2 | 9 | 1 | 3.5 |
| Assimilate | 5 | 23 | 2 | 7 |
| Mixed | 6 | 27 | 3 | 10 |
| Acknowledge differences and suggest strategies | 9 | 41 | 23 | 79.5 |
| *Total* | *22* | *100* | *29* | *100* |

## Parents of minority ethnic origin or mixed partnerships

There were few differences between the ways in which the families helped the children to feel good about their physical appearance, culture and, although less frequently mentioned, religion. For children brought up from infancy in families of similar appearance, and for the older children whose early lives had been spent mainly with ethnically and culturally similar foster families or their birth families, this was not a major issue. We have already noted that some children with two parents of the same minority ethnic groups were placed with mixed partnerships, and some children of mixed parentage were placed with two black parents. The responses of these families were particularly well thought out since, like the white families, they often had to help their children to explain why they were of different appearance from one or both of their parents.

> I know like all people in mixed marriages that I as a white man am treated in the same bank, in the same shop, in the same everywhere in a way which is different to the way my wife is treated. The same shop, the same money, and my wife would have to give her address, and she is terribly affected by this. Some places they don't see her for years because they have the cheek to ask for some form of identification.

This white mother, whose partner was black and whose two children were of mixed race parentage and placed as infants, said:

> White families can just pop into a bookshop and buy a book, or pop into the local toy shop and buy a toy, but for black families it was really hard to get race appropriate stuff. I know things are getting better now, but then we just couldn't see any black children in any of the books. It was as if they didn't really exist. And I think how am I supposed to give these children a positive racial identity? I think I have got to work at it [promoting positive racial identity] because the world out there sees them as different. I just cannot ignore it and I emphasise it by telling them how beautiful they look, how beautiful their hair is, how beautiful their skin is, how beautiful their bodies are, because the world out there spends a lot of time presenting negative traits about them, so I up it, so to speak.

Even when children had always been living with families of a similar ethnic origin, most black families thought it appropriate to reinforce the children's pride in their appearance and culture.

> Whilst you are living in this country, you have to emphasise your racial and cultural identity, and let them know that black is beautiful and that they must be proud of who they are.

As mentioned earlier, going to the Caribbean was important for several children. Others just talked about the 'normality' or 'ordinariness' of being a black family and this task was made particularly easy when they lived in parts of the country where large proportions of the population were of similar ethnic origin.

> The children came into what I would call a black circle. We all in the house were black, and they were black, and I don't think we had to do anything special.

Some families particularly felt that it was appropriate to acknowledge but not to **emphasise** differences of race and culture. Ghita had one Asian and one white parent and was placed as an infant with an Asian adoptive mother and white adoptive father.

> Probably best not to emphasise racial difference because you can't make it go away. We don't feel the need to emphasise it. Ghita is aware of her ethnic origin and obviously the bulk of the family is of Indian extraction, and she appreciates this. She doesn't seem to have a problem. You don't emphasise it but we don't ignore it. The Indian side of the family is not very strict. It's touched upon and it's there but it's not the temple every week and that kind of thing. So I think there is a good kind of balance between the white side of the family and the Indian side of the family.

An African-Caribbean mother also thought that it was not appropriate to place too much emphasis on skin colour.

> We have never really discussed colour so to speak. They are aware of colour and they know that they are black.

Fifteen-year-old Tara (placed in an Asian family) came down on the side of the parents who did think it appropriate to talk about differences.

> Mum and my friend, Savitri, help me to feel good about my colour. Savitri really does help because if anybody says anything to her, she will go up to them and say, 'Have you got a problem?' She really sorts them out. I don't find it helpful when mum tells me to ignore racial abuse. How can you ignore them? I would love to be Savitri, she has got guts. I am a wimp. That's what my friends call me.

For the children who moved from a white to a black environment, the issue was of considerably more importance to the new families who all saw themselves as having an important job to do in helping them feel pride in their appearance and culture. An African-Caribbean mother, whose four year old joined her from an essentially white environment in a children's home, told how she had asked him to close his eyes, taken his hand and helped him to feel a piece of black velvet. She asked him how he felt and when he said it was nice and smooth, she told him that he also had beautiful skin like the velvet.

> Before he came to us he did not really see himself as black, but once he moved into our family he started talking about black being beautiful, and when he was called names at school I told him not to be ashamed of being black. Because he came out of the children's home at that age, and was in a home where we don't see the colour of the skin, and we don't make it a problem, that is the attitude he has from us.

The children who were older when placed had more difficulties to overcome and in making the change. Fourteen-year-old Justine and her half-sister Cathy were of mixed race parentage and moved to live with an African-Caribbean foster mother who was a single parent.

> Cathy thought she was white when she arrived here, and to help her I used to chat with her and give her lots of books to read. I explained that although she was of mixed race, in this country she would be seen as black.

Nicola was a five-year-old girl of Caribbean descent who moved from a white children's home environment into a family where both parents were African-Caribbean. The parents and older sisters made a big attempt, which she greatly appreciated, to improve the condition of her skin and hair which had not been properly looked after.

> She told me that when she was at school in the seaside town they used to call her a golliwog and she asked why did they used to call me a golliwog. So I explained to her about slavery, where we came from, about the West Indies, about Caucasians and Negroid. We had a book which we used. Then she said, 'I hate all white people', and I said, 'No, no, no, you've got good, bad and indifferent in all races'.

A four-year-old African-Caribbean boy moved in with Jamaican adopters who had to provide considerable help to improve his appearance.

> He came to us from white foster parents, and he did not know much about West Indian food so he was given his 'culture food'. His skin was very dry so I took care of his skin, and his hair was very, very dry and I got him hair-cream for his hair. And just more or less made sure that he'd got the right things around him.

*Placements with white parents*

In some respects the responses of these parents were similar to those of the white parents in mixed partnerships. This was especially so where white parents had made a big attempt to learn a great deal about the child's culture and heritage. Many of these were already mixed race *families* when the child in our sample moved in because children of minority ethnic origin had already been living with them. The mothers in particular spoke of being on the receiving end of racist comments.

> In 18 years we have had two bad incidents. Two older ladies were on the bus. One said, 'Some people will sleep with anybody'. Because Mandy was very young I could reply – otherwise I could not have done it. I said very loudly as we walked past, 'The age of miracles isn't past you know'.

Most of the white parents had at least one similar story to tell. They also were extremely upset by the racist abuse about which their children spoke, because of the love they had for them and their distress at seeing them hurt.

Major differences between the white families' responses to race and ethnicity depended on their living environment. It was considerably easier for those living in an ethnically mixed community to help their children have pride in their heritage and culture. This was confirmed by the children themselves who particularly valued having teachers of the same ethnic origin.

This young women of mixed race parentage who was in her early twenties when interviewed spoke of the efforts her white adopters had made to learn with her about her heritage.

> I am very conscious and very interested in black culture. I am still learning today. My mum knows that, she accepts that I'm more into my blackness than my white side - a lot of that is down to my mum because she didn't have to tell me about Guyana and what the capital is and all that, but she did and I respect her for that. I don't find it a problem. I find being black a positive thing. I think I feel more black than white at the moment because of the friends I have got now and the area I am living in now.

Two other factors helped white families to help their children with their cultural and racial identities. First, the young people who were older at placement and had lived for some time with their birth parents or had considerable contact with people of the same ethnic origin had fewer problems around the area of ethnicity. Second, the position was similar if the children had continuing links with parents or relatives. One of the more successful baby adoption placements was of a baby of mixed race parentage whose white adopters kept her in touch with her white mother, who introduced her, when she was slightly older to her African-Caribbean birth father and his family.

Several of the white adopters or foster parents lived in mixed communities and worked as social workers or teachers or in other professional positions which brought them into contact with black people, many of whom had experienced difficulties in other aspects of their lives. Two white fathers, one in a mixed partnership whose partner was a social worker, were much involved in community relations councils and extremely knowledgeable about the cultures of the young people living with them. This knowledge and interest was appreciated by the young people.

There was a small number of white adoptive parents who initially felt that their life was enriched by their closer involvement in the ethnic communities of their adoptive children. However, during the course of these placements there was a shift in public and professional opinion and these parents found themselves being condemned by both black and white professionals, and sometimes by members of the community of their adopted children. This caused distress and led them to withdraw from sources of support for themselves and for the young people.

The foster or adoptive parents of children with severe learning disabilities had the least to say about race and racism. They mostly considered that the young people would not be able to understand the concepts of race and culture and would not be aware of racism.

## Attitudes towards placement policy

Most of the young people who were in broadly ethnically similar placements believed that the policy of placing children in families which were as near as possible to their own ethnic background should be followed if at all possible. Some were more vehement about this than others. Ghita's adoptive mother recalled:

> Recently, I remember her saying to me how daft it was to place an Indian child with white people. I would never do that.

Andrew was not entirely positive about his foster parents, but was clear that he was glad that they were black.

> In the long run being black and fostered with black parents was easier. If they had put me with white folks I would have been in trouble because although I might have been fed, my psychological and social needs would not have been met. If they had put me with white folks I would

have been in trouble because I would have seen the world from a different perspective; from a white perspective.

These two young people now in their twenties were more emphatic:

> I would feel really odd being adopted by a white family. It's really funny. I don't think there's any difference but I would still feel odd.

> Social Services should not place black children with white families. They do not place white children in black families. They should try and place Asian children with Asian parents and black children with black parents. If a child is of mixed race then there is a choice, and Social Services can use their discretion. Perhaps if the child had a black mother then the child should go to a black family; and if the child has a white mother the child might be better off in a white family.

Some of those who were placed as infants, both with parents of similar ethnic origin and with white families, thought the issue was not overly important. A 15-year-old who was placed with a family of the same ethnic background supported her friend's view that placement with a white family was not necessarily a disadvantage.

> My friend is adopted and she is black and she was adopted by a white family, and I don't see anything wrong with that. It doesn't matter what colour they are, it's just how you get on with them. I don't know why people see this thing about black – white being different; there's nothing different about them, we are all the same.

None of the young people who had been placed trans-racially specifically said that this was a policy which should be followed but each was at pains to point out that they themselves had gained a great deal from their white foster or adoptive parents.

The older they were at the time of interview, the more likely it was that the young people would be strongly in support of children being placed with families of similar ethnic origin. A young woman placed with a white family who had subsequently gone to live with her birth mother and was struggling to find her way forward as a black person living on her own said:

> I wouldn't advise any black person to go to a white family. I wouldn't change anything about my family. But at the end of the day I wouldn't advise any black person to go to a white family. Because you miss out on all the culture and everything. But I do appreciate what they did for me. There is nothing I would change about what they have done for me.

In this sample, those who were of mixed race parentage felt least strongly about this issue. This contrast to the findings from some other small scale studies may be the result of the type of sample. Kirton's (1995) study, for example, draws on the experiences of young people of mixed race parentage who had joined post-adoption support groups or sought assistance from professionals, whereas none of those in our intensive sample had approached professional agencies specifically for help with or discussion of identity issues.

A young man of mixed Caribbean and white British parentage said when asked whether it was appropriate for him to have been placed with a white family:

> Yes and no. I suppose it's a roof over your head. If you got no one else to move on to, you have to do that. White parents who are taking on black children need to know about black culture.

Some of the young people placed when older considered that links with their original families were of most importance.

> My dad [birth father] told me when I was little – I was living in a white environment all the time and I used to think I was white. Over the years you realise you are not. You stand out. People see. But my brother, I suppose, has been a big influence and my dad, he's proper African and drills into me about my background and heritage and all that sort of stuff. I already knew by the time I got to the foster family who I was. Any help there would not have made any difference. They were open minded and they had an Indian daughter and they used to live in India. That fascinated me. But at that age (14) being placed with white foster parents probably was the right thing. It didn't really matter because I knew who I was.

Although this adoptive mother felt comfortable in talking to her adoptive son about his cultural heritage, she did not consider that the ethnic background of the adoptive parents was of significance when compared with the importance of them being able to help a very disturbed child.

> Certainly I don't think that he should have been adopted. Now that we have survived, I think we were as good a bet as anybody, and my bet is that if he had gone to a black family who had just been chosen because of their blackness as opposed to their ability to cope with him, they wouldn't have done any better. It probably wouldn't have lasted as well.

However, most of the white parents with different degrees of emphasis considered that it was preferable for children to be placed with families of similar ethnic origin, provided that these could meet any special needs of the children as well as their needs for a sense of ethnic and cultural identity.

The foster mother of two Asian brothers and a young man of mixed white and African-Caribbean descent contrasted the way in which they developed their identities as black people.

> Ashok and Deepak would not see themselves as anything other than black British in terms of culture. I imagine they've all experienced racial abuse but Ashok would just put his head down and walk away. He tried to ignore, appease and smile at them. Deepak fought from day one and Phil has a kind of easy going charm. Phil at about 20 suddenly found his black identity. This followed his experience of racism from the father of his then girlfriend, who was white. And now most of his friends, the people that he finds are in the same situation as him – they are black. He minimises that experience of the girl's father, now, but at the time it felt like a terrible experience for him. But of course he is half white though he's got a lot of friends round here now who happen to be black. He fits in, he fits in wherever he goes. He has such a wonderful personality anyhow.

Phil himself had a similar view, and his comments echo those of most of the young people of mixed race parentage interviewed by Tizard and Phoenix (1993):

> With me being both it depends who I'm with. I can be really posh with my white friends, but with my black friends I'd just be black. Because my dad was black and my mum was white, I am not hundred per cent black or hundred per cent white. Some of the clubs I go to I get taken the Mickey out of me; I've been called 'greyhound'.

This foster mother said:

> I think it is very important for them to feel proud of their ethnic identity, but how you do that is a different matter, especially if they have grown up thinking that they are white. I think it's hard for a white person to do that. It is best for a black child to be fostered with a black family. In this case these decisions should have been made very early on. By the time they came to us they had been in a white environment for most of their lives and to introduce them to an entirely new culture and possibly language would have been hard, especially in view of their learning disabilities which made it hard enough for them to understand what was going on in British culture. But I think they were damaged in terms of their own self-image and culture. So we just did our best with what had already been done. It's a pragmatic thing. I think in a perfect world they would have been placed in families that reflected their racial and cultural heritage.

## Summary

- Our information on the children's experiences of racism is only available in respect of the 51 young people in the interview sample. Fifty-three per cent of the children interviewed lived in areas where there were significant numbers of families of an ethnic background similar to their own. Twenty-two per cent lived in areas and went to schools that were predominantly white. The children's responses were sometimes related to the ethnic background of their new families but more often were about the racial and cultural characteristics of the area where they lived.

- Children placed with families of similar ethnic origin concentrated on describing how they managed to handle racist behaviour and abuse and how their new parents helped them to do so. Those children who had previously lived in predominantly white areas favourably contrasted the move to a black family and racially mixed area. Negative reactions were in the minority and most of the young people felt confident about the way in which they handled racism and were helped by their new parents and schools to do so.

- Children placed with white families were also mostly positive about the help they received from their new parents to deal with racist behaviour. One strategy was humour, which was sometimes regarded by the young people as appropriate and sometimes not. Some young people deployed the 'hard' image. Many emphasised the importance of linking up with other black youngsters. Several young people in white or mixed partnership households noted that racism directed at them was also directed at their white parent when they were out together.

- It was clear that both black and white parents did battle with teachers, employers or neighbours who either racially abused their children or failed to protect them from such abuse.

- The general attitudes towards ethnicity and placement policy as expressed by the young people linked with comments about same-race and transracial placements. Most of the children in same-race placements and most of their new parents believed that same-race policies should be followed if at all possible. The children placed transracially did not argue for transracial placements to be a policy but they took trouble to emphasise that they had gained much from their white parents.

# CHAPTER 8

# Social Work and Other Support Services

There have been many descriptive accounts and a smaller number of research studies (most recently that of Quinton *et al.* 1998 and Lowe *et al.* 1999) of social work practice in the early stages of the family placement process. In some respects practice has moved on since the period in the early 1980s when these children were placed, and this is especially so with the recruitment, assessment, training and support of *black families*. However, these agencies were pioneering new models of practice and tried to ensure that their workers were well supervised and supported and had time to do the work properly. We would therefore not anticipate that, apart from work with black families, and possibly arrangements for birth family contact, the essential nature of practice has changed significantly. Indeed, there are many similarities between the work as described in an earlier account of one of these agencies (Thoburn *et al.* 1986) and the 1990s work of the voluntary agencies described by Lowe *et al* (1999).

Because so much time had elapsed, we did not focus in detail in our interviews on the early stages of recruitment and placement. The little the families did tell us would suggest general satisfaction with the model of placement practice which has already been well documented. Insofar as comments were made, criticisms and words of praise echo those who have spoken to earlier researchers.

Questions about social work focused more specifically on post-placement support for the parents and children, but even here, parents and children were more interested in telling us about other aspects of their lives. Only a minority of those who experienced problems and sought help, or where another child had been placed, had recent experience of social workers. Families and children did, however, have important things to say about placement policy and practice in five areas: choice of placement; choice of social worker for children of minority ethnic origin; links with birth families;

the appropriateness of foster care, residence orders and adoption in different sets of circumstances; and the availability of therapy.

## Overview of the 297 placements

For the full cohort only very basic information was available about the social work service provided. If supervision continued to be provided by the voluntary agency, the information on file was likely to be fairly full until the time of disruption or adoption. If adoption was delayed, or the child remained as a foster child, supervision often passed back to the local authority and the adoption agency's file was closed. Little was recorded after adoption unless the family requested support or other services. However, this gives a false impression of the post adoption service since we were aware that most agencies kept in touch on an informal basis. Whilst preparing to contact the families to ask them to take part in the interview study we were made aware that these informal contacts were extensive. Some families, however, clearly did not wish to stay in touch after the order was made.

In most cases a fairly high level of support was provided shortly after placement, the frequency of visits being at least every two weeks during the first three months for almost 70 per cent of the families. In most cases the major support to children as well as the members of the new family was provided by the worker from the family placement team or adoption agency. The local authority worker usually fell back to take up a less prominent role, but usually attended statutory reviews. This was generally what the new parents wanted at that stage. The pattern for the 16 London Borough placements was different, with the child's worker and the family placement team worker sharing the work more evenly, or with decisions about who did what depending on individual circumstances and already established relationships between social workers, parents and children.

There was less information about the later years after placement. By the two year stage, for the 89 cases about which we had information, the supervision and support was provided by the local authority worker in 25 cases; the placement agency in 43 cases and jointly in 21 cases. Beyond two years we only had information about the frequency of contact with a social worker in respect of 55 cases. In 16 cases contact was at least monthly and in 39 cases it was between six weekly and two monthly.

For those families who adopted, some form of post-adoption service was provided in 54 (57 per cent) of the 95 cases about which we had this information.

## The roles of the family placement specialists and the children's area team social workers

*Family placement workers*

Moving on to the more detailed information from the interview sample, parents had most to tell us about the role of the adoption agency or family placement team workers, and most of what they said was positive. In common with earlier research (O'Hara 1986; Rushton *et al.* 1993; Thoburn *et al.* 1986; Thoburn 1990) we found that the adoption or family placement team worker who undertook the home study and recommended approval had a major advantage when it came to offering support to the family once the child was being introduced and then placed.

> This is where the adoption agency played a great part because I could talk to Nina like I am talking to you. We had already talked about a lot of feelings, mainly to do with me and my mothering because I was brought up by an aunt because my mother was here in England. And I had to look at the fact that I have never expressed any feelings about my mother being away.

Several parents referred back to the positive links made at that earlier stage. A substantial minority were either professional social workers or professionals who worked with social workers. They did not find it easy to go through the home study process and appreciated the sensitivity of the workers involved in that process. This adoptive mother was able to compare the approach of different agencies.

> As an experience it also brought out maybe social workers don't listen, because before we had this particular adoption agency social worker, we were with another adoption agency and they just drove me spare because they did not seem to listen to us as human beings. With this first agency [another voluntary agency], there was an assumption that because there were two social workers in the house we knew everything but we were two social workers who, at the end of the day, were human beings. I really think we were fortunate that we finally ended up with the agency we did.

Those who continued to receive support from the worker who had undertaken the home study tended to be the most positive, and indeed some had the same worker until the child was grown up.

> During our difficulties with her when she was a teenager [ten years after the child was placed] we got hold of our first worker to talk to her. We felt this was the right thing at the time because he knew her inside out.

At least three families remained in contact with their first worker, even after he or she had left the agency, and when problems arose at later stages preferred to go to this person rather than going back to the adoption agency or local authority and having contact with someone they did not know. For some, this was not a possibility:

> The voluntary agency was fantastic. They gave us a great deal of support and we could not have survived without the help of Andrea for the first seven years. When she left it was totally hopeless. We found we had more experience than the new workers.

When a much cherished original worker left after several years, some parents preferred to go for support to self help groups such as *Adoption UK* rather than get to know another support worker either from the local authority or the adoption agency. Some of the parents played important roles on committees of these organisations. Others received continuing support by playing a role in the adoption agency's day to day work, either as an adoption panel member or as a trainer. They greatly valued these roles which provided support for them as well as giving them scope to provide a service to others. Some, especially African-Caribbean foster parents, took pride in the number of other black foster parents they had recruited. For most of the adopters of infants, these contacts were their main continuing link with the agencies.

> In the last 15 years I have not needed anything. But they always write and say you know where we are. They have an annual Mass for adoptive parents and children which we go to. The social workers and I are more like friends. I can always talk to them and they always have time for me.

Local authority adoptive and foster parent groups were also greatly valued by some but not used by others. They were the main source of support for some of the parents who were experiencing difficulties.

There were a few negative comments, mainly about other workers in the adoption agencies rather than the particular support worker who had undertaken the home study and recommended their approval by the adoption panel. There was a sense from some of the adopters who had felt very much a part of the pioneering work of placing special needs children in the early eighties, that workers joining the agencies later lacked the enthusiasm and dedication of the pioneering first wave of 'hard to place' adoption specialists. One problem which did arise for families in relation to the original workers was that they sometimes felt under pressure to live up to expectations and some found it difficult to ask for help.

> I think there is something about adoption and fostering. You go through the awful process of being approved, assessed, and it's quite difficult after that to show any weaknesses – to ask for help if things are difficult.

## The children's social workers

Families tended to compare their support workers with the local authority area team workers. Sometimes they received an excellent service from both.

> The original social services to which the children were in care were also very very helpful. Even though they were miles away, they would come up (there were two social workers) and we would have discussions. The one thing that was particularly helpful was their openness and honesty.

More often the local authority workers were compared unfavourably.

> This is where the adoption agency played a great part because I could talk to Peter like I'm talking to you. I couldn't talk to the local authority social worker like that, because I always thought that they would go and have a meeting and whip her away.

Several of the families commented about the power of the local authority social workers of which these workers seemed often unaware. Thus casual remarks could be pondered over and worried about for the next six weeks or two months until the worker arrived and appeared to have forgotten about the earlier issue which, at the time seemed to be so important (the 'bees in bonnets' problem identified in the earlier study of Thoburn *et al.* 1986). This mother explained that the power of the local authority social workers to remove her child prevented her from seeking advice from them.

> I could talk to them about any areas that I needed to. My own worker and anyone in the team. But the local authority worker, I was always a bit more careful about, because I always felt they had the power to move my daughter without fully understanding the situation. That was my greatest fear.

Some parents were aware that the local authority workers had a difficult role, which was compounded if the young person had been frequently moved and may therefore be fearful that the social workers' arrival might mean another move.

> You could guarantee that if a social worker was coming to visit him, a week before that he would be soiling himself regularly. Although he had a good relationship with her, he always thought she was going to take him away. I couldn't bear to see the hurt in him when she tried to talk to him about his past, because she wouldn't get a sentence out of him. He would just say 'yes', 'no' or 'I don't know'.

The weakness of the local authority most frequently commented upon was the change in workers which often occurred.

> I think we had seven social workers in six years and I believe some of these were agency workers who were hired on a short-term contract, who were seen once and never seen again. The adoption agency was constant. We had the same worker the whole time.

The almost inevitable result of change of worker was that delays were experienced and things which were promised did not materialise.

> The social workers weren't helpful. They have their duty to the children. They should have sent us photos of his dad which they didn't.

Frequent complaints were also made about the poor service around consents to adoption and the court hearing which was often delayed because of social workers having left or not getting papers in on time.

Families had their own explanations for the problems, which were often related to an understanding of the extra pressures which local authority workers were under because of high work loads, and in some cases to lack of specialist knowledge. The lack of time meant that few were able to forge a relationship with the parents. In the later stages of the placement they tended only to see family members at times of stress, and were often seen as being critical rather than providing help and support.

> Social workers were always blaming, it was always my fault. We feel failures and social workers have re-enforced that. The local authority social workers are awful. They have messed everything up. They are less specialised than the adoption agency workers who understand more.

In contrast, the adoptive mother of a young man placed at the age of two who was still 'semi-detached' and clearly going through spells of unhappiness 12 years later gave the local authority worker 'five out of five', even though she felt she ought not to need the help.

> Well, I probably didn't use them enough. They are so far away. But I didn't because he was a permanent fixture our lives. I didn't have a social worker for my other children. Its not social services' fault. Her whole attitude was helpful. She said 'You are being too hard on yourself. You are your own worst critic. You are still looking after him even when he is making himself unlovable. You might think he wants to get away from here but he wouldn't want to be with anyone else. It is not an easy thing you are doing.'

Another problem was confusion between the respective roles of the family placement support worker and the area team worker. One family had to consult their solicitor in an emergency and take action to prevent the child being removed. Having originally intended to adopt, the parents found that relationships remained too difficult for them to take this step. They felt that they would continue to need social work support and were not convinced that they would have got it if an adoption order were made. Their decision not to proceed to adoption was seen by a new worker in the local authority as evidence of lack of commitment to the young person. A review concluded that the problem was 'drift' (she had been a member of the family for almost ten years) and that the young woman should be removed, without her having been consulted. The parents applied for a custodianship order which was subsequently made.

## Social work before placement

*Assessment and preparation*

Most recalled having mixed feelings about the home study and several noted that their anxiety to have a child placed with them got in the way of their hearing what the social workers were telling them. This may be a strong argument for the splitting of training from the home study and approval process, or at least repeating the key training messages once the family has been approved and the anxiety about the possibility of rejection has receded.

> If you are desperate to have children because you can't have your own, you want to be a mummy to a child whatever anybody says. You don't really hear it.

This adoptive mother of an eight-year-old could only remember the good parts of the home study and contrasted it with a poor service later:

> Social work at the approval stage was superb, excellent, wonderful. I can really recommend it. Beautiful people, very very nice. It was very comfortable, very informative. However this was in contrast to the matching stage when a child had been identified but there were then delays and difficulties. In terms of adoption, finding a child – it was the pits, appalling, abysmal, incompetent, criminally stupid.

Another mother was less enthusiastic about the home study, but saw it as a necessary evil.

> I think we realised that the home study part had to be done. We didn't like it but we knew it was official. It was tiresome. But there again, we don't want to criticise the adoption society. We are just so grateful to them.

*Matching and placement*

Families commented about three major areas: the information they were given about the child, including any choice they had at the matching stage; the service provided when the child arrived in their home; and the way any goodbyes, either to birth family members if contact was being terminated or to previous carers were arranged.

A minority of the families did not feel that they were given accurate or adequately full information. Generally parents felt that they had been given sufficient information about the child, although we have already noted that they had complained in some cases about the lack of information on the birth parents especially the birth fathers. 'Adoption parties' were appreciated as a way of getting to know a young person before making the decision about taking an older child into their homes. Parents reported that these were sensitively handled and enjoyable.

> Once I knew her personally, I knew it was this one, because I had actually met a child from my culture and wanted to give her a chance of a family of her own.

Those young people who were old enough to remember were positive in their comments about them as a way of 'breaking the ice' and getting to know each other before they had to commit themselves. These events were the exception rather than the rule, and in most cases parents were given no choice, though some expressly said they did not **wish** to be given a choice. Opportunities to get to know each other better were usually available during the introductory period which again were positively commented on by most parents.

This was not invariably the case and some introductions were fraught. This adoptive mother whose eight-year-old adoptive daughter was reluctant to leave her short-term foster mother considered that she should have been given more help in understanding the psychological impact of separation.

> Given the circumstances we were not prepared enough for some of the difficulties we had. The loss that she felt at leaving her foster mother was touched upon, but it wasn't given the emphasis that it should have been. What would have been helpful was to have had some training about the effect of loss on children. But for some children, and I can't imagine that there would be any children for which this would not be an issue, to know they would go through this process so that we would have been able to recognise it when it happened and not be so confused and upset.

Other adoptive or foster parents thought that social workers had underestimated the sadness the children felt at leaving other children as well as staff in children's homes.

> He missed the other children. The house mother's daughter missed him. Nobody thought at the time that the peer group association was so important.

For some, memories lasted for a long time. This applied particularly to 'goodbye' visits for birth parents. Some seem to have been particularly badly handled as in this case when the prospective adoptive parent was present.

> It's very distressing to see a mother cuddling the child, knowing the child is going to go away. But it was good that we met her, but it would have been better to have met her without our new daughter being there. Even though it is a fleeting meeting, one can tell what she looks like. That helps.

One young man was upset when told that his picture would appear in publicity, but at least he was given the choice of having it appearing in a shop front poster some distance from where he lived, rather than in his home area.

> The reason I was fostered in Seatown was because I didn't want all my mates to see my poster in the shop window. That's why I moved to Seatown. [This had the unfortunate effect of placing him in an area where there were few black people, but he was old enough to keep in touch with friends in the area from which he moved.]

Young people also had their views about choices and generally felt that older children should be given a say on whether they should be placed with a particular family.

> I wanted to go to live with the foster parents but the social workers always emphasised that I didn't have to go if I didn't want to.

Those who were placed after living for a long period in children's homes which were due to close told the researchers that they felt they had little choice. Some of the families and young people were full of praise for the sensitive way in which residential workers handled the move to a new family.

An important decision to be taken at this stage in respect of some of the children was whether this should be a foster placement or a placement for adoption. We have already described the range of opinions of parents and children on the respective merits of these two alternatives. It appears that, once the 'match' had been made, most of the parents and older children in the interview sample had a major influence on the decisions about legal status. However, the anxieties of some of the younger children about the impact of legal adoption on themselves and their birth relatives were not adequately explained or taken on board.

Some parents were able to compare different processes with different children, as was the case with the family where one child was placed directly for adoption whilst another one was a ward of court. The children were unrelated but both placed as infants. The adopters delayed the adoption of the first child until it was possible for both to be adopted together at the completion of the wardship proceeding. In the end this took seven years.

## Social work after placement

### Conveying a 'sense of permanence'

Even those who were placed directly under adoption agencies regulations were often not finally adopted for periods of years. Thus a model of practice which conveys to parents and children a 'sense of permanence' is important for those placed for adoption as well as for those in foster homes.

In a quarter of the cases in the full cohort and one in five of the interview sample it was anticipated that the application for adoption would be contested by a parent. Some of the adopters of infants spoke of their anxieties until the adoption order was made.

> There was always a fear from the time when she came into the house that something would happen and she would have to leave. As far as I am concerned we built up that love from the beginning. When she was adopted she wanted to change her whole name, including her first name. We would not let her drop her first name, we encouraged her to choose a name she really liked, which she could use as another name and she chose the name.

Few of the parents of the older placed children expressed worries that the child might be removed from their care, either by birth parents or by social workers. The young people who were interviewed were asked if they had ever felt that they might be removed from their present placement. Of the 25 children interviewed who answered the question, 21 said they never thought they would have to leave; two thought that they themselves might want to leave; and two thought that something they did might cause the placement to break down. Although one parent described a child's anxieties about the possibility, no young person we interviewed thought that the social worker might take them away unless this was because of something they themselves had done. No young person thought that a birth parent would take them away unless they themselves chose to go back to their birth families.

When the young people were asked whether, as they grew up, they themselves had ever thought they would like to leave before they moved out into independent living, one said 'often'; two said that they had at some earlier stage but not lately; and two said that they did not want to leave at an early stage but did think about leaving in the later stages of the placement. Fifteen said they had never thought of leaving. It thus appears that those who were fostered, and those who were placed for adoption but not adopted until considerably later, were helped to develop a sense of permanence from quite soon after they were placed.

### Facilitating links with birth families

The opinions of the parents and young people about their birth parents and other relatives, and about any continuing contact, have been discussed in earlier chapters. Family members were asked whether the social workers had played any part in supporting links or acting as channels for communication. These placements were made at the time when it was unusual for there to be continuing contacts with the birth family after placement for adoption. Thus, in the majority of cases, social workers had played very little part. In some cases families had themselves arranged contact, and they were sometimes assisted in this by either the local authority social worker or the adoption agency worker. On occasions a parent asked a trusted worker to discuss this issue with the young person, particularly if there was a question of opening up contacts which had been ended at the time of placement. Sometimes a birth parent or (more often) an adult sibling went to the agency and asked them to contact the adoptive parents with a view to re-starting contact. It was clear that, faced with this request, different agencies responded differently, as is still the case (Howe and Feast 2000).

A number of the adoptive parents whose children did not have any contact with birth parents came to believe that this might be helpful but were either dissuaded by the social worker to whom they mentioned this, or did not feel able to ask for help.

> We met the mother. It was very difficult. She was crying and didn't want her daughter to go. The child had been in care for four years so we didn't think we were taking her away from her mother. They didn't offer any contact or ask us about it. They said they thought it would be disruptive for her but she had this rosy picture of her mother. In retrospect I think it's helpful for children to see their birth parents. At the time I thought it would take her longer to bond, but in retrospect it would have helped us.

The subject was never raised until the young person left home during a turbulent adolescence and went back to her birth mother, suffering a further rejection which added to her problems.

In other cases, the adoption worker was positive about contact and encouraged it. In some cases there was disagreement between the local authority worker and the placement agency worker. This adoptive mother, who considered that it was important that she should encourage contact despite the fact that her daughter sometimes was upset by it, went to considerable efforts to take her to her birth mother's home where she also saw her brothers. She told the researcher that she did not discuss with the local authority social workers the difficulties she sometimes had as she feared they would disapprove. She also met disapproval from the post-adoption group she attended.

> When she returned from visiting her mother she would cry and be upset, but I did not want contact terminated and I felt that if I told the social worker this, they would just have said: 'Oh, well it's not good for a child' because they say their first priority is the child. My adoption worker was great over issues to do with contacting the birth family.

As time moved on and there was greater discussion of contact after adoption, one mother felt that she was put under inappropriate pressure to facilitate contact for her son who was experiencing difficulties. She considered that such contact would be unhelpful to him but did not think that the social workers respected her views.

> With regard to contact, the social workers were very bad at the beginning. I mean, I didn't particularly want information about the birth family, but I was happy to send them a birthday card which I gathered was not passed on to her. They didn't, because he found the card in the files. Later they suggested contact with his father. They were putting pressure on us to contact him without thinking whether this was the right thing for the child, which I resisted. They hadn't a clue what they were talking about and we found that they couldn't really give us any help.

### Post-placement and post-adoption supervision, support and therapy

Rather to our surprise, especially since many of the children who were eventually adopted remained as foster children for periods of years, neither parents nor children had too much to say about reviews and statutory visits by social workers. It may be that this was now long into the past and there were other more important things which they wished to talk to us about. Generally the story was of social workers fading into the background or disappearing unless there were problems about which parents wished to consult them. The pattern was similar to that described in an earlier study (Thoburn 1990) with the early practice being essentially about support and practical help, followed in some cases by therapy, often several years after the children first joined the family. In most cases the families either had few problems or turned elsewhere for support. This young person's account reflects the most frequent response.

> We didn't like it much when they came to see us at the foster home because it would mean that we had to come in from playing, and no one else was seeing social workers, so it used to be a bit of a pain. Sometimes I and my brother, we would just go, we just didn't want to see social workers. When they used to come we didn't do anything – we would just sit in the house and talk, and it was quite boring really. We had to stay in for like an hour and talk about rubbish. We didn't have anything to say to them. We were happy where we were. Now could we go out and play? That was it, really.

Families who experienced difficulties after adoption had mixed responses, some having considerable help when they asked for it, whilst others felt that they had to 'go on their bended knees' to get post-adoption services. This was especially so with either practical support such as respite care, or therapy for themselves or the young person. These adopters had a tip for others who take older children into their homes.

> Be assertive with social workers – make sure you know your rights for help. Respite, particularly insist on respite. If your relationship doesn't hold together, the kids have had it. Make sure you get practical help. I don't see why foster parents should have it and not adopters, and make sure that children who have been harmed do get psychotherapy. Get the service for them.

There were mixed responses also to the service provided when young people left home. Unsurprisingly, foster families received a better service than the adoptive families since the local authority retained parental responsibility until they left care at 18. Adopters were dependent on a service being provided under the general provisions of the Part III (family support to children 'in need') provisions of the 1989 Children Act, or as part of any post-adoption services provided under the requirement of the Adoption Agencies Regulations. The adoptive parents of a young person who left home at 16, having been placed at the age of five, thought they were unduly pressured to take her back into their home. The adoptive family continued to provide support as she moved into independent living.

After she left, the social workers at the local Social Services Department were coming down on us very heavy to take her back, but it was as if they were saying that we were not caring enough, and supportive enough of her.

## Social work methods

Parents and young people had little to say about the particular social work or other therapeutic methods used. Like the majority of those who come into contact with social workers and therapists, they concentrated more on the personal attributes of the worker and the quality and reliability of the relationship and practical help provided. In general terms individual psychotherapy or counselling for the different members of the family was preferred, although help to talk through marital difficulties was appreciated by some of those whose marriages came under stress. As with some other studies of adopters, those who were offered or had experienced family therapy tended not to find it helpful.

> The psychotherapist from the Health Authority Young People's Centre was particularly helpful to both me and my daughter for about two years. It really helped us. She reassured us, she made us feel normal, she said 'You are doing a good job'. Tessa liked her a lot. But we had to do all the pushing. If we hadn't we would not have got therapy. The psychotherapist ran groups for foster parents giving ideas about strategies – little things, like saying 'It's not you I don't like, it's your behaviour'. Social workers just sit there and don't think of saying that you must quickly get on to psychotherapists to get the help you need. They were thinking of getting us in for family therapy, but that was very threatening. We didn't want that.

Individual psychotherapy was provided for at least four other troubled youngsters and in each case was found helpful.

One young man, adopted from residential care at the age of six, settled well initially but then, around the age of 11, became sad and worried about his birth mother. Later he was admitted to hospital for tests because of severe stomach pains. Individual child psychotherapy was suggested and found to be very helpful.

> The most helpful thing – the psychiatric help was crucial. If he had not had that help, he may not have been here now. That anger would have got worse and worse. I say that because some families don't ask for help – some adopters. Some have terrible problems and they can't get psychiatric help. Maybe they see it as a stigma. People don't like to feel they need help. They don't see psychiatrists as helpers. They see it as a

failure. People need help when they need it. Not let it get so bad the police are involved. They think psychiatric referrals are about assessment of them as adopters. I don't see his problems as failure. I just see them as part of what had happened to him.

The key characteristics valued in social workers and therapists were those which are described in all consumer studies of social work practice.

With my social worker, I could bounce ideas off – both negative and positive. I did not have to know it all. I did not have to get it right. I could say to her: 'I feel awful', but I wasn't getting anywhere and she would not take this as the end of anything.

In the context of this supportive and caring relationship, practical help and therapeutic help were sometimes valued, but lack of time to listen and reflect diminished the positive impact of much-needed practical help.

My social worker will give me all the equipment that I needed, but time was not one of her strengths. She wasn't bad. It was just that she always seemed to have something more important to do. One day I asked her about this and she said: 'Look I know you can cope and you get on with it, and that's why I don't bother', but sometimes you don't want that, sometimes you want somebody who will come and sit next to you who you can talk to. She was very light on time.

## Financial and practical help

| Table 8.1 Financial support after placement (full cohort) | | |
|---|---|---|
| *Financial support* | *Number of cases* | *per cent* |
| Fostering allowance only | 173 | 64 |
| Adoption allowance only | 3 | 1 |
| Fostering followed by adoption allowance | 7 | 3 |
| Settling-in grant | 5 | 2 |
| Specific practical items | 3 | 1 |
| Fostering, settling-in and practical | 28 | 10 |
| No financial support indicated on file | 50 | 19 |
| *Total* | 269 | 100 |

[Missing data = 28]

Financial support was available to most of the new families after the child joined them, in most cases because the child was placed initially as a foster child. Information on this in respect of the full cohort was sparse, but Table 8.1 gives the details as far as they were known. It almost certainly under-estimates the amount of practical support and one-off payments. The placements were made just as adoption allowances were introduced in certain circumstances. However, there were only eight cases where it was clear from the file or from our interviews that an adoption allowance was paid in respect of these children. Mostly these were paid to those with disabilities or who were older at placement. However, in one case, a child placed when under the age of three was not adopted until problems had developed later, and an adoption allowance was seen to be appropriate.

> We started with the fostering allowance and they paid for bunk beds. We were never told we could get a holiday allowance until the case was transferred back to the first local authority. We were never given the information we should have had. He was very destructive because he was very fidgety. She said: 'He's a big lad – in teenage sizes when he was only ten. I'm going to have to make sure – to ask for more money, because he is so destructive with his clothes and sheets'. And we got a lot more money then. I find it helpful but I find it embarrassing. We didn't want an adoption allowance at first. By the time he was adopted we wanted to finish with them altogether. But by the time we adopted we really needed it.

As far as we could tell, no residence order allowances were paid. Other financial assistance was given in the form of 'settling in' grants for those placed directly under adoption agencies regulations or grants for the adaptations to property or equipment needed by children who had disabilities. Some social workers went to considerable lengths to help families to obtain expensive equipment from charitable trusts. However some parents said that such help was given somewhat reluctantly and only if they asked.

Most of the mothers who adopted infants, as well as some of those who adopted or fostered older children, gave up work at the time that the children were placed, and several of those who did not regretted that they had not done so in order to spend more time with the children and help them to settle in.

Thirty per cent of the adopters but only 13 per cent of the foster parents described themselves as sometimes or often short of cash, a finding in line with that of Gibbons et al. (1995). However some adopters preferred to receive small grants from the adoption agency if they found they needed them rather than have an adoption allowance.

These last couple of years it's been very hard for us financially. It's like three adults. They help us sometimes with small things. But I would not want an adoption allowance.

Foster parents and young people found the foster care payments were acceptable and often essential. Like most of those interviewed by Hill, Lambert and Triseliotis (1989) about adoption allowances, this young woman had no problems with payment to her permanent foster carers towards her keep.

I think May and Bill needed the fostering allowance really. I suppose if it had been one child it would have been all right, but to look after three children and to pay rent, it helped. It helped us as well because we got clothes and goodness knows what else.

## Social work with the children and young people

The young people volunteered very little information on their views about social work and social workers. Most of those who had been placed as infants had had little contact with them other than as friendly and interested adults who visited from time to time and mainly talked to their parents. Only a small minority of the foster children objected to remaining in care, though they tended to find social work visits an unnecessary event which was tolerated with more or less good grace.

In some cases where there were communication problems, parents and young people used social workers as intermediaries, helping each to see that, although the going was tough, there was something worth hanging on to. This model of practice was in line with that described in earlier studies of specialist family placement work, and generally met with the approval of the new parents and children. This comment of a young woman, now the mother of two children, is typical of the responses to a question about tips they would give social workers.

Overall the tip I would give to social workers is to find out what a child really wants – mentally, not physically. Try and see the child's point of view. Tell them what's going on. Don't hide anything. Be honest with the child. The people I've found helpful have been those that have been there for me. They are someone to talk to.

This was a more negative comment from a young person who was maltreated in his foster home and whose placement broke down:

Being a social worker is a treacherous job. You either have it or you don't. There's no tips I can give. Social workers need to be able to read between the lines and observe young people, because they may not tell them everything. That is what I'm saying. You can't teach this sort of thing. Social workers have it or they don't. My social worker didn't, or if she did, she couldn't give a damn.

We have already stated that parents told us that they had valued psychotherapy for the children on the few occasions it had been available, and thought it had been helpful to the young people as well as to themselves. Little mention was made of this by the young people in our interviews. The social workers and therapists appeared to be merged together in their consciousness as either a helpful or unhelpful entity.

The major identifiable piece of work which had been undertaken with the children came under the general heading of 'life story work'. Although there were few accounts of the life story books having been formally updated, several social workers were drawn in to provide more information to the young people, and to act as a sounding board for them, as they grew older and needed to understand more about why they had been adopted. Several of the adopters or foster parents asked for this work to be undertaken and were generally pleased that it had been.

An adoptive mother talked positively about the way in which the social worker came periodically to update the information at important times:

> Our daughter always asked the question: why is it that she is looking after her other two children and she sent her and her brother away. The life story books were very good. We have used them a lot with the children. It is their life history. Our oldest son started attacking the book with knives and compasses and we had to rescue it and hide it.

One mother however felt that life story work had been unhelpful, and was, in retrospect highly critical of the way in which adoption had been held up to a very disturbed young woman as the answer to all her problems.

> The life story book was a glossy view of where she had been with the little stories in it. She knew then that the good thing to do was to have a family. But she did not know what a family was. I don't think she ever settled.

Another mother would also have liked more help, although her criticism was more muted. Her adopted daughter had been placed at the age of five and was still, at 16 when we interviewed her, somewhat confused about the reason why she left her first family.

> She said quite clearly over a period of time that she wanted to talk to somebody privately about her mum and dad. But this never happened. We had her social worker from the local authority until the adoption order but unfortunately she became ill. After that I had an unsatisfactory

experience with the local authority workers and we also experienced more changes with the adoption agency.

As the children grew up, those who were in foster care learned of the possibility of seeing their files and this was another opportunity to update the life story work.

## Social workers and ethnicity

Few of the young people turned to social workers to help them with issues concerning their ethnic background and any experience of racism. In a minority of cases parents and children found an area team worker or a family placement worker helpful, and several of the white and black parents had found that these issues had been well covered in the preparation and post approval training groups. Generally the black parents preferred to have black social workers, whereas the views of the white parents were more mixed.

Black parents in particular commended black workers for their determination to place children with families who could help them with their racial and cultural identity. This was especially so for those children of mixed race parentage who had taken on white identities. A picture sometimes emerged of a partnership between foster family and worker to achieve this end when children were originally placed on a temporary basis.

> They came to me because it was Christmas time and the home was closed. It was undecided whether they would stay and I talked to the [African-Caribbean] social worker and she wasn't happy for them to go back to the home after what I had achieved for them. She said to me, 'You have to try to find a school for them, and if they get a school that is one problem solved because they can't say, "Well, they need schools, so let them go back"'. And then we had the identity work and the social worker says to them, 'Well it doesn't look wise for these children to go back to where they were – a white area – because look at what it is doing to them.' So we were getting more and more ammunition to say that this was a better place for them, getting them to the school and get the social worker to be working with them and their identity.

Black social workers were also appreciated because of their knowledge about living in a black family. For example, their awareness of the importance of financial help to go back to the Caribbean was valued:

> My mum was taken badly ill about three months after they came. I had to go in a hurry to Jamaica and I said to the social worker 'My mum's very ill and I have to go and will Social Services pay for them to go and what about the passports?' They were very good. They jumped round and

sorted the passports and got requests for the fares to be paid and some clothing money for them to go.

Others just talked about feeling more comfortable talking to a worker who shared the same culture.

> Yes, in a lot of ways there were some things you could say, yes, this comes from a black social worker. Talking to her I felt free to say just how I felt about it. But if I was dealing with a white worker, I would probably be wondering 'Now, how do I put this so it doesn't seem as if I'm trying to make trouble, but they do understand what I am saying'. It's not essential to have [a black worker] but it's necessary that it should be made available. I think that's the right way to put it. A black carer could find it quite easy to get on with a white worker without any qualms. But if that is requested, a black worker, they should try to meet that.

Since more of the white families interviewed were adopters, they tended to have less contact with social workers in the later stages of placement. They were less likely to give their views about the race of the social worker than to comment on how they handled the increasingly contentious and sensitive issue of transracial placements.

One family who experienced many difficulties with the child placed with them described how attitudes changed to the placement of black children over the period in question. The adoption agency workers continued to be supportive throughout, but they described how a local authority social worker's comments led them to feel blamed and criticised. Transfer of the father's job to another part of the country came as something of a relief.

> They should have done more cultural work with her early on but they didn't. If you are a black person, you can help a child through that because you have had that hurt, but we did work hard at it. When we came here we asked them if they had a black social worker, and they said yes, which was one positive. With the local authority worker in the first authority we moved from being foster parents to white racists.

Because of the change in attitudes of the placing agency, these parents felt unable to seek help with their difficulties. Fortunately the adoption agency worker continued to be supportive. Other white families had similar though less marked experiences.

The white adoptive mother of a young man placed at four described how, recognising that she lived in a mainly white area, she took great pleasure in going to London with him as often as she could, and wandering around street markets in mainly black areas. When invited to a post-adoption workshop arranged by the adoption agency she looked forward to going to the event with her son, then aged nine. Her memories were not happy ones.

> I thought it would help but it backfired. We were thrown together into this room. This other mother and her black daughter and me and Paul and two other white social workers and the black group leader. By the end of the day I thought 'What am I doing here?' All I felt was anger coming from them that we were white women who had adopted black children. They said 'Had neither of you thought of moving to inner cities so they could have contact with black people?' I felt incredible anger. I said 'It's not our fault that it was decided a few years later that white people shouldn't adopt black children.' It was obvious both of us loved our children to bits, and we would not have trailed down there otherwise. I said 'Don't pour all this anger out on us – pour it out on the people who haven't bothered to come'. Paul was close to tears. He said, 'Mum, don't ever take me to anything like that again'. He said 'I'm all right Mum, I've got black friends here. I'm all right with what I am. I don't need to go up there and sit and discuss it.'

Such incidents were, however, exceptions. The most frequently expressed view amongst white and black parents and those of other ethnic origin was that, provided the workers possessed the other attributes they valued, there was merit in having a social worker of similar ethnic background to the child.

> My daughter did have a black social worker from the local authority. She was very nice and I was able to talk to her about race and cultural issues. This worker did not come in specifically to talk to her about black issues. It was just that she was young, black and trendy and Martine was able to relate to her.

The young people expressed their views also about whether they thought it was a good idea to have a social worker of a similar ethnic background. They tended to be more unsure than their parents about whether this was a good thing or not, generally feeling that what was most important was to have a good social worker, rather than a social worker of a particular ethnic background.

A teenager of South Asian descent placed with South Asian adoptive parents with whom she was well settled said:

> I don't think it would have helped if I'd had an Asian social worker. I think it would have had more effect if the worker had been *adopted* themselves.

## Overall satisfaction with the social work service

Parents were asked about their overall satisfaction with the service provided by the main social work or adoption agency in the pre-placement period, in the early months after placement, and in the later stages of placement. Only one was generally dissatisfied with the pre-placement service; eight had mixed views and 80 per cent were generally positive. Nine out of ten were generally positive about the service in the early months after the child joined the family, with only five parents having mixed reactions and none being totally dissatisfied. In the later years 80 per cent still felt generally positive about the service they had received, with parents of only five children having a mixed reaction and four having a generally negative reaction. As we have noted, the intensity of the service varied, largely depending on whether this was an infant placement or a child who had particular difficulties. These two groups were looking for a different sort of service and generally found what they were looking for.

Overall, there were far more satisfied than dissatisfied customers amongst the young people, the white and black families and amongst baby adopters and those who took children with special emotional, physical or learning disabilities.

> The work I got from the adoption agency worker was unstinting. I could ring her at any time and talk to her but not only to her – to anyone in the team. I could talk to them about any areas that I needed to.

## Summary

Information on social work practice and other support services for the 297 full cohort cases is sketchy, and mainly limited to accounts of the frequency of contact by the child's social worker and the family placement worker. Because they had to cast their minds back a long way, the parents and young people interviewed tended to remember bad or good episodes and have little to say about more routine practice. The majority of the comments made by the family members were about post-placement support and services, or the lack of them.

- In most of the 297 cohort cases a fairly high level of support was provided shortly after placement to both adoptive and foster families. Social work visits were at the level of at least every two weeks for the first three months in 70 per cent of the cases.

- Some form of post-adoption service was provided in 57 per cent of the 95 cases about which this information was available.

- Comments about the service provided by the family placement workers tended to be more positive than those about the child's worker, but there were exceptions, with some in each group being held in very high esteem.

- Of the parents and young people interviewed 80 per cent expressed general satisfaction with the level and content of the social work service.

- Indirect support as well as a sense of a job well done came from playing a part in the adoption service, adoption self-help groups or on race equality or community relations councils. African-Caribbean foster parents in particular spoke of their sense of achievement in recruiting and helping to train the black foster and adoptive parents.

- Few of the young people or adopters turned to social workers in the later stages of the placement to help them to work through any issues about ethnic identity, race or racism. A minority of the parents (white and black) spoke with appreciation of the advice and encouragement of white and black social workers, but the highest praise was given by African-Caribbean foster parents for African-Caribbean workers.

- Apart from early days after placement, when some children showed signs of anxiety lest the social worker remove them, a 'sense of permanence' was secured for all but a tiny minority of parents and children. This was important for those who were placed for adoption as well as for those who remained as foster children since some were not actually adopted for several years.

- Some local authority social workers and family placement workers played an important role in keeping links alive between the birth and the new family.

- Little comment was made about social work *methods* but personal characteristics of workers, including warmth, reliability, availability and honesty, were much commented on.

- Adopters whose children were provided with counselling or psychotherapy at the later stages of the placement spoke about this with appreciation, and regretted that it had sometimes been difficult to obtain and unnecessarily delayed. What they wanted most for themselves was a 'sounding board', encouragement and specialist advice.

- Some young people were particularly positive about help they received to get back in contact with siblings from whom they had become separated. Help to go through their social services files as young adults was also mentioned by the foster children, but did not appear to have been offered to any of those who had been adopted.

# CHAPTER 9

# Families for Life or Ports in a Storm?

## The cohort of 297 placements

There are many different ways of measuring successful or unsuccessful outcomes, most of which can only be understood in the context of detailed interviews with family members. For the full cohort we only had information on intended legal status and on whether the placement lasted for ten to 15 years or until the agency lost contact with the family. Some 210 of the placements (71 per cent) were initially intended to be adoptive placements and 86 (29 per cent) were made as foster placements. Some of the planned foster placements became adoptions and some children placed for adoption remained in the family as foster children. At the time of the records search in 1995, 160 (55 per cent) had been adopted, and 112 (38 per cent) remained as foster children. Some placements in each group had disrupted. Sixty-nine (24 per cent) disrupted in that the children returned to local authority care (27), or left the placement following serious conflict to return to their birth parents (11) or start out on their own when still under the age of 18. Table 9.1 gives this information.

It is likely that the disruption rate will, in the event, have been higher than 24 per cent, because some of those about whom more recent information is not available will have disrupted. Indeed we know from some of the letters we received from adopters who declined to take part in the study that some children who were, according to the files, still in placement had experienced breakdown.

> Please understand that we do not wish to participate in this study because it would be far too painful to reiterate these awful experiences.

### Table 9.1 Young people's circumstances between 8 and 15 years after placement

| Circumstances | Full cohort | |
|---|---|---|
| | n | per cent |
| Living with same adoptive/foster family | 184 | 62 |
| Living independently (planned move) | 41 | 13 |
| Living with birth parent or relative | 11 | 4 |
| Living independently (negative move) | 9 | 3 |
| Other (including residential care, prison) | 49 | 17 |
| Died (including two children with disabilities who remained in placement until death) | 3 | 1 |
| Total | 297 | 100 |

Those away at university or residential employment such as nursing or the armed forces, but still using the family as their home base, were included in the 'living with family' category.

Figure 9.1 shows that there is a statistically significant association between the child being older at placement and the proportion of placements which did not last as needed. The high incidence of breakdown amongst those placed between ten and twelve is most marked, approaching the 50 per cent level.

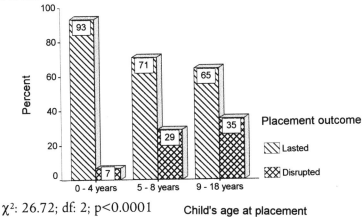

$\chi^2$: 26.72; df: 2; p<0.0001
n = 294; missing data = 3

*Figure 9.1 Outcome by age at placement*

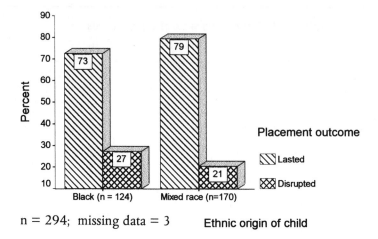

*Figure 9.2 Outcome by child's ethnicity*

Figure 9.2 shows that more of the placements of children born to two parents of minority ethnic origin broke down (27 per cent) than was the case for those of mixed race parentage (21 per cent). The proportion for those with two white parents in the original cohort was 20 per cent (Thoburn 1991). However these differences are not statistically significant and disappear when age at placement is taken into account.

| Table 9.2 Placement outcome by ethnicity of child | | | | | | |
|---|---|---|---|---|---|---|
| *Ethnicity of child* | *Lasted as needed* | | *Disrupted* | | *Total* | |
| | *n* | *per cent* | *n* | *per cent* | *n* | *per cent* |
| Caribbean | 63 | 76 | 20 | 24 | 83 | 100 |
| African | 8 | 44 | 10 | 56 | 18 | 100 |
| South Asian | 15 | 79 | 4 | 21 | 19 | 100 |
| One black/one white parent | 126 | 79 | 33 | 21 | 159 | 100 |
| Other mixed parentage | 9 | 82 | 2 | 18 | 11 | 100 |
| Other ethnicity | 4 | 100 | 0 | 0 | 4 | 100 |
| *Total* | *225* | *76* | *69* | *24* | *294* | *100* |

Missing = 3

Table 9.2 shows that a larger proportion of children both of whose parents were of African descent experienced placement breakdown (more than half did so), and that larger proportions of the children of 'other mixed parentage' and 'other ethnicity' were in placements which lasted as needed. However, because age at placement is so strongly associated with placement breakdown, variables associated with more successful outcomes have to be considered for the different age groups. Of the 18 African-Caribbean children about whom outcome information was available, 14 were over nine at placement, whereas 35 per cent of the South Asians; 35 per cent of the children with one black and one white parent; and almost half of those of 'other mixed parentage'; but only 16 per cent of those with two parents of Caribbean descent were placed when under the age of four.

### Table 9.3 Proportions of placements breaking down where the following characteristics are present (cohort of 297 placements)

| Variable | % disrupting | $\chi^2$ test of significance (two-way analysis of variance) |
|---|---|---|
| Placed child is a boy | 24 | ns |
| No other children in adoptive/foster family | 15 | ns |
| New parent(s) are white | 19 | ns |
| Behavioural difficulties at time of placement | 39 | <0.0001 |
| Emotional problems at time of placement | 35 | <0.0001 |
| Child experienced multiple moves prior to placement | 31 | <0.01 |
| Child described as institutionalised at time of placement | 33 | <0.01 |
| History of deprivation or abuse prior to placement | 33 | <0.01 |
| Previous disrupted 'permanent' placement | 37 | <0.001 |
| Birth mother supports plan for permanent placement | 19 | ns |
| Single parent adoptive/foster family | 25 | ns |
| Adoptive/foster father in unskilled/semi-skilled occupation | 11 | ns |
| Adoptive/foster mother in managerial/professional occupation | 15 | ns |
| Other adopted/foster children in family | 14 | ns |
| Child is placed as youngest child in family with other children | 20 | ns |
| New parent wished to foster rather than adopt | 19 | ns |
| Child placed initially with intention of adoption not fostering | 19 | ns |

Table 9.3 lists variables about which other researchers or practitioners have commented. As with other studies (Rushton *et al.* 1995; and those reported in Sellick and Thoburn 1996, and Triseliotis *et al.* 1997), it appears that it was difficulties in the child's behaviour rather than variables about the placement or new family which were most likely to have an impact on placement stability. We found, in common with other researchers, that having experienced deprivation or abuse was significantly associated with breakdown, a finding which lends weight to the conclusion of Gibbons *et al.* (1995), drawn from a follow-up study of children maltreated when under the age of five, that the experience of abuse or neglect in the early years presents a hazard to successful placement with substitute families.

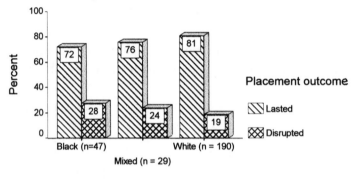

n = 266;  missing data = 31

*Figure 9.3 Outcome by ethnicity of new parents*

This descriptive analysis also showed that, when allowance was made for age at placement, there was no significant difference in breakdown rates between ethnically 'matched' and 'non-matched' placements (Figure 9.3). We examined whether there were any other marked differences between those placed with white or black families or mixed race partnerships. Table 9.4 shows important differences between the children who were placed with the different ethnic groups. Substitute families where both parents were black were more likely to have children aged nine or over, with the youngest children more likely to be placed in mixed partnership or white families. Children who had experienced multiple moves were more likely to be placed with white families, and those who were placed from residential care were more likely to go to new black families. Families with two black or two white parents (or single parents) were more likely than mixed partnerships to be joined by children with many problems.

### Table 9.4 Characteristics of children placed with white parents, mixed-race partnerships, and families where both parents were of minority ethnic origin (percentage of those placed with these characteristics)

| Characteristic known at time of placement | Placed with white parents | Placed with mixed partnership | Placed with one or two parents of minority ethnic origin | $\chi^2$ test of significance* |
|---|---|---|---|---|
| Aged 9+ | 33 | 30 | 55 | p<0.01 |
| Aged 0–4 | 41 | 47 | 15 | p<0.01 |
| Emotional problems | 54 | 50 | 54 | ns |
| Behavioural problems | 47 | 40 | 41 | ns |
| History of deprivation or abuse | 53 | 53 | 65 | ns |
| Multiple moves | 57 | 43 | 46 | p<0.05 |
| 'Institutionalised' | 37 | 40 | 33 | ns |
| Disrupted 'permanent' placement | 21 | 17 | 17 | ns |
| Placed from residential care | 51 | 37 | 82 | p<0.05 |
| Contact with siblings placed elsewhere | 19 | 30 | 40 | p<0.05 |
| Contact with birth parent | 30 | 17 | 61 | p<0.05 |
| Placed with a sibling | 31 | 33 | 45 | ns |
| More than 5 problems at time of placement | 44 | 40 | 56 | ns |

*Significance of any differences when placements with different ethnic groups compared.

These differences in types of problems at placement to some extent balance each other out with all ethnic groups taking a proportion of the children likely to have difficulties after placement. However, a single or two black or Asian parents provided homes for a larger proportion of the oldest age group who were more likely to have complex relationships with the birth family and previous carers.

There was no difference in breakdown rates between children who had physical or learning disabilities and those who did not. These children were mainly placed with white families, although two of the 15 children with serious physical disabilities were placed with mixed partnership families; two children with serious learning difficulties were also placed with mixed partnership families and two with families with both parents of minority ethnic origin.

The overlapping variables made it essential to use more complex statistical techniques in order to consider the effects on success or breakdown of the different variables. The detailed *logit* analysis using LIMDEP version 7 (Greene 1995) is reported in more detail in Thoburn and Moffatt (in press). When other variables were held constant, four variables were independently associated with placement breakdown. These were:

- being older at placement (although the probability of breakdown went down again for children placed over the age of 10);
- having behavioural difficulties at the time of placement;
- being described as 'institutionalised' at the time of placement;
- having a history of deprivation or abuse prior to placement.

For the cohort as a whole neither gender of the child nor the ethnicity of the new parents were associated with breakdown once other variables were held constant. However, when further analysis was undertaken, it was found that boys of minority ethnic origin did better in transracial placements (75 per cent were successful) than in 'matched' placements (57 per cent were successful). This effect is reversed for girls with 72 per cent of those in transracial placements being successful and 82 per cent of those in 'matched' placements. These differences are statistically significant when other variables are held constant.

Explanations for success or breakdown might be found in the new parents and parenting styles or in the reactions of the young people to placement. Other studies of family placement have found differences between the reactions of boys and girls, with boys more likely to experience behavioural difficulties and to be found in clinical populations (see Howe 1997b for a discussion of the research on this issue). It is possible that African-Caribbean or Asian parents have found the behavioural difficulties of the boys more difficult to deal with, or that the more open communication patterns of girls in expressing their opinions and talking about their difficulties might have fitted better with the parenting styles and communication patterns of the new parents in 'matched' placements. There was a tendency for the boys we interviewed to be less interested than the girls in talking about their views on race, racism, ethnic and adoptive identity. Their 'what's all the fuss about and let me get on with my life in this family' attitude might have fitted better with that of the white parents who, whilst not minimising the impact of either 'race' or adoption, appeared more inclined to emphasise the 'ordinariness' of adoptive family life. These highly speculative thoughts are drawn from a small number of interviews in respect of generally successful placements. However, this finding on gender and placement is sufficiently robust to merit further research which **specifically** sets out to explore the relationship between the gender of the child and the ethnicity of the substitute parents. In the UK, few placements are now made of children of minority ethnic origin with white families. It is therefore essential to take these data seriously. If boys are at increased risk when placed in 'matched' families, it is important to learn more about why this might be the case and to take appropriate steps to support the boys and their new parents.

Turning to other variables which have aroused interest in earlier studies, in the larger study of 1165 children, being placed with at least one sibling was found to be a 'protective factor' against breakdown. Face-to-face contact with siblings placed elsewhere and with birth parents were both associated with **fewer** placement breakdowns (Thoburn 1991). However, in this numerically smaller study including only children of minority ethnic origin and with the added variable of ethnicity of new parents, when other variables were held constant, no significant difference in outcome was found between those who had contact with birth parents or siblings living elsewhere and those who did not. From the qualitative data it was clear that some of the most complex placements were of children who would not have allowed themselves to be placed with substitute parents if they had not been assured that contact with their birth parents and siblings would continue after placement.

As with the full cohort, when other variables were held constant, there was no difference in outcome between those placed with 'permanent' foster families and those placed for adoption.

From this analysis of the relationship between outcome as measured by disruption and variables about the child and the placement, we conclude that it is child related factors or less tangible characteristics of the new families rather than variables about the age or family type of the adoptive or foster families which have the biggest impact on whether or not the placement will last as needed. Data on the social work service were not sufficiently robust or easily quantifiable for inclusion in the statistical model.

## The interview sample

Whether or not a placement lasted or disrupted is a crude measure of success, and we had evidence from the interviews that some which did not break down could not be viewed as satisfactory in emotional terms. It was possible to use a wider range of outcome measures for the 51 children in the interview sample. In this section numbers and percentages are used descriptively and no statistical analysis has been undertaken because of the small numbers and non-random nature of the sample. Where we do describe differences between outcomes and the characteristics of children or parents, our comments are tentative and exploratory in nature.

### Table 9.5 Placement of the young person at the time of interviews

| Placement | n | per cent | |
|---|---|---|---|
| Still with family* | 24 | 47 | } 80% |
| Living independently – planned move | 17 | 33 | |
| Living independently – conflictual move | 6 | 12 | } 20% |
| Living with birth family | 1 | 2 | |
| Returned to care, prison, other negative outcome** | 3 | 6 | |
| Total | 51 | 100 | |

\* Includes young people at college, in boarding school or in residential employment (e.g. armed forces or nursing) who return home when on leave or in vacations.
\*\* The lower disruption rate than for the full sample results from the omission from the interview sample of placements which broke down within the first two years.

Table 9.5 gives information on the placements of these 51 young people at the time of our interviews, and gives the researchers' conclusions about the overall success of these placements using a broader definition of outcome. Some of those who were living independently as a result of a planned move were no longer, in the light of additional data from the interviews, in the 'success' category, even though we did not record the placement as having broken down. However, all except four of the children appeared to have gained something from the placement, including some who had left their adoptive or foster families in less than happy circumstances. Table 9.6 shows that 72 per cent were rated as successful in most respects. These ratings take into account the extent of the difficulties experienced by the children before they were placed. In other words, there is a 'value added' element in our overall 'success' rating which is not present in the 'well-being' rating where the notional comparison was with an 'average' child having a similar level of mental and physical ability and living with averagely competent parents.

### Table 9.6 Overall success of interview sample placements – researcher rating

|  | *n* | *per cent* |
|---|---|---|
| Highly successful – needs met – young person succeeding in life | 8 | 16 |
| Successful. Most of young person's needs being met. Doing well in most respects (in the light of his/her abilities/ disabilities). Substantial progress made on problems identified at time of placement. | 16 | 31 |
| Successful in most respects. Most needs being met 'well enough'. Good progress made on problems identified at time of placement. Still some problem areas. | 13 | 25 |
| Evidence of some benefits but some important needs not met by placement and serious concerns for young person's future well-being remain. | 10 | 20 |
| Unsuccessful. Placement broke down and no/little evidence of child benefitting from placement. Important needs not met. Serious concerns about young person's future well-being. | 4 | 8 |
| *Total* | *51* | *100* |

Table 9.7 lists and gives the researchers' ratings of outcome for the 29 measures which contributed to the overall ratings of success. They are based on the Department of Health's *Looking After Children* indicators of good parenting (Ward 1996). Reliability checks were made by a second researcher on a proportion of cases, and more complex cases were discussed by all three members of the research team.

## Table 9.7 Summary of outcome indicators

| Outcome* | n | per cent |
|---|---|---|
| Placement did not disrupt (n = 51) | 42 | 82 |
| Educational achievement in line with potential (yes or only slightly below) (n = 50) | 40 | 80 |
| Educational achievement improved (since time of placement) (n = 50) | 35 | 70 |
| Achieved GCSE passes (excludes 16, under 16 and those with severe learning disabilities) (9 of these 22 had A Levels or were in Further/Higher Education) (n = 35) | 22 | 63 |
| Young person in regular employment (excludes those in education or severely disabled) (n = 21) | 11 | 52 |
| In generally good physical health (allowing for any disabilities) (n = 49) | 44 | 90 |
| Improved physical health (n = 49) | 35 | 71 |
| Not involved in criminal activity (excludes 5 with some involvement as children but not later, and those with severe disabilities) (n = 36) | 25 | 69 |
| Not abusing drugs or alcohol (excludes 12, too young and those with disabilities) (n = 36) | 27 | 75 |
| Has no serious emotional or behavioural difficulties (n = 51) | 40 | 78 |
| Improvements to earlier emotional and behavioural difficulties (young children with no problems at placement omitted) (n = 41) | 31 | 76 |
| Has adequate self care skills (allowing for disability) and excluding those with very severe disabilities (n = 41) | 37 | 90 |
| Has adequate social skills (n = 45) | 37 | 82 |
| Does not show signs of emotional immaturity (those with serious learning disabilities omitted) (n = 36) | 21 | 58 |
| General well-being overall (in light of above variables) is rated at least average (n = 51) | 34 | 69 |
| Overall well-being has improved (includes good at placement and allows for disabilities) (n = 51) | 37 | 73 |
| Self-esteem appears to be at an average level (n = 39) | 30 | 77 |
| Realistic sense of biography and abilities (self-concept) (omits those with severe disabilities) (n = 33) | 27 | 82 |
| Has appropriate contact with birth parent (including cases where contact is not appropriate) (n = 51) | 24 | 47 |

### Table 9.7 continued

| Outcome* | n | per cent |
|---|---|---|
| Has some contact with siblings (n = 40 who had a sibling) | 23 | 57 |
| Has a good knowledge of identity as adopted/fostered person (n = 42) | 36 | 86 |
| Has a positive view of self as an adopted/fostered person (n = 37) | 22 | 59 |
| Has clear sense of self as a person of his/her own heritage, race and culture in most respects (n = 41) | 36 | 88 |
| Values his/her own ethnic and cultural background and heritage (n = 45) | 35 | 78 |
| Has emotional bonds with at least one member of the adoptive/foster family (n = 50) | 32 | 64 |
| Young person was mainly satisfied with the placement (n = 30) | 22 | 73 |
| Adoptive/foster family provides a 'family for life' for the young person (n = 51) | 39 | 76 |
| All or most of young person's needs met (n = 51) | 25 | 49 |
| Placement rated overall as success in light of problems at time of placement (n = 51) | 37 | 72 |

* Researcher ratings' using all data sources. Notional point of comparison is a young person living in a similar environment with similar physical and learning disabilities.
** Missing data cases excluded in calculation of percentages.

*Education and employment*

Some 50 per cent of the children appeared to have achieved educationally in line with their potential and 30 per cent slightly below. Excluding those where educational achievement was good at the start of the placement and remained so, and those who were placed when under the age of five, 70 per cent appeared to have made progress in their educational attainment. One young person had already acquired a degree and at least three others were at university; six had further educational qualifications, and two more had A levels. However, some started from a low base and 37 per cent of the 22 who were of an age and ability level to have taken GCSEs left school with no GCSE passes. Although there were the usual tensions between parents and young people over homework and sometimes over behaviour in school, generally parents expressed satisfaction with the efforts that all but a minority of the young people had made with their schoolwork.

When it came to the exam time, GCEs/CSEs, she wasn't bottom of the heap – no, she was just about average, and ended up quite good.

Of the 21 who had left school and were not in further education, 11 had regular work, eight had had some irregular work, and (leaving aside those with severe disabilities) only two had never gained employment. Some of the parents went to very considerable lengths to help their youngsters find work. Two of the young women were full-time parents, and another was expecting her first child. The information was not available in respect of three young people who had left the family and were no longer in touch.

### Physical health

Some 90 per cent were in generally good health or there were only minor concerns. One young person's health was still causing concern because of life-style problems including misuse of drugs and alcohol, and this had applied to others in the past. There had been improvements in the health of 73 per cent of the young people but a quarter, who had problems at the time of placement, still had health problems. Amongst those whose health was poor at placement and was still poor, there were serious causes for concern. This young women had serious asthma throughout her childhood.

> Sometimes I wake up and I think, God, I don't want to die and leave my kids. And another thing I worry about is, if I die tomorrow, who is going to have my kids. I don't want them to go to foster parents, or anything. Not that I'm saying my experience was bad. Asthma is life-threatening and the medication I take affects my heart rate and could lead to death.

A young man whose physical health was rated as 'worse' had a very troubled life, including physical maltreatment within the children's home over a period of years, before he was placed at the age of 11. In most other respects this was a highly successful placement. He was well-settled with a partner, buying his own house and had been in employment ever since leaving school. However, he described himself as a worrier (confirmed by his partner who was present at the interview) and had a severe stomach ulcer which required regular treatment and careful attention to diet.

### Emotional health and behaviour

Other studies of adopted young people have identified a pattern of emotional and behavioural difficulties during childhood which has become less marked as the young person moves into adulthood (Tizard and Hodges 1990; Triseliotis and Russell 1984; Howe 1997a). The Kovacs and Beck (1997) depression inventory was used with the teenagers, and the Rutter malaise inventory (Rutter *et al.* 1981) with the young adults. For those already in new partnerships the Gibbons' family problem checklist was used (Gibbons *et al.* 1990). These, alongside the opinions of the young people and parents, contributed to ratings of emotional and behavioural difficulties and general well-being. Twenty-eight of the 51 children had had some emotional or behaviour difficulties earlier in the placement. For eight of these, the problems were no longer apparent; for five there were still problems of a similar magnitude, and for five the problems had got worse. At the time of the interviews, 21 (41 per cent) had no apparent emotional or behavioural difficulties and a further 19 (37 per cent) had only minor difficulties. Eleven, however, had serious behavioural difficulties. With other researchers, we concluded that behavioural and emotional difficulties became less severe for some of the children as they got older. Encouragingly, this was the case for some who did not become fully attached to their new families, as well as for the majority who did.

The incidence of substance abuse and delinquency also fed into our conclusions about well-being. A quarter of the 36 who were over 14 at interview, and did not have severe physical or learning disabilities, had abused glue, alcohol or drugs at some stage, though four of these nine no longer did so. Emotional and behavioural difficulties were associated with involvement in crime for 16, but for five of these, after a turbulent period, these problems had abated by the time of the interviews. Not untypical was the young women who joined her adoptive family at the age of five and moved out at 15 to live in a hostel. Prior to this her parents felt that her behaviour had deteriorated to a point which they could no longer manage. She got into serious fights which involved the police, although there were no convictions. She refused to do homework and truanted from school. Her mother said:

> Her behaviour was freaking me out. I nearly had a nervous breakdown.

At the time of the interview she was still living away from home but in close touch and leading a more settled, if not unproblematic, life. For others the problems were more severe and led to the total breakdown of relations with the foster or adoptive parents.

> He came to us when he was eight and he left when he was 16. For me, his leaving was a relief, but for him it was difficult. But he began to steal and get in trouble with the police, and there were all sorts of little things he would get into. On one occasion he threatened to shoot me. He was going to get his gun from his uncle and he was going to do this, and it was at this point that I said that I'd had enough. I rang the social services

and asked them to take him away today. It actually took six weeks for him to leave. And the social services were trying to bring me round, but I had got to the stage where I was thinking of me – I had just had enough – to the extent that, if his sister had wanted to go too, I would have let her go as well.

Some of those who continued to attempt to provide 'a secure base', despite earlier difficulties, were still aware of serious problems.

She had left and then came back again and stole things from the house. Again she nearly broke the marriage up. She said at that time that she was depressed, she felt alone, she was old before her time. I think she realised that if she didn't say sorry, and give us some of the things back she had stolen, she could never come back into our house. As the years pass, I might find it impossible to live with her, but I am very fond of her. When I heard she was on drugs, in a way I was relieved, at least I could understand what she had done to us that weekend – stealing our belongings.

A young women, whose problems were by no means so severe, also talked to us about her worries.

I don't really make friends. I just stick to the ones I already have. I don't trust people and I get on better with guys, I suppose because there is no competition.

### Self care and social skills

All the foster and adoptive parents we spoke to placed emphasis on helping the young people to acquire social and relationship skills, and to take care of themselves. This was confirmed by most of the young people we interviewed, and much appreciated by them. Indeed, a point to which we shall return in the conclusion, it seems likely that writers on adoption and fostering, and the parents themselves, may overemphasise the importance of the 'chemistry' – love, attachment, bonding – and underestimate the importance of helping the young person to acquire the skills to cope with the outside world. Even when placements broke down, there was evidence that the social and self care skills, which these essentially caring and competent parents had passed on to the young people, were helping some troubled youngsters to keep their heads above water. Only eight were rated as below average in social skills (excluding four very severely disabled young people and two about whom we had insufficient information). Reliable information was available on some of the young people who were no longer at home and whom we were unable to interview since their parents were able to describe examples of their ability, for example, to get jobs for themselves or generally negotiate difficult situations. On the information available, 90 per cent were rated highly in this respect. When there were problems in this area they tended to be around relationships with friends and acquaintances, a finding which is in keeping with that of other research on the adoption of children who have had difficult early lives (Tizard and Hodges 1990; Howe 1996).

### Sense of permanence and attachment

Emotional well-being was also affected by whether or not the young person was secure in the knowledge that he or she had 'a family for life' – which could be their family of origin or the substitute family. At least one member of the adoptive or foster family was likely to remain available to provide both emotional and practical support in 39 (76 per cent) of the cases, although, in 13 of these, relationships were not good with either the extended family or members of the nuclear family. This included those cases where the parents' marriage had broken down. There were a further five cases in which the adoptive or foster parents would be likely to provide advice or practical help in difficult times, but were not emotionally close and unlikely or unwilling to provide emotional support. There were seven cases (14 per cent) where the adoptive or foster family was no longer available to provide either emotional or practical support. In 6 of the 12 cases where emotional support was no longer provided, the child had originally been placed for adoption, and in six the child had been placed as a foster child. This outcome measure was linked with the question of whether affectional bonds had been established between the young person and the different family members. Here the 'success' rate is lower, with 7 (14 per cent) appearing to be unattached to any member of the new family and 11 (22 per cent) having only weak emotional ties. This is not surprising given the age at placement of several of these young people.

> I can remember saying to Fred, 'I would like you to feel as if you are a part of this family', and he sort of said, 'That can't happen really'. He didn't sort of say, 'You are not my mother', but that was his attitude. 'What are you on about? I know my history, and I am not part of your family'. I think that what he needed was a comfortable roost, a port in the storm sort of thing, where he could come and go from, but he really wasn't going to build his allegiance to it, and sort of feel family.

Other parents who had in the earlier stages thought that all they wanted to do was to survive until the young person could be encouraged to leave home and 'stand on their own two feet' found themselves becoming more attached as some of the worst problems decreased.

> I could not see myself as being a grandparent to her child. But that has changed now.

A young person also felt that he came closer as he was able to look back at his experience of joining the foster family at the age of 14:

> When I was under 18, I might have said the family didn't care, but now I am out of care and have left the foster family, I am grateful to them for helping me. So I suppose I do see them as my family. I always describe them as foster parents.

The young people were asked what they thought their parents would say when asked whether they were glad they got together as a family. This was a fairly typical response from those who had gone through difficult times but felt sure that they were still full members of the family.

> I think Elaine would say, 'Yes', that she's pleased I came to live with her. Sometimes we go through patches where we don't get on at all, but she is still very much a part of my life.

### Identity, self-concept, and self-esteem

These three concepts are linked and much has been written about them in the child development and adoption literature. The key texts on identity which influenced the focus of our interviews were by Erikson (1968), Honess and Yardley (1987) and Kroger (1996). Coopersmith (1981), Harter (1985) and McGuire (1994) were the main texts used to guide the discussions and ratings of self-concept and self-esteem. Banks (1992), Maximé (1986) and Burnell (1993) have discussed these concepts in the context of social work policy and practice. For young people of minority ethnic origin, there are the additional dimensions of racial identification and racial pride which we consider in the next section. In asking whether the young people had a realistic sense of who they were and of their own abilities and vulnerabilities, we included a question about whether they had appropriate contact with members of the birth family, or, if this was not appropriate, reliable information about their biographies and how they might seek further information. The question of links with members of the birth family is also relevant and has been discussed earlier.

In their teenage or young adult years, 17 (33 per cent) had contact with at least one birth parent, and for seven, contact was not possible or likely to be harmful. This leaves just over half the sample whose needs in this respect had not been adequately met. Some 57 per cent had appropriate contact with at least one birth sibling. This contact contributed to their sense of identity, as well as increasing the number of people who might be available to provide emotional or practical support as they moved into their adult lives. Even where this support was not forthcoming, there were advantages for the young person in terms of their sense of identity. An adoptive mother whose 17-year-old son had had a very troubled life, and was presently living with his birth mother, said:

> Any child would rather have the idealised 'let me into my own lovely family'. But I think that now he has gone back and found out how chaotic and wild his family are, he now has a more realistic picture of what his family is like. He totally identifies with us and would be very upset if someone said he was not part of this family.

Those young people who had had regular contact with a birth parent were as likely as those who did not to feel attached to their adoptive or foster parents.

We asked the young people whether they thought they were like their adoptive or foster parents or like their birth parents. Some referred to physical attributes, others to talents or personality. Whilst only 6 per cent saw themselves as different from, and over 90 per cent saw themselves as like at least some members of their birth families, half of those who answered this question about members of the adoptive families thought they were different from all of them. Six of those who thought they were different from all members of the adoptive or foster family were placed with white families and five were placed with families where both parents were of similar ethnic origin as was the case with this young woman of Asian descent:

> It's weird, but I don't feel similar to anybody [in adoptive family]. If you were to compare me to my birth family, I'm like everybody. I look like them; I act like them; I'm funny like my brother.

**Self-concept** was also related to whether the young people had a realistic sense of their abilities and of what the future might hold for them. At the end of the interview each young person was asked if they could tell us three things about themselves that they were proud of, and three things which they were less pleased with. They were also asked what their three wishes would be, and where they saw themselves being in five years' time. The answers to these questions contributed to a rating of self-concept. It was concluded that 80 per cent had accurate self-knowledge and an opinion of themselves which was close to the reality of their situation.

The question of **self-esteem** is a slightly different one in that a young person might appraise themselves realistically but not value themselves. The Coopersmith Self-Esteem Inventory was used with 21 of the young people and rated by a clinical psychologist. 'Average' was scored by 29 per cent; 33 per cent slightly below average; and 38 per cent low. Five of the seven who had average or above average scores were placed as infants but one was placed at the age of 11 and one at 14. Other data on these two young people (one placed as a foster child and adopted at 17; the other remaining as a foster child) suggest that they were resilient children who had come smiling through many adversities and seized the opportunity to become part of their new families. Two of the four with very low scores were placed at the age of 5, one at 8 and one at 11.

The Coopersmith scores, where available, and other information from the young people and the parents, contributed to a rating of self-esteem for 39 of the young people. (There was insufficient information on the other 12). At the start of the interview the young people were asked to describe themselves. Their responses were overwhelmingly positive with only five of the 24 giving mixed or neutral responses. The early responses were returned to at the end of the interviews when they were asked to talk about their positive and negative attributes. The general picture on self-esteem from all the data is more positive than that which emerged from the Coopersmith ratings on the 21 young people with whom that instrument was used. However, there was a large measure of correlation between the Coopersmith results and the researcher ratings, with none of those rated low on the Coopersmith scale given a positive rating on the basis of the interview data, four being given a fairly positive rating and four being rated as low in self-esteem.

As with other aspects of outcome, those who were high in self-esteem said so in very similar words, whereas those who had problems tended to have problems in different ways and this is represented in the quotes below. A young woman placed at two from a residential nursery had not been without problems as she grew up. However, she had a high 'Coopersmith' score at 18 and this came across in the interview.

> I'm happy. If I want something I go for it. I'm a popular person with friends. I am very straightforward. The worst thing for me, growing up, I didn't have confidence in myself. My main ambition now is to be happy. Go back to college. Get a good job. Have a long engagement and get married and have children. I want to work, I don't want to take things for granted.

Several adopters or foster parents and young people talked about improvements in self-esteem as the young people moved into their late teenage and young adult years.

Difficulties in forming relationships with friends or partners as young adults were associated with low self-esteem. This young woman felt that she had been greatly harmed by having to come into care in the first place, and then by a long spell in residential care. She was, however, still fully supported and had a close emotional relationship with her adoptive family.

> My confidence is a bit low at the moment. It has just gone at the moment. I don't know why, not having a boyfriend, and things like that. As I say, how you start off in life is how you are going to carry on.

A determination to always look well was described by several of the parents, to some extent as a 'positive' survival tactic but also, because it was taken to great lengths, as an indication of low self-esteem. It was nevertheless a defence mechanism which they encouraged.

> Other people tend to see her as happy, cheerful, not very bright. Outwardly she presents very, very well and would describe herself as happy and cheerful. Outwardly the hair has got to be perfect. She has to have the right shoes on even to go to the local shops. She looks as though she is off for an office job. But inwardly she never feels pretty enough, I don't think. And anything can be interpreted as a negative. She always picks up on the negatives.

Behind these comments is the question of maturity, a question which has been raised by other researchers (Tizard and Hodges 1990) The data from a range of sources contributed to a rating on the maturity of the young people. Fifty-eight per cent appeared to have a level of maturity which was age appropriate; almost a quarter showed some signs of immaturity, but about one in ten of those about whom it was possible to reach a conclusion showed clear signs of immaturity. Again some of those who had experienced the greatest difficulties were not interviewed, and it was not possible to make a rating because there was no recent information from their adoptive or foster parents.

Identity as a member of a particular minority ethnic group, or as an adopted or fostered person, also contributed to the question of self-esteem, but because of their centrality to this study they are discussed separately.

*Ethnic identity and ethnic pride*

As with the more general assessment of self-concept and self-esteem, knowledge about ethnicity and culture was rated separately from the question of pride in being a member of a particular ethnic group. The views of the young people and their parents which contributed to our conclusions on this dimension of outcome have been reported more fully in Chapter 7. Twenty-five of the young people (36 per cent of the 41 about whom there was sufficient data) were rated as having a clear sense of their ethnic and cultural identity with a further 11 being considered to be fairly clear about their ethnicity and cultural heritage. Five were rated as experiencing some confusion or lacking important information about their ethnic identities, biographies and culture. The disabilities of four children were so severe that it was clear that they would have no understanding of the issues concerned, although parents of some of those with moderate learning disabilities went to some length to help them to understand issues of ethnicity and heritage.

Because of the importance of this aspect of the research, the outcomes for individual children were considered in the context of the characteristics of the young people and their parents. However, attention is drawn to our earlier reminder about the small numbers and non-random nature of the interview sample.

The children who were older at placement were clearer about their ethnicity and cultural heritage, only two of those aged over five at placement being rated as having some confusion. The birth father of a young man of mixed race parentage was described on the file as Asian, but the young man told the interviewer that he was of Caribbean descent. Three of the 16 who were under the age of four at placement had important information missing which would have helped them to make sense of their ethnic and cultural identities.

All except one of the 32 children born to two black parents had a clear sense of their ethnic origins whereas four of the 19 with one black and one white birth parent had some confusion or lack of information. All the children placed with new families where both parents were of minority ethnic origin were clear about their ethnic origins and cultural heritage whilst two of the nine placed with mixed partnerships had some uncertainty as did three of the eighteen placed with white parents.

Three of the 15 children whose families had adopted mainly for self or family-directed reasons such as having a child, or enlarging the family, had some areas of confusion compared with only one of the 18 whose parents' main motivation was altruistic or child-focused.

A further dimension explored during the interviews was that of **racial pride and the extent to which the young people were rated as feeling positive about their ethnic and cultural heritage**. With 30, there was evidence of a sense of self-worth and pride in their heritage and appearance. Five showed little interest in the subject but did not attribute negative qualities to their ethnic group. Three were ambivalent, expressing some negative views either about their own racial characteristics or appearance, or about other members of the ethnic group to which they belonged. One young person of mixed race parentage, who was placed with a white family, described himself as white, and one had generally negative views about his ethnic background.

Although more likely than those with one black and one white parent to have accurate and full knowledge about their ethnicity, six of the 32 children born to two black parents, were either **ambivalent or negative** about their ethnic background or showed no interest in the subject of ethnicity. Only one of the 19 children of mixed ethnic origin was ambivalent or negative about membership of a particular ethnic group, and two showed no interest. The numbers are small, but the finding is in line with that of Tizard and Phoenix (1993) and the recent survey (Modood *et al.* 1997) that the younger generation of young people of mixed racial parentage may be taking more pride in their dual heritage than appears from earlier studies to have been the case in the past.

Those placed when aged nine or older were most likely to feel positive about their heritage. Some 20 per cent of the young people placed when under the age of four and a third of those placed between five and eight held ambivalent or negative views about their ethnicity. As with self-knowledge, more of those whose parents had adopted or fostered for altruistic reasons gave indications of feeling positive about their ethnic background than was the case for those placed with families whose major motivation was self or family-focused.

As we saw in Chapter 7, some of the black foster parents took particular pleasure in their achievements in this respect. Two of the six young people placed with mixed partnership families were rated as ambivalent about their ethnic origins as compared with only one of the 18 who were placed with a single parent or two parents of minority ethnic origin. Only one of this last group appeared to show no interest in her ethnic origins and culture. Ten of the young people placed with white families (59 per cent) evidenced a sense of pride in their ethnic background, whereas four (24 per cent) had areas of discomfort or were negative and three said they had no interest in their ethnic background, but did not appear to have negative views about people of the same ethnic origin.

The strongest expressions of **positive racial identity and racial pride** came from young people placed with black families or mixed partnership families. It was obvious from their conversations and the similarities in the way in which parents and young people expressed themselves that race and culture had been firmly on the agenda in most of these families.

A black adoptive mother said:

> My daughter now is very much into being a young black woman. She buys *Ebony* and black hair-care magazines. She is very much aware of herself as a black, young woman.

Her daughter said:

> If I was white I would want to be black. I think people who say negative things about being black only want to be black themselves.

Some of the children placed with white families also made very positive comments about themselves as black people or people of mixed race parentage, and about others of similar ethnic origin in their communities. They were unhesitating in their expressions, but less fulsome in the way they expressed themselves than those brought up in black families. When asked to describe herself this young women of 18, brought up in a rural and essentially white community, but who made friends with people of a similar mixed parentage background when she moved away to work, said she described herself as 'black' even though in the adoptive family she knew that her parents preferred the term 'coloured'.

When asked to describe herself she said:

> As far as I am concerned, I've got my family here in Hilltown. I know I am black and have been brought up in a white family.

Her half-sister, also of mixed race parentage, spoke in very similar terms and the impression was gained that, although neither explicitly said so, having another black person in the household had been important.

> Me and Mandy, she is exactly like me – in her looks and in her ways – even though we have different dads. In our temperament too, we are alike. It's funny.

Some of the young people interviewed who were brought up in white families tended to be more mixed in their views about ethnicity. They did not express themselves in overtly negative terms but rather indicated, by showing disinterest or disinclination to discuss the subject, that this might be a topic with which they were not entirely comfortable.

### Identity and esteem as an adopted or fostered child

In earlier chapters we gave some of the views of the parents and young people about adoptive and foster family life. As with the question of ethnicity, we divided outcomes on this dimension into: **knowledge** about their biography and legal status as adopted or foster children, and their sense of **self worth** as young people who grew up in adoptive or foster families.

Thirty-six (86 per cent of the 42 young people about whom we had adequate information) had a reasonably clear understanding of their biographies and legal status, but eight were still confused about important aspects of their identities as young people living with parents other than those they were born to. However, a smaller proportion (22 of the 37 about whom we had reliable information) gave evidence that they valued themselves as adopted or fostered young people, or were comfortable with that aspect of their identities. Eight felt some discomfort about their adoptive or foster status and four had a negative view. There was no difference between the different placement groups, with similar proportions for those who were placed as foster children and those who were placed for adoption; and for those in ethnically 'matched' and those in 'non-matched' placements feeling comfortable about their adoptive or foster status in the family.

This teenager, who joined her adoptive family at the age of five and retained contact with her first family said in a matter of fact way:

> I really feel part of this family - they didn't chuck me out - they didn't say 'Oh she's an outsider, she's not part of our family'. They treat me like I was born into the family. I think even they treat me better than the other kids in the family. They treat me with respect and love. Its been different, being adopted, because most kids don't have what I have – two families.

A more neutral comment was made by a young man in higher education.

> It's not the first thing I tend to say to people I meet. If the conversation turns towards the family, then yes, I will mention that I am adopted. I'm not ashamed of it. But if its irrelevant, then I wouldn't bother. I wouldn't talk about it to people I hardly know.

This comment from an 18-year-old placed at the age of two represents the views of those who were adopted at an early age.

> I've got no regrets. Absolutely no regrets. I've had a very easy life. I didn't realise how lucky I was till I went away to work. We are all friends as well as family.

When asked for a quick response to sum up her adoptive experience she said:

> Family – that's it, really.

The more negative comments, reported already in Chapter 6, tended to be around not being treated as a full member of the family; negative comparisons with birth children, and adverse reactions of relatives. This teenager used the word adopted in a negative sense as being different from the other member of the extended family.

> There are times when I feel adopted and that I don't belong.

## Well-being overall

Family placement is about meeting the needs of children, preferably at the same time as providing a service to their birth parents and adoptive or foster parents. However, meeting the needs of some of these children was a 'tall order' as some of the young people themselves admitted as they looked back over their placement experience. A minority of the placements appeared straightforward, but most of those placed past infancy presented difficulties beyond the average 'own grown' child. These were compounded by the need for the parents and children to get to grips with the complex issues around being an adoptive or foster family, and, in some cases, by having a child who was visibly different and of a different cultural heritage. It comes as no surprise, therefore, that despite the progress which most made, most or all of the needs of the young people were met in only 25 of the cases. Several important needs were not met in 25 cases and in one case the placement clearly made things worse.

| Table 9.8 Changes in well-being of young person since time of placement | | |
|---|---|---|
| *Changes* | *n* | *per cent* |
| Much improvement | 16 | 31 |
| Some improvement | 12 | 23 |
| Always good | 10 | 20 |
| No change/problems at placement | 7 | 14 |
| Somewhat worse | 3 | 6 |
| Much worse | 3 | 6 |
| *Total* | *51* | *100* |

Putting together all the data from a range of sources, a rating was made of the young person's well-being at the time of the interviews and of any changes in well-being (Tables 9.7 and 9.8). In considering well-being our notional point of comparison was a young person of a similar age brought up by their birth parents and living in a similar environment as that in which he or she was brought up, with broadly the same physical or learning disabilities. Thirty-four were rated as of average well-being (27 young people) or above average (seven) young people). However, the well-being of 17 of the 51 still gave cause for concern (including five rated as 'poor'). This finding is in

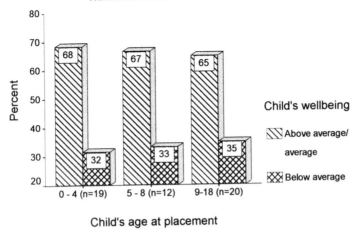

n = 51 children in interview sample

*Figure 9.4 Well-being by age at placement*

keeping with earlier studies (Thoburn *et al.* 1986; Gibbons *et al.*1995) which have noted that, whilst family placement can provide many advantages, and is often successful in providing long term stability, it cannot be expected to 'cure' earlier harm. However, of the 41 children who were of below average well-being at the time of placement, 16 showed much improvement, and 12 some improvement. The well-being of seven appeared to be neither better nor worse and that of six appeared to have deteriorated.

It was interesting to note that well-being (unlike disruption) was not associated with age at placement. Figure 9.4 shows that, contrary to expectations, there was concern about the well-being of an important minority of the children in each age group. The particular difficulties of the 'latency' age group in foster care were highlighted by Berridge and Cleaver (1987). Our findings in this respect are in line with theirs, and also with those of Gibbons *et al.* (1995), Howe (1996) and Quinton *et al.* (1998) in that we concluded that all children placed beyond infancy are potentially vulnerable to problems in placement. Two children placed at the age of one, a three-year-old and three four-year-olds were included in the 'below average well-being' group. On the positive side, 11 children placed at 12 or over were amongst those rated as of average well-being. One possible explanation is that those placed when younger were also younger when interviewed and problems which appear serious in the teenage years may, as Howe (1997b) suggests, become less so for some of the young people as they mature. If this is so, we may anticipate that fewer of those in the 5–8 age group will be of below average well-being by the time they reach their mid-twenties.

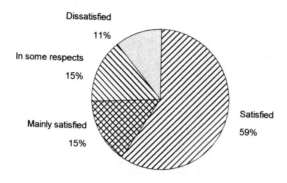

n = 35 cases for which adequate information available

*Figure 9.5 Young person's satisfaction with placement (interview sample)*

## Young people's satisfaction

The outcome measure with which we conclude this chapter is the level of satisfaction of the young people (Figure 9.5). There was evidence that three-quarters of the 35 young people about whom we had adequate information were either satisfied or mainly satisfied with the placement decisions which had been made about them ten or more years earlier and with their growing up experience. Only four (11 per cent) held entirely negative opinions. There was no difference in the numbers of those with two black parents and those of mixed race parentage in terms of satisfaction. More of those placed with two white parents or those in mixed partnerships were either satisfied or mainly satisfied, but the older age at placement and more complex birth family relationships of those placed in black families need to be borne in mind. All five who were satisfied only in some respects had been placed with two white parents; two of the four who were dissatisfied were placed with two black parents; one was in a mixed partnership family, and one was in a white family. It must be remembered that variables other than the ethnicity of the new parents are likely to be influencing satisfaction. Those who were satisfied in only some respects were aged 4, 6, 9, 12 and 14 at placement. Those who were dissatisfied were aged 1, 8, 11 and 14 at placement. The general views of the young people have been given in Chapter 5. The range is covered by the following quotes, but with the last two being more representative:

> I don't remember any good times, hardly any. I just remember bad times, that's all I've got in my mind.

> We just sort of clicked. I was happy to be here.

As they shared these narratives with us, we were made conscious of how much more complex the journey towards an adult identity is for those young people who have to make sense, in different combinations, of loss; rejection; an adoptive or foster family; a biological family which may or may not be part of their present reality, their membership of an ethnic group which is not that of the majority in the UK, and from which some of them have become separated; and the racism to which all were exposed to a greater or lesser extent. To deal with these extra life tasks they had devised different and changing strategies. Some concentrated on getting on with being teenagers and getting a good education, putting 'on the back burner' a serious consideration of adoption and their first families, but knowing that at some time they would come back to what they recognised to be important parts of their identities. Others – mainly those placed with white families – did the same for issues of race and cultural heritage. For some, one or other of these 'differences' or both were up front throughout their childhood and teenage years, and had to be dealt with, sometimes in ways which appeared to be harmful and destructive, before they could go on to develop their full educational and social potential and allow family members or friends to become close to them. For another group, mainly those in touch with their families of origin and those of similar ethnic background, their growing up period was one of constantly working towards integrating the different parts of their identities. They tended to have fewer calm periods than those in the more traditional adoptions but also avoided the dramatic spells of turbulence or the depressions which occasionally overwhelmed some of the children as they moved through their teenage years.

These complex narratives support our conclusion and that of other researchers that it will take longer for most adopted or fostered young people to reach maturity; that those who have been harmed will have a steeper road to climb; that some will not make it and will need a high degree of continuing support (which most were getting from members of their first or their substitute families); but that the majority will take their place in society and will have something very special to offer which comes from their experiences of growing up in adoptive or foster families.

## Summary

In this chapter limited information has been provided on the outcomes for the 297 children in the full cohort and more detailed information is given about the outcomes for the 51 children in the interview sample.

- Some 55 per cent were known to have been adopted and 38 per cent remained as foster children, though some in each group subsequently broke down (the legal status of 7 per cent was not known).

- There was evidence that 24 per cent broke down, in the sense that the young person left the placement earlier than planned.

- When age at placement is held constant, there is no statistically significant difference in breakdown rates between those with two black parents and those of mixed race parentage.

- When other variables were held constant, statistically significant associations were found between placement breakdown and: having a history of deprivation or abuse prior to placement; being older at the time of placement; having behavioural difficulties at the time of placement; and having a history of deprivation or abuse prior to placement.

- There was no statistically significant association between family variables, including whether this was a 'matched' or 'transracial' placement, and disruptions. However, breakdown rates for boys in 'matched' placements were higher than for girls.

- There was no statistically significant difference, when age at placement was held constant, between foster placements and placements for adoption.

For the 51 children in the interview sample, because of the small numbers and the uncertainty about the extent to which these placements can be regarded as representative of the cohort as a whole, caution is required when looking for associations between variables and outcomes. However, the rich interview data give a fuller picture of the outcomes for these 51 young people, and throw light on some of the findings from the full cohort.

- All except four of the young people appear to have gained something from the placement, and 72 per cent were rated as 'successful' in most respects.

- The words of the young people and the parents were used to provide a commentary on the ratings for self-concept, self-esteem, racial and adoptive identity. The picture they present is complex. Most of those who were in their twenties appeared to have constructed a sense of themselves as adopted or fostered young people and members of a particular ethnic group with which they were at least fairly comfortable. Those who were still teenagers were mostly working hard, with signs of success, on putting together a narrative which included their complex biographies and patterns of relationships.

# CHAPTER 10

# Our Findings Reviewed

Most of the children described in this book were placed from care, and most had suffered one or more adversities in addition to having to leave their families of origin. With the full cohort of 297 placements, the only measure of 'success' available was whether or not the placement lasted or broke down. For most children we had these data up to the records search ten years after placement, but for a small number of adopted children, where it was not possible to locate the file and the family was no longer in touch with the agency, we have made the, possibly erroneous, assumption that the child is still a member of the family. Thus, our 'lasted as needed' rate of 76 per cent is likely to err on the side of optimism.

However, the opportunity to interview some of the adoptive and foster parents and young people has allowed us to learn about other aspects of outcome and to present the complex reality which lies behind the 'disruption' statistics.

Using the additional information on the 51 children in the interview sample (which we re-emphasise cannot be regarded as representative as they are a small, non-random proportion of the total cohort) we concluded that, whilst 82 per cent of these did not break down, only 72 per cent had been successful in most respects. However, the young person had gained at least something from the placement in a further 20 per cent of cases, even though important needs were not met, and only 4 of the 51 could be regarded as completely unsuccessful or harmful. On the other hand, our conclusion that only 69 per cent of these young people could be regarded as being of at least average well-being, combines with earlier studies in demonstrating that it cannot be assumed that early harm will be reversed even by very loving, competent and stable parenting.

Perhaps more importantly, we concur with Gibbons *et al.* (1995) in concluding that, whilst placement breakdown is fairly unusual for children placed under the age of five, this may conceal a less optimistic picture in terms of the well-being, even of young children placed for adoption after experiencing neglect or maltreatment as infants. This note of caution is particularly important for those placed at primary school age who comprise the majority of those presently being placed for adoption. It lends yet more support to the weight of argument in favour of a routinely available, flexible and 'adopter and child-friendly' post-adoption service. We did not interview birth parents but conclude from the comments of the young people that a post-placement service is also necessary for birth parents, both for their own sakes, and for the sake of the young people placed for adoption and any siblings still at home or placed elsewhere. There was actual contact with at least one birth parent at some stage in the majority of cases, and even when there was no contact there were few young people who did not feel at the very least, curiosity, and often concern about what had happened to them, and especially whether they had had any more children.

For the full cohort, a range of variables (about the young people, their early histories, the families they joined, and the placement decisions and practice) was considered as possibly associated with placement breakdown. The findings in respect of these young people of minority ethnic origin are very similar to those in earlier studies of predominantly white populations. We concluded that it was child-related factors which had the biggest impact on whether or not the placement lasted as needed. Neither policy nor practice variables (such as whether the placement was for adoption or fostering), nor family related variables (such as whether or not there were other children, or, more central to our study, whether the new parents were of a similar or different ethnic background to the child) were significantly associated with placement breakdown. From the interview data we saw that some very experienced parents of all ethnic groups struggled, and sometimes failed, to turn around the lives of some very damaged young people. Others in all groups succeed with children who appeared equally needy. The information from our detailed interviews does, however, throw additional light on these findings and supports one of our early hypotheses that parents of different ethnic origin to the child have additional obstacles to overcome as they nurture and guide the child towards maturity. It is clear that, despite the best endeavours of their parents, some of the transracially placed children suffered additional stress from being separated from their ethnic and cultural heritage as well as from their birth families.

A key question to be asked, when considering the relevance of our study to contemporary child placement policy, is whether placement practice has significantly changed since these young people joined their substitute families in the early 1980s. All the social work teams responsible for the work with the adoptive or foster families were specialist family placement teams and had pioneered the methods which are still regarded as 'best practice'. From our knowledge of present day family placement work, we would not anticipate that, in most respects, practice with young people, their birth parents or the substitute parents has changed significantly. However, in three respects there have been important changes in practice, which are relevant to this particular group of children. These are around issues of ethnicity; deciding about and facilitating appropriate contact with members of the birth family; and the provision of post-adoption support, including financial support through the payment of adoption allowances (an issue discussed in Chapter 8).

## Family contact

We have considered the question of contact in earlier chapters, and concluded that practice in this respect was often ill-thought out and generally based on a 'total severance' model of adoption, irrespective of the wishes of the child, the birth parents or the new parents. In this respect the foster parents were better served since there was an assumption that social work help should be available in facilitating appropriate contact.

The more usual pattern for the adopters was to accept the ending of contact as the norm, most would say with some relief. But for most of the children placed past infancy, the issues around links with birth parents were not off the agenda for long. Many of the young people had significant relationships with members of their birth families which they were unwilling to give up despite the maltreatment which they may have suffered.

Encouraged by the provisions of the Children Act 1989, much has been learned about the importance of preserving and nurturing links when children are looked after and, in appropriate cases, maintaining these links when children join substitute families. Practice has moved forward, with the development of contact agreements and 'letter box' facilities. The distressing, and, in the opinions of some of the adopters, harmful 'goodbye visits' with birth parents are less frequent, though they still occur. 'Indirect contact' has been more carefully thought about although it is an area of practice which is not without its problems, as some of the parents told us, and has not yet been adequately researched. It can at least be hypothesised that decisions about, and the practicalities of, contact with birth parents and siblings for some of these children would have been better handled today than it was in most of these cases 15 or so years ago.

## Ethnicity and child placement

A survey of placements of infants might have had a better chance of unravelling the specific impact of the ethnicity of the new parents on the progress of the placement. The number of infant placements in our cohort and interview samples is small, especially when subdivided into the four different placement groups based on the ethnicity of the children and the new parents. With older children placed from the care system, only careful sifting through the interview data can give clues as to why some placements, with black families and with white families, ran into such intractable and distressing difficulties. For many of the children, the harm which resulted from parental neglect and maltreatment was compounded by the adverse impact of racial abuse and by placement in children's homes and communities which often failed to provide them with positive black role models.

Before turning to the question of whether lessons can be drawn from our study about the impact of placement policy and practice on the different ethnic groups and age groups, it is important to consider the changes in social work practice with black children and families, since these families were recruited and the children placed.

In the early 1980s, as more black workers moved into the social work profession, often specialising in family placement work, black families were encouraged to come forward as adopters or foster parents. But most of the children's area team workers and most of the adoption workers were white. Some of the black workers were unqualified trainees, bringing much enthusiasm, but lacking the knowledge, skills, self confidence and status which a professional qualification in social work would have given them. There was very little post-qualifying training for either recruiting, assessing and supporting black families, or in assessing and helping children who had been placed in an all-white environment and taken on white identities. On the other hand, black and some white workers, joined by some of the black families they recruited, were fired by a deeply felt sense of sadness and injustice at the additional harm done to black children in care by racial abuse or the lack of respect shown to their heritage.

Over the same period, white families who had applied to foster or adopt a black child, often motivated in part by compassion on hearing that there were many black children in care, found that, almost overnight, they were blamed rather than valued for their actions. Some perceived themselves as being labelled as racists by the social workers to whom they might have turned for help. These years, then, can be seen as unusual and this should be borne in mind when our findings on ethnicity are considered.

We set out essentially to provide descriptive information about the lives of the young people and their parents, their coping strategies, their joys and frustrations, their support systems and the services they found helpful or unhelpful. Many of our questions focused on race, culture and racism, yet it is difficult to do justice to the richness of the information and opinion which parents and young people shared with us. The messages were complex, and at times contradictory.

Our data show that, for the group as a whole, there was no difference in disruption rates between placements with black families and placements with white families for either children with two black parents or those of mixed race parentage. We cannot know what impact the lack of experience in making placements with black families had on this result, and could identify cases where mistakes made then would probably have been avoided now. Some of the black parents told of their struggle to make some white workers understand their point of view and their attitudes towards parenting. Some of the white families held back from seeking help because of lack of mutual trust and confidence between them and some of the social workers (white as well as black) who took over the child's supervision at a later stage.

The conclusion from our survey of breakdown rates and from the detailed interviews is that parenting children who have suffered adversity, whatever their age, is a special task requiring personal strength, commitment and parenting skills of a high order. High priority must be given to finding families from a wide range of ethnic communities who possess these attributes and skills so that children can have the best possible chance of having their complex needs met. Most of the parents we interviewed, including the successful and the less successful, gave ample evidence of possessing these qualities.

The race of the parents has an important bearing on how they fulfil the specific parenting tasks of helping children develop a positive racial and cultural identity, and confronting racism. The task is particularly difficult and complex when young people have been socialised into thinking of themselves as white and have absorbed racist attitudes from previous carers or relatives. From the interview data we conclude that the requirement in the Children Act 1989 to seek to place children with parents who can meet their identified needs as individuals, and who are of a similar cultural and ethnic background, provides a sound basis for policy. This would be the view of all but a tiny minority of the parents and children who gave their opinions on this question, including members of ethnically mixed and ethnically similar families. But we also conclude that some white families can successfully parent black children and those of other ethnicity, and would agree with other writers that the optimum environment for them to do this is one where there are many role models, including some in high status occupations, who are of the same ethnic origin.

The Children Act guidance has to be applied in the context of the detailed information available about each child's history, current circumstances and attachments, as well as the expressed wishes of the young people, their parents and carers. When this is done, there will be a small minority of cases where a new placement with, or remaining with, a family of a different ethnic origin will be the placement choice (in UK society, most likely, for reasons of prevalence, to be a white family). In saying this we are mindful of the complexity of racial identities as explored by Gilroy (1993) and Modood *et al.* (1997). Class, culture, religion, special needs as a person with a disability, and language as well as ethnicity should each inform the placement decision.

We stress in particular the importance of a full assessment of the child's attachments in the context of any information as to whether this is a resilient or a particularly vulnerable child. The possible impact of separation from parents or previous carers must be carefully assessed since the evidence suggests that, whilst children **can** overcome the stress and sadness of loss and form new attachments, some will be unable to do so. It is rarely possible to be clear as to which will be the resilient children who will get over the temporary harm of separation, and which will carry the emotional scars for the rest of their lives. There were examples of both in all age groups and we could not easily see why, for example, one four-year-old settled in and bonded with the new parents, whereas another four-year-old carried on grieving and failed to fully attach after the move to new parents. Our study gives many clues about how such decisions can be made and how, if it is right for a child to remain with a white carer to whom he or she is attached, his or her special cultural needs can be met, and pride in belonging to a particular ethnic group encouraged.

The views of the birth parents and of the children themselves must also be carefully weighed and links with the birth parents and extended families nurtured wherever possible. This issue is usually straightforward when both parents are black, or it is the black parent who wishes to stay in touch. The question is more complex if, for example, a white birth mother holds racist views and does not wish the child to be in contact with the father or his relatives. There were examples in our study of black and white birth parents working in partnership with black and white adopters or foster parents to seek to ensure that all the child's needs were met, especially their need to have good self knowledge and pride in being an adopted black young person.

But the many advantages which adoptive or foster parents of the same cultural and ethnic background bring to the task lead us to conclude that placement with a family of a different ethnic background, including one from a minority ethnic group other than that of the child, should be unusual and should be clearly linked to specific reasons in individual cases. Whilst some white families can successfully parent black children, they have additional tasks to negotiate, and the job they have to do in parenting a child who has already suffered adversity and at least one separation and rejection is difficult enough without making it more difficult.

## Special parenting for special children

In earlier chapters have we tried to convey something of the love, care, reflection, skill, determination and indeed dedication which most of the parents put into the task. The respective emphasis placed on **skill** and **love** differed depending on the age of the child at placement and the reason for undertaking this special sort of parenting. Those whose motives essentially sprang from altruism, a religious calling or a determination to help black young people, tended to talk more about the way in which they tackled the job and the rewards they got from a job well done, even if the outcome had not been as successful as they had hoped. Those who adopted a child in order to experience the joys and fulfilment of parenting or to add to their families spoke more of love and intuition and less of skill. But to be successful, it was clear that skill and intuition, head and heart, love and determination, altruism and meeting a need of their own, had to be present in all the families. Above all, at least one of the parents, and preferably both if it was a two parent family, had to enjoy and feel fulfilled by the every-day routines of parenting.

Not all children placed with substitute parents will become fully attached to them. Sometimes they have been too harmed, or too frequently moved, to allow themselves to trust; sometimes they are still too emotionally caught up with a birth parent or a previous carer and don't want another parent; sometimes it is just that the 'chemistry' of personalities is wrong. If the only reward lies in loving and being loved, some families will be bitterly disappointed and there will be nothing there to keep them going.

The young people themselves greatly value good parenting, which, for black young people, must include help to deal with racism and with issues of identity and racial pride, but also includes help with school work, personal care, getting jobs, negotiating a different role with birth relatives, moving into your own flat and being there when things are not quite working out. Those families who took pleasure in being good parents had the reserves to carry on through troubled times when others, for whom the only reward lay in being able to give and receive love, gave up. The most positive message from the study is that things often took a turn for the better and relationships improved when this was least expected.

The last word is left to a young woman who represents the majority. When asked if she had any messages for social workers about how the placement service could be improved she replied:

> Tips: I don't know really. The chance I have had has been marvellous. Full marks. Thank you.

# References

ABAFA (1977) Association of British Agencies for Fostering and Adoption. *Soul Kids Campaign: Report of Steering Group.* London: ABAFA.

ABSWAP (1983a) Association of Black Social Workers and Allied Professions. *Black Children in Care: Evidence to the House of Commons Social Services Committee.* London: ABSWAP.

ABSWAP (1983b) Association of Black Social Workers and Allied Professions. 'Give the black child a chance'. *First National Conference on Black Children in Care.* London: ABSWAP, 15 November.

Ahmad, B. (1990) *Black Perspectives in Social Work.* Birmingham: Venture Press.

Ahmed, S. (1988) *Defining and Assessing Black Families in Family Rights Groups Planning for Children.* London: Family Rights Group.

Alexander, C.E. (1996) *The Art of Being Black: The Creation of Black British Youth Identities.* Oxford: Clarendon Press.

Alexander, R. and Curtis, C.M. (1996) 'A review of empirical research involving transracial adoption of African American children.' *Journal of Black Psychology 22,* 2, 223–235.

Arnold, E. (1982) 'Finding black families for black children in Britain.' In J. Cheetham (ed) *Social Work and Ethnicity.* London: George Allen and Unwin.

Arnold, E. and James, M. (1989) 'Finding black families for black children in care: a case study.' *New Community* 15, 3, 417–425.

Bagley, C. (1993a) 'Transracial adoption in Britain: a follow-up study with policy considerations.' *Child Welfare 22,* 3, 285–299.

Bagley, C. (1993b) *International and Transracial Adoption: A Mental Health Perspective.* Aldershot: Avebury.

Bagley, C. and Young, L. (1979) 'The identity, adjustment and achievement of transracially adopted children: a review and empirical report.' In G.K. Verma and C. Bagley (eds) *Race, Education and Identity.* London: Macmillan.

Baldwin, J.A. (1979) 'Theory and research concerning the notion of black self-hatred: a review and re-interpretation.' *Journal of Black Psychology 5,* 51–78.

Banks, N. (1992) 'Techniques for direct identity work with black children.' *Adoption and Fostering* 16, 3, 19–25.

Banks, N. (1995) 'Children of black and mixed parentage and their placement needs.' *Adoption and Fostering* 19, 2, 19–24.

Barn, R. (1993) *Black Children in the Public Care System.* London: Batsford with BAAF.

Barth, R.P. and Berry, M. (1988) *Adoption and Disruption: Rates, Risks and Responses.* New York: Aldine de Gruyter.

Beek, M. (1997) *What Does it Mean to be Black? A Study of Adoption through the Eyes of Adopted Adults.* Norwich: UEA MSW Dissertation.

Berridge, D. and Cleaver, H. (1987) *Foster Home Breakdown.* Oxford: Basil Blackwell.

Berridge, D. and Smith, P. (1993) *Ethnicity and Child Care Placements.* London: National Children's Bureau.

Borland, M., Triseliotis, J. and O'Hara, G. (1990) *Permanence Planning for Children in Lothian Region.* University of Edinburgh.

Brah, A. (1992) 'Difference, diversity and differentiation.' In J. Donald and A. Rattansi (eds) *"Race", Culture and Difference.* London: Open University and Sage.

Braithwaite, E.K. (1962) *Paid Servant.* London: Bodley Head.

Brodzinsky, D.M. and Schechter, M.D. (1990) *The Psychology of Adoption.* Oxford: Oxford University Press

Brunton, L. and Welch, M. (1983) 'White agency, black community.' *Adoption and Fostering* 7, 2, 16–18.

Burnell, A. (1993) 'Open adoption: a post adoption perspective.' In Adcock *et al.* (eds.) *Exploring Openness in Adoption.* Croydon: Significant Publications.

Butt, J. and Mirza, K. (1996) *Social Care and Black Communities: A Review of Recent Research Studies.* London: HMSO.

Charles, M., Rashid, S. and Thoburn, J. (1992) 'The placement of black children with permanent new families.' *Adoption and Fostering* 16, 3, 13–19.

Coopersmith, S. (1981) *'Self-esteem Inventories, Palo Alto'.* The Consulting Psychologist Press.

Cross, W. E. (1971) 'The negro to black conversion experience: towards the psychology of black liberation.' *Black World* 20, 13–27.

Cross, W.E. (1980) 'Models of psychological nigrescence: a literature review.' In R. L. Jones (ed) *Black Psychology,* 2nd edition. New York: Harper and Row.

Cross, W.E. (1991) *Shades of Black: Diversity in African-American Identity.* Philadelphia: Temple University Press.

Dale, D. (1987) *Denying Homes to Black Children: Britain's New Race Adoption Policies.* London: Social Affairs Unit.

Department of Health (1998) *Adoption – Achieving the Right Balance.* LAC (98) 20. London: DH.

Department of Health (1999) *Adoption Now.* Chichester: Wiley.

Divine, D. (1983) 'Defective, hypocritical and patronising research.' *The Caribbean Times* 4 March.

Erikson, E.H. (1968) *Identity: Youth and Crisis.* London: Faber.

Fanshel, D. and Shinn, E.B. (1978) *Children in Foster Care.* New York: Columbia University Press.

Fratter, J., Rowe, J., Sapsford, D. and Thoburn, J. (1991) *Permanent Family Placement: A Decade of Experience.* London: BAAF.

Fratter, J. (1996) *Perspectives on Adoption with Contact: Implications for Policy and Practice.* London: BAAF.

Gaber, I. (1994) 'Transracial placements in Britain: a history.' In I. Gaber and J. Aldridge (eds) *In the Best Interests of the Child: Culture, Identity and Transracial Adoption.* London: Free Association Books.

Gambe, D., Gomes, J., Kapur, V., Rangel, M. and Stubbs, P. (1992) 'Improving Practice with Children and Families: A Training Manual.' *Anti-Racist Social Work Education* 2. London: CCETSW.

Gibbons, J., Thorpe, S. and Wilkinson, P. (1990) *Family Support and Prevention: Studies in Local Areas – Purposes and Organisation of Preventive Work with Families.* London: HMSO.

Gibbons, J., Gallagher, B., Bell, C. and Gordon, D. (1995) *Development After Physical Abuse in Early Childhood.* London: HMSO.

Gill, O. and Jackson, B. (1983) *Adoption and Race: Black, Asian and Mixed Race Children in White Families.* London: Batsford in association with the British Agencies for Adoption and Fostering.

Gilroy, P. (1987) *There ain't no black in the Union Jack.* London: Routledge.

Gilroy, P. (1992) 'The end of antiracism.' In A. Rattansi and J. Donald (eds) *'Race', Culture and Difference.* London: Open University and Sage.

Gilroy, P. (1993) *Small Acts: Thoughts on the Politics of Black Culture.* London: Serpent's Tail.

Greene, W. (1995) *LIMDEP Version 7.0, User's Manual.* Bellpart, New York: Econometric Software Inc.

Grotevant, H.D., McRoy, R.G., Elde, C. and Fravel, D.L. (1994) 'Adoptive family system dynamics: variations by level of openness in adoption.' *Family Process* 33, 125–146.

Grotevant, H.D. and McRoy, R.G. (1998) *Openness in Adoption: Exploring Family Connections.* New York: Sage.

Harter, S. (1985) 'Processes underlying the formation, maintenance and enhancement of the self-concept.' In J. Suls and A. Greenwald (eds) *Psychological Perspectives on the Self* 3, 137–181. Hillsdale, NJ: Lawrence Erlbaum.

Hill, M., Lambert, L. and Triseliotis, J. (1989) *Achieving Adoption with Love and Money.* London: National Children's Bureau.

Hodges, J. and Tizard, B. (1989) 'Social and family relationships of ex-institutional adolescents.' *Journal of Child Psychology and Psychiatry* 30, 1.

Holman, R. (1980) 'Exclusive and inclusive concepts of fostering.' In J. Triseliotis (ed) *New Developments in Fostering and Adoption.* London: Routledge.

Honess, T. and Yardley, K. (eds) (1987) *Self and Identity: Perspectives Across the Lifespan.* London: Routledge and Kegan Paul.

Howe, D. (1996) *Adopters on Adoption.* London: BAAF.

Howe, D. (1997a) 'Parent reported problems in 211 adopted children.' *Journal of Child Psychology and Psychiatry* 38, 4, 401–411.

Howe, D. (1997b) *Patterns of Adoption.* Oxford: Blackwell.

Howe, D. and Feast, J. (2000) *Adoption, Search and Reunion: The Long-term Experience of Adopted Adults.* London: The Children's Society.

Hutnik, N. (1992) *Ethnic Minority Identity: A Social Psychological Perspective.* Oxford: Clarendon Press.

Jackson, B. (1976) *Family Experiences of Inter-racial Adoption.* London: Association of British Adoption and Fostering Agencies.

Katz, I. (1996) *The Construction of Racial Identity in Children of Mixed Parentage: Mixed Metaphors.* London: Jessica Kingsley.

Kirk, D. (1964) *Shared Fate: A Theory of Adoption and Mental Health.* New York: Free Press.

Kirton, D. (1995) *'Race', Identity and the Politics of Adoption.* University of East London: Centre for Adoption and Identity Studies.

Kovacs, M. and Beck, A.T. (1997) 'An empirical approach towards a definition of childhood depression.' In J.G. Shulterbrand and A. Raskin (eds) *Depression in Childhood.* New York: Raven Press.

Kroger, J. (1996) *Identity in Adolescence: The Balance Between Self and Other* (2nd edition), London: Routledge.

Ladner, J. (1977) *Mixed Families.* New York: Free Press/Doubleday.

Logan, J. (1999) 'Exchanging information post adoption: views of adoptive parents and birth parents'. *Adoption and Fostering* 23, 3, 27–37.

Lowe, N. with Borkowski, M., Copner, R., Griew, K. and Murch, M. (1993) *Freeing for Adoption Provisions.* London: HMSO.

Lowe, N., Murch, M., Borkowski, M., Weaver, A., Beckford, V. with Thomas, C. (1999) *Supporting Adoption: Reframing the Approach.* London: BAAF.

Macey, M. (1995) 'Same race adoption policy: anti-racism or racism?' *Journal of Social Policy* 24, 4, 473–491.

MacLeod, M. (1996) *Children and Racism – A ChildLine Study.* London: ChildLine.

Maximé, J. (1986) 'Some psychological models of black self-concept.' In S. Ahmed, J. Cheetham and J. Small (eds) *Social Work with Black Children and Their Families.* London: Batsford in association with BAAF.

Maximé, J. (1993) 'The importance of racial identity for the psychological well-being of black children.' *ACPP Review and Newsletter* 15, 4, 173–179.

McRoy, R.G., Zurchev, L.A., Lauderdale, M.L. and Anderson, R.N. (1982) 'Self-esteem and racial identity in transracial and inracial adoptees.' *Social Work (USA)* 27, 522–526.

McRoy, R.G. (1991) 'Significance of ethnic and racial identity in inter-country adoption.' *Adoption and Fostering* 15, 4.

McGuire, S. (1994) 'Measuring self-concept in children.' *Association of Child Psychology and Psychiatry Newsletter* 16, 2, 83–87.

McWhinnie, A.M. (1967) *Adopted Children: How They Grow Up.* London: Routledge & Kegan Paul.

Modood, T. (1988) 'Who's defining who?' *New Society* 4 March 4–5.

Modood, T., Berthoud, R., Lakey, J., Nazroo, J., Smith, P., Virdee, S. and Bershon, S. (1997) *Fourth National Survey of Ethnic Minorities in Britain: Diversity and Disadvantage.* London: Policy Studies Institute.

Neil, E. (1999a) 'The sibling relationships of adopted children and patterns of contact after adoption.' In A. Mullender (ed) *We Are Family: Sibling Relationships in Placement and Beyond.* London: BAAF.

Neil, E. (1999b) 'The contact after adoption study'. *Family Studies Newsletter.* Norwich: UEA, School of Social Work.

Nelson, K.A. (1985) *On the Frontier of Adoption: A Study of Special-needs Adoptive Families.* Washington: Child Welfare League of America.

O'Hara, G. (1986) 'Developing post-placement services in Lothian'. *Adoption and Fostering* 10, 4, 38–42.

Owen, M. (1999) *Novices, Old Hands and Professionals: Adoption by Single People.* London: BAAF.

Owusu-Bempah, J. and Howitt, D. (1997) 'Socio-genealogical connectedness, attachment theory and childcare practice'. *Child and Family Social Work* 2, 4, 199–207.

Parham, T.A. (1989) 'Cycles of psychological nigrescence.' *The Counselling Psychologist* 17, 2, 187–226.

Ponterotto, J. (1989) 'Expanding directions for racial identity research.' *The Counselling Psychologist* 17, 2, 264–272.

Quinton, D., Rushton, A., Dance, C. and Mayes, D. (1998) *Joining New Families: A Study of Adoption and Fostering in Middle Childhood.* Chichester: Wiley.

Rattansi, A. (1992) 'Changing the subject? Racism, culture and education.' In J. Donald and A. Rattansi (eds) *"Race", Culture and Difference.* London: Open University and Sage.

Raynor, L. (1970) *Adoption of Non-white Children in Britain.* London: Allen & Unwin.

Raynor, L. (1980) *The Adopted Child Comes of Age.* London: Allen & Unwin.

Rhodes, P.J. (1992) *"Racial Matching" in Fostering.* Aldershot: Avebury.

Robinson, L. (1995) *Psychology for Social Workers: Black Perspectives.* London: Routledge.

Robinson, L. (1997) 'Nigrescence.' In M. Davies (ed) *The Blackwell Companion to Social Work.* Oxford: Blackwell Scientific Publications.

Rowe, J. and Lambert, L. (1973) *Children Who Wait: A Study of Children Needing Substitute Families.* London: Association of British Adoption and Fostering Agencies.

Rowe, J., Cain, H., Hundleby, M. and Keane, A. (1984) *Long-term Foster Care.* London: Batsford.

Rowe, J., Hundleby, M. and Garnett, L. (1989) *Child Care Now – A Survey of Placement Patterns.* London: BAAF.

Rushton, A., Treseder, J. and Quinton, D. (1989) *New Parents for Older Children.* London: BAAF.

Rushton, A., Treseder, J. and Quinton, D. (1993) 'New parents for older children: support services during eight years of placement.' *Adoption and Fostering* 17, 39–45.

Rushton, A., Treseder, J. and Quinton, D. (1995) 'An eight-year prospective study of older boys placed in permanent substitute families.' *Journal of Child Psychology and Psychiatry* 36, 4.

Rushton, A. and Minnis, H. (1997) 'Annotation: Transracial Family Placements.' *Journal of Child Psychology and Psychiatry* 38, 2, 147–159.

Rutter, M., Tizard, J. and Whitmore, K. (eds.) (1981) *Education, Health and Behaviour.* London: Longman.

Ryburn, M. (1994) *Open Adoption: Research, Theory and Practice.* Aldershot: Avebury.

Sellick, C. and Thoburn, J. (1996) *What Works in Family Placement.* Barkingside: Barnardos.

Shireman, J.F. and Johnson, P.R. (1986) 'A longitudinal study of black adoption: single parent, transracial and traditional.' *Social Work (USA) 31,* 172–176.

Silverman, A.R. and Feigelman, W. (1981) 'The adjustment of black children adopted by white families.' *Social Casework* 62, 529–536.

Simon, R.J. and Altstein, H. (1977) *Transracial Adoption.* New York: Wiley.

Simon, R.J. and Altstein, H. (1981) *Transracial Adoption: A Follow-Up.* Lexington MA: Lexington Books.

Simon, R.J. and Altstein, H. (1987) *Transracial Adoptees and Their Families: A Study of Identity and Commitment.* New York: Praeger.

Small, J. (1986) 'Transracial placements – conflicts and contradictions.' in S. Ahmed, J. Cheetham and J. Small (eds) *Social Work with Black Children and Their Families.* London: Batsford in association with BAAF.

Stanfield, J.H. and Dennis, R.M. (1993) *Race and Ethnicity in Research Methods.* London: Sage.

Stubbs, P. (1987) 'Professionalism and the adoption of black children.' *British Journal of Social Work* 17, 473–492.

Thoburn, J. (1990) *Success and Failure in Permanent Family Placement.* Aldershot: Avebury.

Thoburn, J. (1991) 'Evaluating placements and survey findings and conclusions.' In Fratter *et al.* (eds) *Permanent Family Placement: A Decade of Experience.* London: BAAF.

Thoburn, J., Murdoch, A. and O'Brien, A. (1986) *Permanence in Child Care.* Oxford: Blackwell.

Thoburn, J. and Moffatt, P. (in press) 'Outcomes of permanent family placement for children of minority ethnic origin.' *Child and Family Social Work*, 4.

Thomas, C. and Beckford, V. (1999) *Adopted Children Speaking.* London: BAAF.

Tizard, B. and Hodges, J. (1990) 'Ex-institutional children: a follow-up study to age 16.' *Adoption and Fostering* 14, 1, 17–20.

Tizard, B. and Phoenix, A. (1993) *Black, White or Mixed-race? Race and Racism in the Lives of Young People of Mixed Parentage.* London: Routledge.

Triseliotis, J. (1983) 'Identity and security in adoption and long-term fostering.' *Adoption and Fostering* 7, 1, 22–31.

Triseliotis, J. and Russell, J. (1984) *Hard to Place: The Outcome of Adoption and Residential Care.* London: Gower.

Triseliotis, J., Shireman, J. and Hundleby, M. (1997) *Adoption: Theory, Policy and Practice.* London: Cassell.

Ward, H. (ed) (1996) *Looking After Children: Research into Practice.* London: HMSO.

Wedge, P. and Mantle, G. (1991) *Sibling Groups and Social Work.* University of East Anglia: Department of Social Work.

Weise, J. (1988) *Transracial Adoption: A Black Perspective.* Norwich: University of East Anglia.

Wilson, A. (1987) *Mixed Race Children: A Study of Identity.* London: Allen and Unwin.

# Subject Index

# Author Index

Learning Resources
Centre